The Fisherman's World

The

by Charles F. Waterman

Photographers:
Frederick C. Baldwin
Erwin A. Bauer
Bill Browning
Patricia Caulfield
Wallace O. Hughes
Bernard Kreh
Karl H. Maslowski
Paul D. McLain
Leonard Lee Rue III
Charles F. Waterman
Joseph Van Wormer

isherman's World

Ridge Press Book | Random House, New York

The Fisherman's World
by Charles F. Waterman
First printing.

Published in the United States by Random House, New York,
and simultaneously in Canada by Random House of Canada, Limited, Toronto.
Prepared and produced by The Ridge Press, Inc.
Library of Congress Catalog Card Number: 71-176122
ISBN: 0-394-41099-8
Printed and bound in Italy by Mondadori Editore, Verona.

To my wife, Debie,
who buys fly rods the way some
women buy hats.

Contents

Acknowledgments

These people have shared their fisherman's world with me and thus have added greatly to this book: Captain Ted Smallwood, oracle of the mangrove coast; Louis Nordmann, student of bass and panfish; Ray Donnersberger, master angler of bluegill to tarpon; Milton Culp, wader after saltwater trout; Joe Brooks, who started me after bonefish; Stuart Apte, follower of the shimmering flats; V.M. Gowdy of the fly rod and popping bug; Art Hutt, who bought my first fishing article; Bob Budd, casting champion; Dan Bailey and Chester Marion of the western trout; John Walker of the cold steelhead waters; Les Allen, who knows the ways of Yukon pike and grayling; Pete McLain, who races striped bass with a pushpole; George Archer, the Gulf Stream captain; Paul Fournier of the silent Maine canoe; Don Buck of Kansas, who showed me how to catch my first bass; Charley Barnes, who ran the Ozark rivers long before the dams; Walter Dineen, airboat biologist of the Everglades; Jimmy Addison, who knew where the snook lived; Bob and Stuart Ramsay, who had the bluefish marked; the late Merton Parks of the Yellowstone; W.S. Steerman, who watched the black bass schooling grounds; Dorothy Miller, who gets bass messages from monofilament; Don Williams of the high golden trout; Ben Williams, who knows the perfect beaver ponds; Bud Gaffney and Richard Vincent of the Montana Fish and Game Department; and, with particular gratitude, Forrest Ware, fisheries biologist, who served as special ecological advisor.

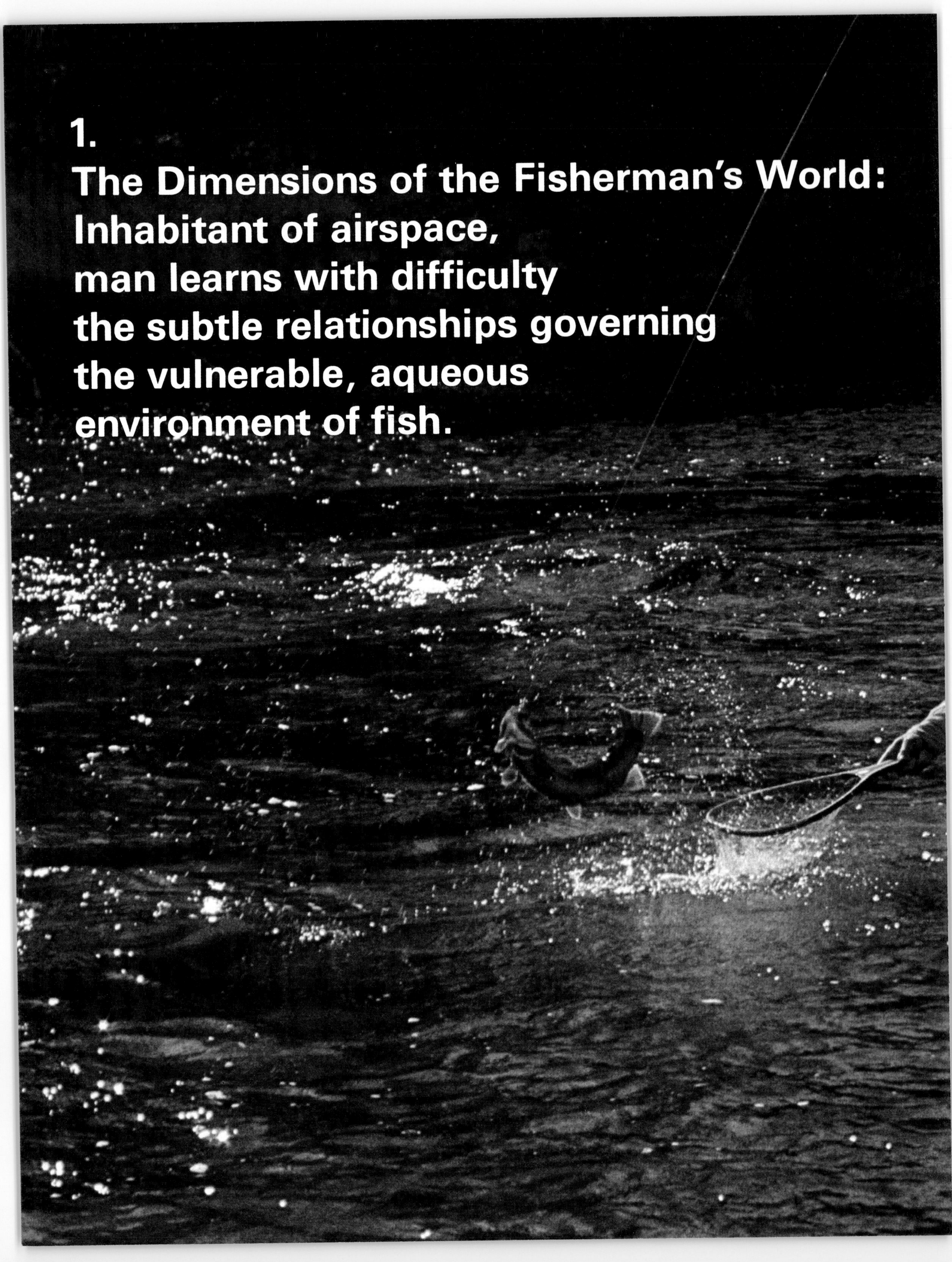

1.
The Dimensions of the Fisherman's World:

Inhabitant of airspace,
man learns with difficulty
the subtle relationships governing
the vulnerable, aqueous
environment of fish.

Preceding pages: Brown trout leaps in heavy water of swift river. Opposite: Divided by bars and islands, great stream gives angler choice of speeds and depths of trout water.

 The successful fisherman is a student of his favorite waters, whether they be the endless blue world of the open sea or a brook he steps across. In either place the chain of life must be complete or there is no quarry for the fisherman, and no success.

In the fragile food chains that connect all living organisms, the place of the game fish is close to the microscopic beginnings. The fish subsists delicately in its vulnerable environment, whether it swims in a few inches of meadow brook or in the fathoms of the continental shelf. Knowledge of fish and their lives comes with great difficulty to man, who is a land creature, bound to a different element, and a clumsy interloper when he invades the world of fishes, a world larger than his own. At best, the fisherman tends to view his subject in terms of the land.

The angler's true skill or knowledge is not measured by the size of his quarry; some of the greatest fishermen have been masters only of the learned trout of small streams, fish smaller than the baits used for tuna or marlin. And although the general public takes no notice of his efforts, the catcher of educated trout has become a hero and legend among those who understand his achievements. There has been more written and studied about these smaller fishes than about any others. In their intimacy with civilization they have become more difficult subjects than wilderness fish or fish of distant seas. The trout of brook and pond lacks the variety of forage available to fish of bigger waters and knows its limited foods so well that their effective imitation becomes both art and science. In this book we endeavor to give the reasons the trout behaves as it does. Such fish are not for the casual or hurried angler.

Not only does each species have its separate ecology and environment, it has its own temperament which we must try to interpret—in human terms if necessary—for by this means we can see the contrasts among the species and even the differences that exist among individuals. These are the things a fisherman studies, aware that among individuals the factor of luck becomes smaller as knowledge and expertise increase. There are forms of angling so exacting that luck is of little consequence. Whereas the fisherman of small streams studies the underwater insects and their timed emergence, the offshore angler is attuned to the color of his waters, the sweep of changing currents, the subtle narrative of the fathometer, the simmering pattern of surfacing bait-fish, and the telltale turns of distant gulls.

The masters of such things are good anglers, but the study often eclipses the end result, producing fishermen who seek new situations when one has been solved: the bass angler who turns from his deadly bottom lure in order to catch a single fish with a surface counterfeit; the fisherman who leaves his home pond and the bass he has learned to deceive and crosses a continent to challenge other bass, no larger but different in behavior; the Atlantic-salmon fisherman, who spends a fortune on a difficult river when he could catch many more fish on a wilderness stream simply by being there at an easily predicted time.

Whatever his chosen sport, the naturalist-fisherman educates himself in every aspect of it. He becomes a judge of the shores, the currents, and the water's texture. He learns about the creatures that share the element with his quarry or live on the water's edge, creatures large and small that consume or are consumed by his game fish, and those that compete with it for food. Moreover, the fisherman's task is not simply to learn a single set of interrelationships, for the fish's habitat is often an abruptly changing thing; some environmental change may occur that shifts favoring circumstances from one species to another.

In the farm pond tiny black bass grow well if the spawning bottom is proper and their microscopic food is present in sufficient quantities. But their enemy, the bluegill, must be present also to take his regulatory toll of the thousands of eggs and reduce the overabundance of the teeming fry. And, at a later time, the bluegill again enters the

1

Maine brookies (1) hide in brushy trickle, brown trout (2) in heavier water. Angler wades both sunny creek (3) and pushing surf (4). Smallmouth bass (5) is inland prize. Mayflies (6) crowd streamside bushes and egret (8) leaves shore at angler's approach. Where ocean meets the land (7), a bonefish ghosts across wide flats to be hunted by wading caster with tackle similar to that used in tiny brook and wider river.

2

3

4

5

6

7

8

During salmon-fly hatch, fisherman works dry flies over cutthroat trout in border eddies of big river tumbling through mountain canyon.

chain, now as prey instead of predator.

In the pond's shallows the statuesque heron is enemy, competitor, and friend. As an enemy he devours small bass, he competes with larger bass for minnows of other species, and as a friend he consumes a surplus of rough fish that might form the deadly margin in a time of low water, heat, and dwindling oxygen. The bass itself is a benign cannibal, turning on its own progeny in a regulatory campaign that may halt a disastrous population explosion, an explosion that can occur within a single season and leave thousands of starving and stunted bass where dozens might prosper and grow large. The bluegill that helped to control the pond's bass population may find spawning conditions too nearly ideal and thus become a deadly competitor with bass for food, space, cover, and oxygen. And then the bluegills can overcrowd their own kind and become swarms of dwarfed fish.

The pond must be fertile, but overabundance destroys the balance as surely as scarcity. The pond can become a soup of algae or a thatch of unwanted weeds, neither of which will permit the growth of game fish. The farm pond is hardly a treasure for the polished and sophisticated angler, although he sees there the problems of angling in concentrated form, applicable in varied scale to a thousand other situations where the end result may be steelhead or a sailfish.

The running waters of the earth present a different scene. As water reaches the sea it may undergo a thousand miles of changes from a beginning in glacier, snowbank, spring, or rain. As a glacial water it comes forth milky with the fine-ground sediment of relentless pressures. From spring or snowbank it comes clear, often of almost distilled purity, not yet affected by the thousands of elements that will act upon it before it becomes salt. On the way it will be host to millions of unseen organisms and thousands of fishes, birds, reptiles, and mammals, each of which will make its own use of the stream and contribute to it in its own way, for good or ill.

The beaver alone can be an important influence, building his businesslike catch basins to hold water for larger fish in time of drought, but curbing and slowing other streams until their usefulness for cold-water fishes has ended. Farther downstream the muskrat tunnels the sod banks and makes a haven for resting trout, but when he does his task too well the bank caves in and a stream loses its boundary. It becomes slow and shallow, and its fish disappear. So the sporting fishes are only part of the scheme.

It is time for the fisherman to study not only the wild world, but also the influences of man, for his sport faces destruction in many ways, and the study of fishes must encompass a study of the industries that endanger them. Such a study is a complex one, for, as in the fish's natural world, the factors that may help in moderation can become destructive when present in the extreme. In the timbered hills and mountains the mature forest may strangle a stream, for where the sun never reaches the insect life dies, leaving a sterile watercourse. Where the sun reaches the shallow riffles the insect world thrives beneath the surface, but still the water stays cool in summer as it traverses shady glens and here the trout live in heat of day. Then when the trees are cut the stream warms and the trout cannot live. When the hillsides are bare the snows melt quickly and the water comes down in muddy floods that destroy the bottom homes of a million creatures and erode the natural banks until the stream is a sluiceway carrying water off and leaving tepid pools in a dead stream.

The big rivers are composites of the small streams and are also the avenues of migration. Much of their game-fish traffic is dependent upon the tributaries where large fish spawn and small fish grow. A given species of fish may travel thousands of miles through its life cycle, only to meet an unnatural end if at some point the route of travel is blocked, the food chain broken, or the spawning area damaged.

Migrants must travel the broader valleys where man drives his logs and floats his tons of pulpwood, sometimes in rafts that hide miles of river. In some streams the bark peels off the floating logs and sinks, smothering the fertile bottom and killing the river. Yet these are elementary destructions. Farther down, the river may meet the complex disease of pollution—not always a simple poisoning that can be halted by turning a valve, but sometimes an insidious enrichment that kills the river through overfertilization, a plague of plenty that grows like yeast and takes the river's life. Or the river meets the man-made thermal curse from riverside use which returns the water pure but warmed above the game fish's tolerance.

The fisherman learns that the fishes of the great man-made reservoirs may be different species whose value must be weighed against that of the wild river's original population, and that they exist at the expense of migratory species blocked by concrete walls. Then the estuaries enter the sea, carrying the accumulation of man's sins against the river—the silt of erosion, the pollution from the cities, and artificially generated heat.

However, there are waters where the conservationist is winning his battle for the environment and other waters where the battle has not begun.

When the egret and green heron are guarding the shoreline gap the fisherman knows small bait-fish are entering the lake, for there has been little rain and the water is lowering in the marsh. Where the bait-fish enter he looks for the bass that have come to meet them. In the surf he watches for the glint of gold that means moving channel bass along the flank of a wave, or the funnel of noisy gulls that betrays a school of bait and the striped bass beneath them. At night in the salmon camp he awakens briefly to the roar of drought-breaking rain and knows the freshet will stir the waiting salmon at the river's mouth and there will be new fish in the upstream pools.

A single mayfly bobs unsteadily in the breeze over an eastern trout stream and the fisherman recognizes it as vanguard of the hatch he has waited for and he knows that within the hour the stream's now placid surface will dimple with rising trout. The angler sees the slack, low tide has begun to build with small rivulets on the coastal flat, and he watches for the wake traces of bonefish preparing to leave the green swash channels. He stands in the cold push of a steelhead river and reads the pattern of bubbles and dead leaves to learn that on the bottom of the heavy river there is a break in the flow and there may be a broad fish there, resting before it continues its journey.

It is the study of the sport that means more than the number of fish caught, and it is the knowledge of his surroundings that makes the skilled and happy fisherman. We hope to remind him of the things he sees and feels about his sport and we hope to point out some such things he may have missed. All of this adds to the conclusion that "happiest is the fisherman who counts not his fish."

2. A River Begins:

Steep-sided mountain lakes nourished by melting snow are the uppermost homes of sporting fishes and a source of streams below.

At high altitude the beginnings of a river are cold but already filled with life. At the very source only algae, fungi, protozoa, and bacteria live in the old banks of snow.

Only a little lower down are small, busy, cold-water fishes, making the most of their short growing season and limited food. Their life chain begins in the dingy snowbank above, from which water trickles down rough stone faces; the flow is intermittent, slowing or stopping at night when the melting ceases. In winter there is no flow at all and the surface snow is powdery and white. In summer the snow is stained and rotten, partly darkened by dust blown from the bare ridges of the peaks, partly from algae that can live in snow and tinge it red, orange, or green. Mountaineers often leave brilliant red tracks, their boots compressing the snow with each stride so that the algae-color is concentrated.

Above timberline, where sunlight is plentiful, the algae usually are red; where snow is shaded most of the day they are green. It is the liquid within the snow deposits that fosters growth, for metabolism ceases when water freezes. Hence, it is late spring before microorganisms develop in the high mountains of western America.

The topmost lakes, set among the peaks of the high ranges, draw most of their water from snow run-off and are the uppermost homes of sporting fishes. A mountain lake, like those of lower elevations, begins to die the day it is formed, but its life is generally long because the erosion that will eventually fill it is very slow. Cirques, those small cup-like lakes high in the mountains, form where snow has collected and changed to ice, marking the heads of glaciers. When the glacier begins to melt, a small lake is created. These cirques sometimes occur in a shining sequence of steps, leading to lower altitudes, connected by small streams that fluctuate wildly as warm weather increases snow run-off or as cold weather halts it. The high lakes are most frequently caused by glacial action—some of them scoured out and "destructively formed." Others are the result of glacial obstruction, as when a moraine arrests the flow of water and makes a natural dam. "Kettle" lakes are produced when ice blocks are buried in moraines, then melt to leave water-catching pits.

Glacial lake formation is not confined to the heights, of course; even the Great Lakes were formed from glacial gouging. Earthquakes also have formed high lakes, sometimes damming small streams or even large rivers in a matter of moments. The already famous Quake Lake, northwest of Yellowstone National Park, appeared a few years ago when a great landslide crossed the Madison River, one of the best-known trout streams in the world. At a much lower level, Reelfoot Lake, in Tennessee, was formed by an earthquake as recently as 1811-13. The bed of Crater Lake in Oregon was left by an extinct volcano.

Most high-mountain lakes have steep sides in keeping with their rugged surroundings and their fishes are specialized in conformation to exist in the shallow shelves and great depths.

The golden trout, originally found only in isolated streams and lakes of the Sierra Nevada, appears as a brilliant splash of color in numerous Rocky Mountain lakes and streams today, a gaudy prize gained only after a long climb, for when the golden is introduced to lower levels it hybridizes freely with less exotic species and the magic reds and golds dim and disappear. The original goldens were protected from crossbreeding by impassable falls.

The high-lake fisherman may see the golden as a shadow against deep blue, which turns to show its flashing colors in a deliberate rise to a small insect, often near the edge of the lake's drop-off. Between it and the shore is a sloping bottom of sediment, studded with boulders, and if the lake is below timberline there may be sunken gray hulks of long-dead tree trunks. The water growth is scarce, providing scant cover for the water insects and minute crustaceans that are the golden's diet. An occasional audacious grebe is a competitor,

Preceding pages: Cutthroat trout moves in mountain stream near snowy origin of flowing water, yet has a home in deep, protective pools.

entertaining the observer with jack-in-the-box appearances on the still surface.

Where the cliffs rise steep on the lake's south shore, the sun seldom strikes. There are slow-thawing scabs of dirty snow, and where the bank has crumbled to a natural ramp there are tracks of thirsty mountain sheep and occasional goats. In summer, mule deer eye visitors from among dwarfed pines, both parents and fawns in tawny, warm-weather coats. When fall comes they will be lower down and wearing darker tones.

The fish leave gently fading circles on the surface and search the bottom with tails angled steeply upward, for most such mountain lakes afford limited food and the foraging is almost constant. In the swirling weather patterns of the high country the lake turns from placid blue to ominous purple in minutes as a crashing thunderstorm arrives.

All species of high-mountain trout live much the same way. High western lakes may contain native cutthroats, or implanted eastern brook trout, or rainbows, and high country is a home for the grayling with its trout-like habits. Brown trout prefer warmer waters.

When not connected the high lakes are truly individual, some of them crowded by stunted fish, others containing only a few giants, the population dependent upon the spawning facilities and the degree of cannibalism.

Somewhat lower down are swift streams, some of them leading from lakes, others fed by high-mountain springs in a series of falls. Some high streams flow from small mossy caves where icicles appear like stalactites in chilly weather. In summer, watercress switches in the clear, cold flow, and where a dozen rivulets enter one natural pool there are brook trout. The pool does not freeze; it is only fifty yards from where the water leaves the mountainside, and in summer watercress fills all but a narrow streak of open channel. The competitive brook trout take insects in darting rushes, indistinct streaks against the green watercress and yellowish bottom. When a pair of mallards alights on the pool the fish disappear instantly, only wriggles of the watercress showing where they have gone. In minutes they are back in the pool's center, racing each other for almost invisible midges. Most of the trout are only 6 inches long, but they have learned the ways of their little world. In the West they are adaptable replacements, more favored than the Dolly Varden or the bull trout, which is an original western char.

Their patient enemy, the great blue heron, is hard put to catch a trout off guard. He stands rigid for an hour while the fish strike midges just out of his reach. A passing high-country snow shower aids his camouflage, clumping wetly on his back and lowest crook of his neck, but his vigil results only in an unwary frog. As a human fisherman arrives, the heron's widespread wings and irritable croak instantly halt all trout activity. But these fish are susceptible to almost any small fly if they can be approached quietly, a difficult task where nothing diffuses the intruder's silhouette, where a footstep may vibrate along a rod of bank, and where the very smallness of the stream makes a close approach mandatory.

Two thousand miles away the same kind of fish live in a stream about the same size but vastly different in appearance. The New England brook is hemmed and roofed by willows and begins at a much lower altitude. Here the brook trout is a native and its chill habitat is shared by only a few small rough fish and no other trout species at all. Most of the brook flows at modest speed down from wooded mountains, and it winds against willow and alder roots. The fisherman wades it in a stooped position, seeking a spot unobstructed enough to present his fly or bait. Here most of the open areas are shallow and fishless. The trout feed perversely in narrow runs where a few streamers of dead grass cling to willow stems and make additional cover along slightly undercut banks. There are sandy bars with swirls of current around their ends, and trout rest there in the willow shade.

1

2

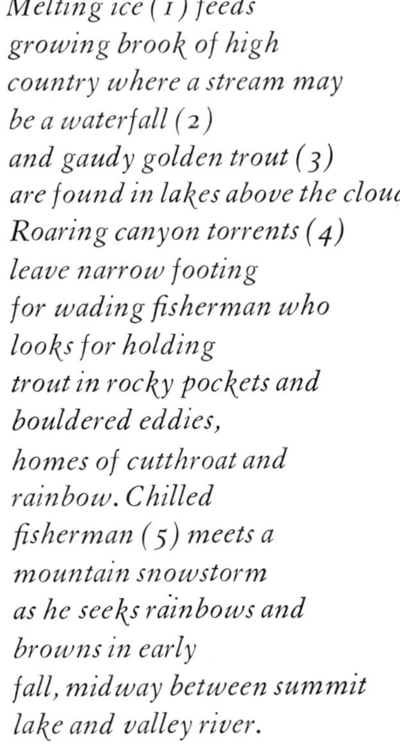
Melting ice (1) feeds growing brook of high country where a stream may be a waterfall (2) and gaudy golden trout (3) are found in lakes above the clouds. Roaring canyon torrents (4) leave narrow footing for wading fisherman who looks for holding trout in rocky pockets and bouldered eddies, homes of cutthroat and rainbow. Chilled fisherman (5) meets a mountain snowstorm as he seeks rainbows and browns in early fall, midway between summit lake and valley river.

3

4

The eastern brook trout lives in ponds as well as in streams and delights in cold, mucky bottoms which—in Maine—it shares with moose. In summer a moose feeds in deep ponds with his head submerged and a dark cloud of black flies attends him, hovering, even when the great beast submerges completely.

In late summer the small Maine brookies often rise at dusk to hatches of mosquitoes and other small insects, making a raindrop patttern on a shallow pond formed by an ancient dam; the fisherman's canoe barely skims the tops of water growth as he finds them thick in the shallows. They have spent the heat of the day in deeper water, but now forage in areas only a few inches deep, moving a little away from the gliding canoe and returning to the surface almost immediately to take an imitation mosquito with abandon.

Brook trout, the original wild trout of the East, are found from northern Canada (where they are often called "speckled trout") to the hill creeks of northern Georgia, and although the smaller ones are not considered difficult quarry for the angler once he has stalked them, the species generally requires habitat difficult to provide in thickly settled country. Water warmer than 75 degrees is commonly fatal to brook trout, and as streams have eroded as a result of lumbering and farming along their route they have slowed and widened. More exposure to direct sunlight has warmed the waters until the brown trout takes over, leaving the brookie only his spring-fed brook, his backwoods lake, and some cold coastal waters.

The brookie, like the lake trout, is a char with a smaller complement of teeth on its upper jaw as compared to true trouts. It is a fall spawner, moving upward to colder gravels as October approaches. Lake residents will seek feeder streams, but where they are lacking the lake fish will often spawn successfully over bottom debris, eventually overpopulating a lake until flashing swarms of stunted fish are competing wildly for what food is left. In other areas less ideal spawning conditions may result in an opposite condition: only a few very large fish.

The fish of the smaller brooks tend to be small. Sea-run brook trout may run to several pounds, but the largest of all brookies are found in large lakes and big northern rivers—and are usually fished for with metal lures. Although it has a reputation for preferring sunken food, the brook trout rises willingly to floating insects when they are plentiful. As with other trout the largest specimens turn more to bait-fish as a staple diet.

The brook trout, driven from its ideal homes by warm water, pollution, crowds of fishermen,

Winter is not yet gone in high country when horsemen travel narrow trails and wind-cleaned ridges to approach mountain lakes at ice-out, when trout begin brief period of surface feeding. Near timberline ambitious angler (left) tours a small lake in inflated boat he carried along rough trails, through conifer forests, and past more accessible fishing waters.

Beaver ponds (1) are small communities of life, changing with the years, and brook trout must be approached from below dam. Brookies (2) are caught from snowbanks. Dolly Varden (3) is pirate of chilly trout waters where great blue heron (4) fishes silently and moose (6) grazes on shallow bottom, feeling for submerged growth that also attracts mallard (5), summer resident of mountain valleys and high marshes.

1

2

3

4

5

6

and the more adaptable browns and rainbows, has, nevertheless, traveled far to be stocked in cold mountain lakes and streams in South America and Europe, as well as in America's western mountains, strongholds where it is unchallenged. In many locations man-built dams, usually a curse of trout propagation, have actually fostered a divided habitat where brook trout live in the cool upper stretches, protected from the brown or rainbow trout living below the barriers.

In much of its range the brook trout lives among the works of that persistent engineer, the beaver, which sometimes aids the trout and sometimes brings about its destruction. A stream prefers its own course, its meanderings determined by the easiest gradients, and even over smoothly sloping terrain a stream winds in geometric regularity. It is these meanders that, for better or worse, the back-country beaver changes. In a brushy Michigan stream, already near the upper limits of a brook trout's usable water temperature, a beaver family stops the flow and forms a pond that spreads wide and catches the sun. As the pond ages it is likely to fill rapidly, for the beaver's impoundment may be subject to immediate siltation. In months or years it may be only inches deep, floored by several feet of decayed matter and mud—and without a trout.

Where summer temperatures are lower in the Rockies, a beaver pond may be a prime objective for the fisherman who knows it can be a holding spot for brook trout. He approaches it cautiously from downstream, addressed coarsely by magpies, and if he is overly attentive to his approach he will not see the coyote that perks its ears beside a nearby rock outcropping, watches him intently, and then drifts into the sage, its route marked only by a mildly disturbed meadowlark that rises briefly and alights again.

Below the beaver dam the creek is very narrow and cut deeply, in places deeper than its two-foot width. There are trout to be caught in the creek, quick strikers ready for terrestrial insects that drop helplessly from the overhanging grass. In sections bordered by sedgy seeps they may find an occasional frog or small crayfish. Days of high wind bring a variety of scrambling land residents to the narrow surface.

But if the fisherman is intent upon the beaver dam above him, he hardly notices the small, darting forms of trout that flee his shadow as he goes upstream. One larger trout of almost two pounds has foraged a long way from its favorite undercut and because of a crook in the channel sees the angler only as he appears almost immediately above it. Its escape throws a little spurt of water and it squirts downstream, running shallow in plain sight, caution abandoned and leaving a boiling wake.

It is an old pond, already half-filled with silt, and there is a thick growth of willows around its shallow end, opposite the dam. Below where the seemingly haphazard logs have made an efficient barricade there is a mucky area where the brisk creek seeps before becoming a faster current again. Braced awkwardly on a log and half-hidden from the pond's surface the fisherman surveys the entire pond and finds it a typical beaver design. There is no surface movement near the dam itself, but the trout are busy only a cast away, where the stream enters the pond forming a small delta of silt and decaying vegetable matter. The trout are active there, dimpling constantly for small midges or near-surface nymphs. Now and then a larger fly drifts down on the slowing current and a small trout will show most of its length as it lunges at the insect.

The fisherman casts a small dry fly almost across the pond, careful to reach only the nearer fish and hoping not to alarm those farther up the little delta. The trout takes with a chug and is brought across the pond without ceremony. The brookie does not jump deliberately when hooked, although occasionally it may swim into the air in its effort to escape. The fish is cold to the angler's hand, more slippery than the true trouts, for it has

With high dorsal fin
like a gleaming, iridescent flag,
grayling lives only
in cool, clean waters and takes
fly with a shining rush.

even smaller scales. Its white-bordered fins, vermiculated back, orange sides, and bright spots are almost gaudy. Only the golden trout competes with it in brilliance.

As the trout strikes and is hauled from its feeding station, its neighbors disappear in quick swirls and puffs of bottom mud. Some of them hurry to deeper water. Most of those upstream from the strike simply drop abruptly to the bottom and vanish. Within three minutes, however, there are feeding dimples again, most of them above where the first fish was taken, and the angler measures his line once more.

The Arctic grayling is almost a novelty fish in the northwestern part of the contiguous states. It lives in the high, cold waters over much of Canada and Alaska, a dainty feeder of transparent brooks and seen as a school of shadows in deep lakes where food is too scarce for most of the grosser fish. The grayling is found at altitudes and temperatures similar to those of the brook trout. Although the record fish is a five-pound behemoth from Great Slave Lake, most anglers seldom see one over a pound.

Hurrying travelers pass miles of grayling water in search of larger species, and many a fisherman from the "lower states" has fished Alaska and returned without seeing a grayling, for long travel means big fish to most anglers.

In British Columbia the Pine River is near the frontier, running through timbered valleys, followed much of the way by a main highway and a railway. It has very deep pools and very shallow riffles, and the broad gravel bars have multicolored stones, mixed by centuries of mountain freshets. There are black-bear tracks on the patches of damp sand and one grizzly print, deeper and much larger. Only the brown coastal giants are larger than the denizens of Pine River.

It is late summer and the river is low, but there are smashed log and brush jams left from the spring run-off. One such heap is strewn by the current on a bend of the river, lodged haphazardly

1

New England streams (1) can be made of pools and falls. Brook trout (2), fight ended, swings in swift current. Insect forms (3) are staple of trout; coyote (4) is western shoreline hunter. Hooked grayling drives downward after strike, carrying fly that betrayed him (5) and spreading his giant dorsal fin in alarm.

2

3

4

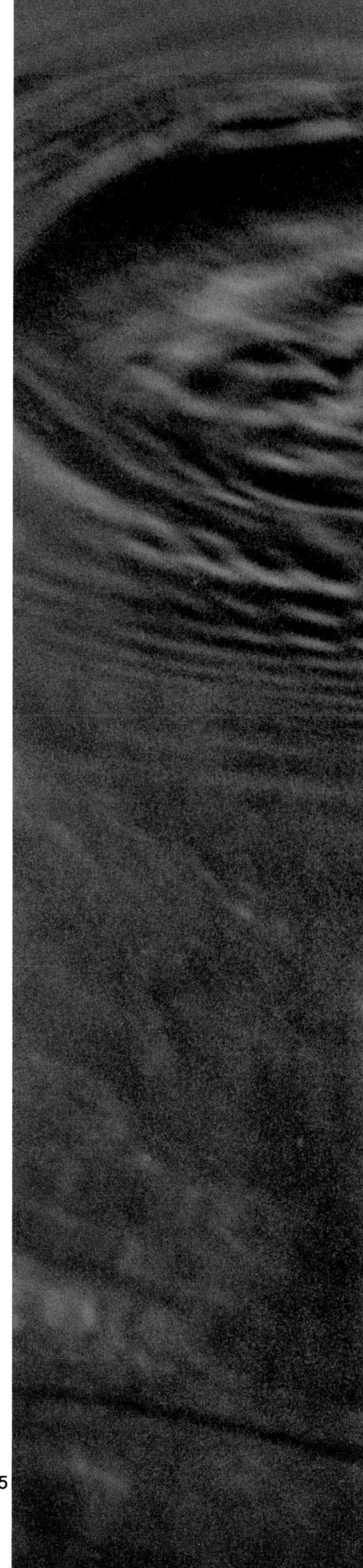
5

In western mountain country bull elk watches intent fisherman where grassy meadows are traced by clear trout streams.

on the deeper shore so that the river is narrowed. Where ragged log ends divide the water there are small eddies and a little added depth due to the gouging of the diverted current. Most of the bottom is seen as yellowish gravel, distorted by wrinkles of the current, but where the stream deepens next to the log heap the color changes abruptly to blue. Grayling, more than a dozen of them, lie in the shallow part, their gentle fin motions mingling with the current's boiling so that they are invisible except to a very careful observer, and then seen only intermittently. They are on the bottom, each of them shielded from the full current by irregularities of the stone and gravel. The insects they take occasionally are invisible from above, but the fisherman locates them by a sucking rise, and after he has watched several such strikes he catches a glimpse of light through a great flowing dorsal fin, an iridescent banner, fully displayed for an instant as a fish turns, and he has identified the risers. At other times he might have taken whitefish for grayling. His first cast brings a response, a gentle splash near his fly, but he feels nothing as the fish follows it downstream, for the grayling has great curiosity, examining a variety of floating objects with care, even when it takes none of them.

On another cast the angler is sure that he has a strike, but he strikes back too quickly. The grayling often turns slowly as it takes. When he finally catches two of the fish the others disappear. Five minutes later they are rising regularly again, fifty feet downstream, but the fisherman has gone the other way to look for a new school.

Commonly associated with high creeks and small ponds, the grayling also lives in great lakes and giant rivers if their waters are cold and clear enough. The Teslin River of the Yukon Territory fulfills the grayling's requirements, flowing from big Teslin Lake through big-game country, followed by trappers and prospectors. It is large enough to offer a variety of fish. In early summer the Lake Teslin trout are near the surface, but by late summer they have gone deep and are difficult to attract. In some of the sluggish eddies of the river are inconnu, or sheefish, a northerner that migrates long distances in fresh water, a favored food fish of Eskimos and Indians. And farther on, in the weedy sloughs of the backwaters, slow swells mark the evening search for food of great northern pike. But the grayling has its special places, too.

The long, high-bowed river guide-boat is beached where a gravel bar runs far out and downstream, piercing the deep current and turning a bit of it into a gurgling ripple at the bar's tip, a strip of broken water more than forty feet long, streaming down over a shallow ridge of built-up gravel. The grayling are bunched there. They follow insects, taking them in rolling turns. The delayed rise comes all the way from the bottom, which is typical of the species. When dry artificial flies are presented from above and drifted down the rippling run, the fish follow them and sometimes attack long after the fly is dragging. As the sun warms the gliding main river there is an occasional rise in deep smooth water and it becomes time to fish there. The rising grayling comes at an uptilted attitude, seeming to grow as it nears the fly. Sometimes it breaks the water from its momentum, hooked, coming down and twisting wildly.

The slower risers often turn as they come, riding down the current in more typical grayling fashion, their small mouths inches from the fly, deciding deliberately whether to take it or not. When the sun goes below a timbered ridge the grayling disappear and the swift surface is flat except for the gentle wrinkles of the current.

Residents of the small streams that begin our rivers have a tenuous existence, confined for life to a ribbon of water that is acutely vulnerable to the whims of man and nature. Some such brooks can be destroyed by a single beaver in a single night, or permanently altered by a spring freshet that forms in hours or minutes. Drought may leave dusty rocks and stagnant pools where a lively creek and its occupants have thrived for years. The friendly murmur of the smallest trout stream

Gentle, wooded river (opposite) swings in easy curves to form shady runs and bright riffles. Long, stiff hackle (1) supports small dry fly. Rising fish (2) leaves silent rings as angler seeks the proper pattern. Brilliant cutthroat (3) takes a tiny fly in fertile valley stream of lush submerged growth. Long-abandoned stonefly shucks (4) cling to streamside branches.

1

2

3

4

 is less reliable than the crash of heavier waters.

The most obvious enemies of little fish in very small streams are the winged predators: the herons and kingfishers, and even the little water ouzel, a gray wren-like swimmer which busily patrols the stream edges, usually at high altitude; but none of these act as more than population balances. Along normally flowing wild streams the chief fish diet of such birds is made up of nongame species, especially the sluggish surface feeders, although in the unnatural circumstances of hatchery confinement it is necessary to control predatory birds which can be deadly to small trout in close quarters. When drought strikes the small stream, game fish are exposed in crowded areas but are likely to perish from other causes if not thinned by birds. Even in the smallest creek, cannibalism is a factor in the survival of fry, yet it is a factor of nature and seldom needs the interference of man.

The well-populated trout stream, regardless of its location, must have its quota of sun, shade, depth, and shallows, even if on a miniature scale. A small and completely unshaded stream is at the mercy of a summer sun that can drive temperatures to the danger level within hours if its work is not tempered by cold springs. Conversely, the brook roofed and walled by native forest and sealed from the sun becomes nearly lifeless, for the trout's food depends partly on sunlight.

Ideally, the trout requires depth and shade for concealment and resting, but it is in the sun-nurtured riffles and shallow runs that insect life, the foundation of trout life, abounds. Most of the sustaining trout stream organisms are the various stages of mayflies, stoneflies, dobsonflies, caddisflies, and two-winged flies, all of which depend upon current, bottom, and air for their existence.

Most often seen of the small trout stream's inhabitants are those with strong locomotive powers of their own, such as the trout themselves, rough fishes, the crayfish, scuds, and nymphs that move rapidly above the bottom with a variety of propulsion methods. Some insects, designed as flattened shapes to offer less resistance to the current's power, are mobile, yet can cling with suction cups or sticky substances, and some forms can hold a position against the battering of waterfalls. A few such mobile clingers move with the aid of muscle-driven pistons. The slow creepers include some small snails, water pennies, flatworms, and caddisfly larvae. The caddisfly-larvae cases are homes, camouflage, armor, and even ballast in some forms, and are made sometimes of wood splinters, often of sand and stones. A neat case of fine sand may be attached to a pebble to hold the occupant against the current. Into most of these cases the growing larvae can retreat in turtle fashion. The trout may swallow case and all. In a larval stage some caddisflies spread nets to capture minute water animals and build a pebble shelter into which they can retreat from danger.

There are many organisms with permanent attachments, like the mosses, river weeds, and the streaming filamentous algae, and there are little animals that live in the moss blankets or among the algae filaments. Some of them are too tiny to feed trout in themselves, but they are a fragile beginning of the food chain. Some of the nymphs are burrowers and a few of the insects important in the trout's diet are predators as well as prey. The dragonfly, taken by the larger trout, is itself a consumer of very small fish.

Trout food is most plentiful, and most strenuously pursued, in the sun-sparkled riffles of the stream. This is its most stable environment, for the bottoms of the deep, slow pools are more likely to be formed of easily moved materials, bottoms that can be hurled downstream by freshets, ripped out by flood-driven timbers, or destroyed by grinding ice; the riffles are less precarious because they are founded on larger stones that may have withstood centuries of ice-outs and cloudbursts. The principles of stream formation are the same whether observed in the ladder-like little cascades of the High Sierras or in the silt-laden rivers of the plains —warmer waters with different fishes, though with the same principles of life and movement.

In dense and unbroken forest the wilderness stream may have scant trout life, yet most such primeval habitat has its open stretches where sun strikes much of the day, and the riffle community thrives while the larger trout lie almost motionless in deep pools or beneath undercut banks, unafraid of any underwater hazard and awaiting evening for a venture into shallower and more productive water.

It is the varied features of its meanders that make the productive trout stream; straight current loses much of its living community. When channels are straightened for agricultural efficiency stream life is temporarily destroyed by the excavation and the trout stream becomes a canal to which life returns slowly. If banks retain their firmness and some shade is left, nature promptly begins renovation through flood and ice, although it may be a task of many years.

With removal of forests, flood dangers increase, both because roots hold soil that could otherwise be eroded, and because shade delays snow melting. A few hours of warm sun on treeless hills can change a heavy snowpack into a dirty torrent. Snow above timberline can be a hazard as well, but the altitude moderates the heat and runoff is less likely to be sudden. Most of our higher streams are threatened more by lumbering and grazing than by cultivation. As trees are cut away, banks may be held by faster-growing shrubs. If these do not appear or are cut back by wild or domestic browsers, only sod remains to retain the earthen banks, and that may be grazed away or crumble through current undercutting. Inevitably, the result is a widening, slowing, and shallowing stream. At the lower altitudes or in the warmer climates the water may become too warm to accommodate any cold-water fishes. Where the atmosphere is dry, evaporation has a cooling effect; where it is humid a stream warms more quickly.

An erratic course is nature's system of stream engineering, and management studies of moderately high creeks show that fish populations are concentrated in the erratic section of short turns and much broken water. In a mountain valley the river changes its position constantly, the outer bank of each bend continually being eroded, and the deposits made in the form of bars upon the inner bend. Usually it is a flood that begins a completely new course, cutting across meanders to leave islands, dry channels, and sloughs as high water subsides. But such procedure occurs normally in only small sections of the stream at any one time and the river never straightens.

From the peaks the stream comes in crooked trickles to gather in pools and falls, to run smoothly across mountain meadows where the course is noticeably different from last year's, and to compress in a roaring gout through a rock canyon where course changes are measured in thousands of years. Beneath a falls there is a blue pool, lined with gravel to a shallow tail where current gathers for another steep descent. In the deep hole is a big native cutthroat trout that avoids the direct sun but glides to the shallow end only ten feet away when evening shadows arrive suddenly. A marmot moves from the boulder where he has sunned during midday and is roundly insulted by an ill-natured pine squirrel in a stunted tree. Most of the marmot's life is spent in hibernation and his summer enjoyment of the canyon sun is brief.

Farther down the valley where the creek is wider the small rainbows have fed much of the day in a noisy riffle. When dusk begins, a bulky shadow slides from a deep undercut and the lesser fish make room for it in their aerated shallows. A thousand miles to the north the fly hatch has stopped and the grayling have disappeared from their riffle in a Yukon creek. It is moonlight in Vermont and a big squaretail leaves a silent wake in a wilderness pond.

Below the small streams the brooks become rivers and broaden in wide valleys. Their fishes are different, but they live with similar friends and enemies.

3.
Valley Streams:
Broader now and slower, the rivers swell with the tribute of spring creeks, where lie those connoisseurs of insects, the rainbows and the browns.

The river has traveled a hundred miles and it is going slower now. The fisherman can see its sources on very clear days, but even then the white peaks have a blue cast from the intervening haze, and much of the view is blocked by lesser mountains darkened by timber. In the foreground are foothills where the conifers are irregular dark patches with lighter areas of green aspen, and the small tributaries show as willow streaks that seam the narrow canyons, adding their hundreds of tinkling flows to larger brooks that feed the river. It still booms in occasional steep and rocky places but spreads more quietly into the valley.

The fertile valley land supports livestock, grain, and hay. In winter the sheep and cattle that have shared the summer's high pasture with mule deer and elk, and occasionally with bighorn sheep and mountain goats, come down to the valley where the snows are less insistent and where native grass is supplemented by alfalfa and timothy. The valley is threaded by roads and even a superhighway; it is a developed agricultural community although bordering primitive country. The speeding tourist who passes the ranch houses will seldom see the mule deer that feed on the foothills at dusk. He will almost never see the whitetail deer that live in the river bottoms.

In this valley is a special kind of trout stream, unique in many ways, but offering the attractions that draw master anglers to the limestone streams of the East, the teeming chalk streams of Britain, and the nurtured waters of continental Europe. Here are the perceptive trouts, the difficult currents, the verdant growths, and the delicate insects that have challenged the studious fisherman for centuries. In the West such water is simply a "spring creek." There are dozens of them. Some are still undiscovered for what they are and others have been dammed, destroyed, or otherwise diverted from their destinies as proving waters for angling's elite. Many flyfishermen have given up financial success to live by such streams.

The springs come forth in some spots as muddy seeps among sedge that continues to be green after other grass turns in the fall, producing rivulets that join the trickle. There are other springs, unseen in the stream's bottom, and there are springs that pour white from rocky banks. The tempering influence of springs encourages heavy water growth, but during the winter months most of the vegetation will disappear. There will be only a remaining fringe of green near the actual spring outlets. In summer the creek will be deeper than in winter, for plant growth has a damming influence.

Only a mile of the creek is a testing ground of the true angler, with the proper insects and with trout that may grow to considerable size still preferring insects to darting clumps of bait-fish. Insect bodies are filled with fats the trout desires, and are far more nutritious than an equal weight of small fish. The spring creek itself is only a long cast across. The water is very clear, with shoals of green showing on its surface and avenues of current curving about the low plant clumps. Nearly all of the creek is less than three feet deep and the emerging water that forms the stream is a little warmer than 50 degrees, cool enough to be within the trout's favorite temperature range, and warm enough to favor the mayflies that help to make the creek a compact and self-reliant community of trout life. Another factor bears strongly on the stream's population: It has an even flow, regulated by the springs and only slightly affected by its minimal surface drainage. In Britain the chalk streams have that same characteristic, rain water being absorbed quickly into spongy soil which feeds it into the stream evenly. There are no muddy freshets.

It is the difficulty, delicacy, and complexity of such fishing that obsesses the expert, but it is the predictability of the trout's feeding habits that adds to the stream's attraction, for the fisherman can see the fish feed and knows they can be caught if his approach is carefully correct. His failures can hardly be attributed to bad luck.

In such waters the insects are mainly prod-

Preceding pages: Big rainbow, brilliant fighter and most adaptable trout of all, nears the end of typically stubborn battle.

ucts of the stream itself, beginning as eggs on the surface or in the depths, living as nymphs beneath the surface, and emerging as true flies whose airborne existence lasts only a matter of hours. Throughout this cycle the insects furnish the bulk of the trout's diet, and in such a stream the terrestrial insects of smaller brooks have little importance. A swimming grasshopper will be ignored while fish are rising to miniature mayflies.

Whether he uses an underwater nymph as the predictable mayfly emergence begins, or casts a dry fly to imitate the mature insect, the fisherman's approach involves a delicate interrelation of method and equipment in which each element is vital.

First he must locate his fish—and the master prefers to fish for the individual, not because this is easier or necessarily more productive, but because it leaves little to chance. It is a test of his expertise, beginning with study of the fish and its lie and ending with the delicate business of landing a trout on a hairline leader despite the hazards of underwater vegetation.

There are times when a fish actually can be seen before it rises, holding easily in curling current. The trout may be sharply outlined against a sand bottom, a bottom shaped in sweeping curves by ceaseless water movement. Or the fish may be an indistinct shadow with traces of color over a clear-washed rocky stretch, resting where bottom friction slows the stream. Most obviously it stands out against the bright green of submerged plants, appearing brown or golden. A rainbow's pink side seldom shows against gravel but is seen plainly against green. Busy suckers, deliberate in their motions, appear relatively awkward and are of a lighter tone than the trout.

A flicker of white may be the inside edge of the trout's jaw as it feeds or breathes, even when the rest of the fish is invisible. A fish may be located by the small bubbles sent up as it works the bottom for nymphs, but usually it is the fish's feeding rise that gives it away, and study of the rise is a science in itself, the surface disturbances being allocated to definite classifications of purpose and execution.

Even when its target is the true dry fly, either in the emergent dun stage or in the final spinner phase, the trout's rise takes several forms which are important to the angler. The matter is made more complex by the variation in nymph forms and behavior.

A mayfly nymph, ready to become a true fly, comes upward toward the light, almost helpless in the weaving current, and involved in the business of emerging from the drab husk it has occupied for months. The trout takes it inches below the surface, perhaps showing tail and dorsal fin lazily, or at least making a broad swirl that can be falsely interpreted as surface feeding.

For the small, free-floating mayfly, the trout simply allows the surface flow to go through its open mouth while the insect is adroitly separated from the water and goes down the throat. Large trout may suck the fly noisily or make loud gurgles at the take, sounds easily separated from the splashy strikes of juvenile upstarts small enough to consider so tiny a fly worthy of an all-out attack. The feeding plop of larger fish is caused by the roof of the mouth as it is brought down on the surface in taking the fly. That sound must be distinguished from tail splashes made by nymph feeders.

The mayflies of our spring creek are small but of several varieties, the smallest ones bringing rises that are hardly more than dimples, a simple matter of the fish barely breaking the tension of the surface film to take a few small insects with as little exertion as possible. A placid dimple, spreading for a few inches before disappearing on a glassy pool, can mark a large trout.

There is a prolonged rise, really a tour of the surface, in which a fish makes a sustained wake as it moves about to take several flies before returning to its lie. A fish may move energetically about the bottom, searching for nymphs, and releasing a chain of bubbles. That can hardly be termed a rise although it is a subtle indication of a feeding

1

2

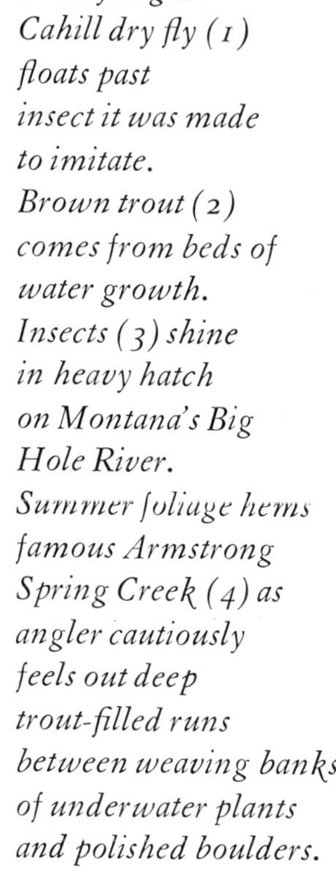

Dainty Light Cahill dry fly (1) floats past insect it was made to imitate. Brown trout (2) comes from beds of water growth. Insects (3) shine in heavy hatch on Montana's Big Hole River. Summer foliage hems famous Armstrong Spring Creek (4) as angler cautiously feels out deep trout-filled runs between weaving banks of underwater plants and polished boulders.

3

4

trout, but a muskrat or a sucker can cause bubbles, too. Trout bubbles are usually few and intermittent. There are bulging rises in which the fish takes something beneath the surface but almost breaks water, forming a momentary mound that sends out telltale waves. Occasionally the flies dancing above the waters of our spring creek may attract a leaping rise, but it is almost always a smaller fish. For the most part the small flies of our creek are the objectives of a gentle approach by both fish and fisherman, and the fishing is thus more difficult and more attractive to the expert than when cloudy hatches of huge insects are being charged recklessly by trout of other waters.

The studious angler observes the hatch with care, and he watches to learn which flies are preferred if more than one variety are showing. On a given day a little gray fly may receive all the attention, while the yellowish insect that was eagerly gulped yesterday is ignored. The trout establishes a feeding pattern and can be single-minded in his foraging. The angler's art may be challenged by too heavy a hatch when his fly is only one of a veritable carpet of insects, his imitation almost impossible to discern among live flies —a simple case of too many choices for the temporarily overfed trout. Perhaps in this unusual case the angler will offer a "stranger," a fly just a bit larger than the hatch or of a slightly different color, near to the hatch yet different enough to attract special attention.

On our spring creek the midday hatch is most reliable (in other waters it may be the evening or morning rise the angler waits for). In some streams the emergence of mayflies is predicted by a concentration of birds, especially agile citizens such as swallows which take the insects in mid-air. On some streams with late evening hatches, bats take up the patrol when the birds have left.

The veteran dry-fly angler on our creek seldom casts until he sees rising fish and then he chooses his first station with care. He is concerned both with where the fish holds in its feeding lie and where it is actually taking flies, usually an area a little upstream. He may study his fish for some time, not only to learn the exact spot where he expects his fly to be taken, but to discover the pattern of the trout's feeding, even the rhythm with which it surfaces and sinks when the hatch is heavy. It is not necessary that he actually see the fish itself as long as he can read the bulges, swirls, or dimples, and envisage the underwater scene, perhaps well enough to guess the exact spot where the fish is lying between its rises.

The fish sees above the surface only through a "window" of area directly above him, an area that increases with the fish's depth. Beyond the perimeter of its window the fish sees the surface only as a mirror, reflecting objects from below. A mayfly alighting on the surface outside the cone of vision can be marked only by the glistening flash of its tiny intrusions on the surface film. The fish's excellent vision, which is known to interpret colors invisible to humans at the ultraviolet end of the spectrum, means very little when it focuses upon a floating object outside its window. Objects beneath the surface can be studied minutely but floating flies are poorly seen, even in the area of clearest vision.

The fisherman must study the pattern of his own effort, the vagaries of the current which may cause his fly to drag instead of floating naturally, the wind that will influence his cast, and the position he must take to show only the fly and no gleaming leader, slashing line, or waving arm as the fish inspects his counterfeit. So he takes his position by wading gingerly, spending careful minutes reaching his casting station, near enough to the fish's feeding station that his cast will be accurate, yet far enough that the fly can alight with the tiny surface tick of a true insect. His high false casting is done in another direction, and then the fly is presented upstream, possibly in a deliberate curve or with a slightly slack line, just enough above the feeding point that it will appear in the trout's cone of vision in a natural float, preceding

Handsome brown trout
from Oregon's Deschutes River.
Bottom: Wearied by tug of
leader, brown is led
into shoreline shallows.

1

Above: Dry fly is inspected over lush growth. Killdeer (1) wades in clear shallows. Busy muskrat (2) ignores intruder. Brown trout (3) holds shadowed feeding station. As river widens, angler (4) gathers line for long cast to midstream boulders. Wilson's snipe (5) probes for food in shallow backwater.

2

3

4

5

a leader made up of twelve feet of tapered monofilament tipped with a wisp of material testing less than two pounds. The tiny fly slips down beside two or three naturals, pleasing the caster when it neither lags nor gains on its fellow travelers. It matches them well in color and size, sitting high on dainty feet of hackle, supported by surface film, a tough carpet for such delicate objects.

If the fish does not take, the fly goes across its feeding plot, then over the fish itself, and begins to trace a little telltale groove of drag in the glassy surface. The fisherman allows it to go well downstream, an inanimate something being pulled by a leader, and then picks it up for another cast, drying it with brisk flicks of the wrist. His victory comes if the fish takes the imitation the same as it has been taking live mayflies, with no special motion or extra splash; possibly the greatest compliment to his deception would be the trout's seizure of a natural insect in continuation of the same rise after the little fraud is already in its mouth.

Although the browns, rainbows, and cutthroats may have different individual characteristics elsewhere, their feeding habits are almost identical on our spring creek where all take the same food in a type of water that pleases all.

When the surface hatch ends, the curling surface is unbroken by fish movement. Fish or frogs may cause convulsive twitches in the shoreline watercress and a loud splash there may startle the fisherman, but often it is only a muskrat. After his steep dive the muskrat's route is traced by a few surface bubbles, and when he passes the fisherman's waders two feet below the surface his outline is sometimes fringed with smaller bubbles, captured by his thick fur. He swims in flowing motions and under water he has no fear of the angler's feet and legs.

The muskrat, primarily a vegetarian, is a constant resident of the creek and especially in evidence in the fall when the roly-poly individuals sit in furry balls atop midstream clumps of pondweed and nibble as if winter were only hours away. Occasionally a muskrat will be angered by an intruder and make splatting noises with his tail, a small-scale imitation of the thunderous warning sounds of his cousin the beaver. Muskrats eat very little animal food and are neither predators nor competitors of the trout, but their work influences the fish's life. Muskrat tunnels contribute to deep shoreline undercuts, which are good hiding places for trout; however if the digging is overdone the bank may cave in and lead to erosion, an important trout-stream problem. Muskrat thoroughfares along the banks are wet highways of flattened grass.

Above the silent stream are magpies, glossy and vocal, often sitting on matted water growth or moving about the tops of tall cottonwoods that line the creek, flying in slow-winged, up-and-down patterns. In the tangled rosebushes along the shore there is the occasional tuneless cackle of a pheasant, hard to locate precisely. In a miniature cove where the current is very slow a pair of resident mallards gabble softly to each other around mouthfuls of greenery, and tip up or paddle in irregular patterns with their heads submerged. There will be occasional moving patches of pondweed, broken loose and drifting downstream, dislodged by a muskrat or a drinking deer, or possibly coming from a cattle crossing far upstream.

There are cottontail rabbits in the rosebushes and the fisherman has seen a whitetail doe and fawn approach the shore at dusk. He has watched the less cautious mule deer along the stream, deer that live in the foothills a mile away and sometimes stray into the river bottoms. The whitetails are residents there, moving among the rosebush tangle almost as easily as the undulating and unhurried skunks.

Raccoons and Wilson's snipe share a seepy area beneath an old dam that diverts the stream. The raccoons go about their searching hurriedly as if the seep might be turned off at any moment. Killdeers come and go in small, uncertain flights.

In a deep backwater, almost clogged by the trailing green streamers of filamentous algae and

Tall conifers and fallen tree trunks shade sections of Deschutes River, and caster works riffles where trout find summer oxygen.

partly fed by a small boggy spring, there is some trout movement, fish that seem to carry on lives separate from those of the mainstream fish. Although the brisk current runs only a few yards away there seldom are mayflies on the backwater, and the fish that feed there seem to be concerned with other insects they find in the strands of algae. Where the backwater meets the stream there is a busy party of fish that seems to use the fast water for adult flies, and then turns back to its slough when a hatch ends.

But there is little motion on the creek's surface once the fluttering little flies are gone. Now and then a tiny trout flicks a few drops of water. Occasionally there is a V marking a bigger fish's route as it slides across a shallow spot—an indication that the trout are not all asleep or resting—and the unseen underwater life goes on. The brief flurry of surface feeding is but an incident that lasts an hour or two each day, and the thousands of insects that may become flies tomorrow or next year are crawling on the bottom, buried in mud or gravel, or clinging to the underside of stones or to the stems of rooted plants. It is these things the nymph fishermen hopes to duplicate, and since his delicate effort is made beneath the surface, he can watch neither his successes nor his failures.

Dry-fly fishing has a special dramatic appeal, for the whole process can be viewed. Even when there is no strike the angler can judge whether his fly floats properly, matches the hatch, and covers the best water. The nymph fisherman may see no telltale bulge or rise, may never see or hear his strikes, and feels with practiced hand for a fish he only suspects is present. It may be the same trout he or another angler has fished to with a dry fly at another time of day, but now the fish is interested in other things.

The blizzards of flies that sometimes appear as backlighted golden clouds about rivers and brooks may coat the windshields of passing cars, and the motorist wonders why the swarms are always near streams; he seldom realizes that the

3

2

4

Leaping rainbow (1) shatters placid surface of pool. Brown trout (2) is taken on large, bushy dry fly during a stonefly hatch in midsummer. Broken current (3) sweeps against snags and brushy shore to compound caster's problems on swift section of trout water. Brown (4) leaps frantically only a few feet from protection of overhanging bushes along shoreline.

 insects are a part of the river's life, in many cases the dominant factor in the trout's food chain. The nymph is a seldom recognized subsurface phase of an insect, generally a dull, sluggish creature with little similarity to the delicate mayflies that dance over the waters in their mating rites, ride the surface film briefly in dry-winged grace, or swirl in helplessness with high winds.

The amount of underwater life is dramatized when today's thousands of mayflies are known to have been so many nymphs yesterday, and the millions of flies which will emerge in the weeks to come are, even now, living in the stream despite the endless searching of thousands of hungry trout, fish capable of scooping immature nymphs from the bottom or taking them in an easy turn as they rise toward the surface to leave their shucks.

A stream's insect life is greater beneath the surface than above it, and there are nymphs too small to be sought by trout which are, nevertheless, a part of the food chain for larger insects. In Maine, there are few outdoorsmen who know that some of the dark mossy growth on waterfall stones is made up of the nymphal beginnings of the dreaded black fly.

There are more than five hundred species of mayfly, the best known of trout-stream insects, and the life cycle varies greatly among them, but there are special stages important to the angler. Mayfly eggs are laid in the air above the stream, on the surface, or, with some species, beneath it, the adult female penetrating the surface film to labor down a plant stem or other route that enters the water itself. Eggs, free floating, caught in obstructions, or resting on the bottom, hatch to nymphs which grow toward maturity, often doing so in a series of moults as each succeeding shuck becomes too small. From the time the eggs are laid to the moment of emergence may be a few weeks, or as much as three years in some species.

Anyone who would imitate a nymph must know how it moves, whether under its own power or as a victim of the current's whim. There are nymphs with flattened shapes, designed to cling to rocks in sweeping currents. There are nymphs that cling with their legs and catch passing food with raised forelegs, held rigidly like tiny forceps; there are those that move with their own systems of jet propulsion; there are some that spread tiny nets to capture drifting diatoms. All of this is in streams of moderate depth, for the insects are partly land creatures and need sunlight. There is a myriad of sizes and shapes, and to match them the angler must either study live specimens or know from the emergent insects what the appropriate nymph is. Matching in itself is a controversial process and some of the more successful artificial nymphs are simply impressions, exact copies of nothing, vague shapes of hair of nearly the right color, nearly the right size, and nearly the right outline. There have been some masterpieces of duplication, laboriously fashioned from casts of the living creature, that have failed miserably. Many fine anglers, on the other hand, use nearly exact imitations with success.

Those of the impressionistic school will say that a hint of legs, a hint of thorax, and a suggestion of feelers can invoke a strike, while efforts at exact imitation may cause more careful study and a rejection. The trout, they say, is a creature of instinct, hunger, impulse, and no great sagacity. His activities, they say, are triggered in simple ways, and human reactions to a fly are simply human reactions and nothing more, for humans see things differently and try to fit their reactions to a creature far down the scale of life. The same argument—whether an impressionistic offering or an exact imitation is most effective—goes on with regard to other game fish as well.

The fisherman must select the proper runs for his presentation. He knows that his best chances are likely to be where fish have fed actively on emerging flies, and he knows that clean sand makes an unlikely bottom for nymphs. Most of all he must know what sort of action his nymph should

Spinfisherman uses his long casts and gleaming hardware to reach rainbows in wide pools where he wades over slippery stone bottoms.

take, whether moving along the bottom as if under its own power, drifting free, or squirming upward toward the light as if escaping the nymphal shuck to appear as a fly. In strange water he tries all of these manipulations, but on a familiar stream he knows his way and the polished nymph angler is likely to be the most successful trout fisherman of all.

It is true that the nymph is fished wet but its master will tell you that it is not a "wet fly." The difference is in the subject represented and the presentation, and the three classes of artificial flies—dry, wet, and nymph—endeavor to span the life of the insect.

The typical species of mayfly nymph leaves its underwater home after a growing period, then works its way upward to the surface where it sheds its nymphal husk, emerges as a true fly, and dries its wings for flight.

In that first stage as a fly it is a dun, or subimago, and when its wings are dried it goes to a perch on a streamside bush or tree to undergo another transformation, shedding one more shuck to become an adult. Then as an imago, or spinner, the fly mates in reckless maneuvers over the water, and both male and female die soon after the fertilized eggs are deposited. The dying fly, its wings useless and no longer erect, floats temporarily on the surface and is imitated by a spent-wing artificial. Then when drowned by broken current or sucked down by an eddy it is truly imitated by a wet fly.

The complete fisherman may use imitations of all of these stages, but the nymph is frequently recognized as the most advanced tool of all, and Edward R. Hewitt, fly-fishing immortal, has said that the casual angler can have little hope of doing better with his nymphs than he can with his other flies. The dry fly must move in a natural drift. The streamer, which imitates a small fish rather than a fly, can make all the moves of a self-propelled minnow. The nymph may move in several ways as a crawler, swimmer, or drifter. The dry fly strike is plainly seen, the streamer or wet fly

1

2

3

4

His fish beaten but unnetted, fisherman (1) splashes toward landing spot. Red variant (2) barely creases surface film. Undercut grassy banks (3) and watercress edges (4) are trout sanctuaries. Right: Rainbow (left), brown trout share valley waters.

strike is urgently felt; the take of the nymph is likely to be almost an abstraction, a hesitation in the drift, a tick that resembles a thousand contacts the fly makes with the bottom or with vegetation. The angler's reaction is a specially developed sense and he will never know how many strikes he has failed to notice at all. It is said that most nymph strikes go unnoticed but in this case the word strike is poorly chosen for there is seldom haste or violence in a fish's approach to a nymph.

In a carefully worked single cast the nymph expert can use several approaches. Probably the most delicate maneuver is the free-floating nymph, cast upstream and followed down the flow with the line and leader almost taut, but with the nymph showing no sign of the leader's restraint. The fisherman closely watches his floating line for a sign of a strike, and then visualizes what his fly must be doing, now and then making his own gentle strike to feel for the tug of a trout—and moments later he cannot tell why he set the small hook.

As the nymph comes downstream and passes the fisherman's station it changes from a free-floating lure as it is snubbed by the leader, then swings below the angler, and finally dangles directly downstream. To alter the drift the fisherman may mend the line in a gentle flip of the rod, thus extending the free-drift nymph movements that are often followed in detail by a cautious trout. The fisherman may feed a little line to give the extreme downstream drift a different look, and he may retrieve the fly with gentle twitches, or even quick jerks. Even while the fly is well upstream he may move it toward the surface by lifting his rod tip to mimic the surface rise of the mature nymph in its final underwater movement. All of these manipulations are imitations of specific movements by living insects as carefully observed, and are more easily described than executed, for the result of each move is unseen, although guessed at with increasing accuracy as the angler learns.

In spring-creek fishing the tackle is light, with the fragile leaders demanded by clear water and sophisticated trout; once a fish is hooked it must be played with conscious restraint to the limit of the leader test, a coaxing, guiding procedure to keep the prize from darting into the gently waving clusters of streaming water growth. If it reaches the cover the angler will feel only the blunted tugs of a fish trussed in greenery and he will wade to the spot and cautiously slide his fingers down the thread of tippet through chilly water, hoping to feel the trout's nose at the other end. This is a critical and dainty movement for one who has so nearly won a difficult game, but the trout will be released anyway.

All resident trout of the spring creek feed very much the same. The characteristic cannibalism of large trout is greatly postponed in streams of heavy insect population, for a fish that in other waters would have long since turned to meatier prey continues to live from insects in such streams. There is, of course, a size limit to the regular taker of small flies and nymphs. Even in a stream crowded by insects, fish of more than three pounds seldom take very small floating flies, although much larger ones sometimes do so, great fish that take a tiny thing probably through some faint memory of their youth. It is doubtful that the shred of nourishment can replace the energy burned in the rise, but the fisherman hopes for such performance. There are some anglers who feel that all extremely large trout should be removed by some means, deciding their cannibalism more than offsets their potential to the fisherman, but most anglers prefer to have the monsters present, even though they are unlikely to catch them.

Our spring creek contains mainly brown, rainbow, and cutthroat trout with a few eastern brook trout, and all of these except the native cutthroat have been introduced to the West. In similar eastern streams the newcomers are browns and rainbows; only the cutthroat is missing. In our creek the three main species rise together and their individual characteristics are minimized for the water temperature is satisfactory to all. The rainbow, noted as the greatest leaper of the trouts, jumps little if any more than the brown in our spring creek. The brook trout and the cutthroat are not jumpers, although they may clear the surface occasionally in a dash for freedom.

For the most part, the brown trout, or Loch Leven, is the mainstay of our spring-creek type of angling, and he is a prized introduction, generally accepted as the wariest and most resourceful breed. Although the rainbow is usually credited with more power and agility in fighting the hook, the brown seems wiser and survives in waters where the rainbow fails, even though the rainbow has a slightly better tolerance for warm water.

And when he has survived more pollution, more fishing pressure, and more civilization than the other trouts, the brown's reputation for wariness is enhanced, since only the selected few fish still live and the fisherman must try his skill on them. It is not quite a fair measure but the brown trout undoubtedly has an edge in intelligence and in some cases has taken over from other species, a bitter fact for those loyal to the displaced fish.

The brown trout is native to Europe and Asia but has spread over much of the world as an adaptable and easily managed planter. It was first brought to America in 1883, a fish of less gaudy color than the rainbow but of a muted beauty preferred by some fishermen. Depending on water conditions it varies from a golden brown to a much darker shade and carries small but brilliant red spots. In spawning season the colors brighten, the males showing a great deal of orange that displaces the gray-white of the belly. Older males develop a hooked kype and take on a crocodilian expression, beautiful only to the true lover of the brown.

The brown is a fall or winter spawner and some of the largest fish are caught then, still willing to take dry flies, although most of the bigger ones succumb to large streamers or metal lures, things that would fail miserably in our spring creek. Spawning is preferably done on gravel with shallow redds, and there is often a migration to smaller streams for this purpose. There are other occasions when the fish spawn within the very area they have occupied the rest of the year.

When they are found in the same stream, the brown trout holds in somewhat quieter water than the rainbow, a bit deeper into the quiet eddies and generally farther from the full-bore main current. Although he is not alone there, the brown is a special lover of the gurgling, undercut grassy banks, the weedy sloughs that border the stream, and the fallen trees and aging stumps that cause the busy current to dig pits and grooves, those dark blue holes that break the pattern of rocky or pebbled bottoms.

Most of all, the brown can adapt, the characteristic that has enabled it to spread from Siberia to Argentina, to New Zealand, to the meadow stream in rolling Pennsylvania farmland. But all of our fish in the spring creek are very nearly alike in shape, although they come from different ancestry, and rainbow, brown, and cutthroat live well in a nearly self-sufficient community where water comes in regulated temperature from seeps and rocky springs, forming a long growing season and hosting a world of life beneath a sliding, weaving current of friendly gurgles, going down to the great river only a little distance away.

And as the fish come to the spring creek through preference, most of them descendants of those that have turned from the broad river, so do the fishermen come to such a shrine, speaking eagerly to those of their kind, having less to say to cruder fishermen.

They park their expensive cars and battered pickup trucks at the weathered wooden gate and dismount in their faded jeans and English tweeds, and stand for a moment to watch the placid surface for the beginning of a hatch. They are very different people, even yet, but then they struggle into waders and vests and slip their felted feet gently into the stream, and somehow they all look very much alike.

4.
Big Rivers:
In early summer, tumultuous, swift-running western water descends the slopes, and great trout and salmon rest beside the current.

All winter the northern river has been clear and low, running part of the way under a sheath of ice that breaks and piles in some places but generally covers only the fringe, the sloughs, and the slow-moving side channels. In some places, where the water is friction-slowed over a shallow bottom, there will be streamlined cakes of anchor ice.

The trout of the river and its tributaries have been sluggish during the cold weather, holding near to the bottom and preferring to take easily caught nymphs or sculpins, leaving little surface sign that they are there at all. The winter trout has slowed all of its processes, and even when it takes food its digestive organs are inefficient, for the fish's body chills with the water and waits for a proper operational temperature when growth and vigor will be resumed.

Most of the local summer fishermen have been hunting or fly-tying. Some of the river lovers are far away but will return when summer comes. During the winter there have been a few bait fishermen in parts of the river that are open to angling, and on warmer days there have been occasional flyfishermen working with imitations of the tiny midges that hatch at around 40 degrees or warmer. On some western rivers these midges are known as snowflies (although they may hatch in summer as well as winter), and the drowned adults are sometimes gulped in clumps when washed against driftwood or banks. Some fishermen have used weighted, woolly worm artificials, allowing them to roll with the current on the bottom, resembling large and ungainly nymphs. All year the larger trout have pursued freshwater sculpins, small bottom-living fish that rest under and between stones, and are called bullheads by some fishermen.

Most of the anglers wait for warmer weather and there is a sequence of events, easily forecast by the river watcher, that governs the fishing year.

Sometime in the spring the weather will warm enough to clear ice from the lower river, although higher elevations may still be locked tight. Then comes a period of clear-water fishing which is interrupted by the arrival of muddy torrents, as the mountain snowpack gives way before a warming summer sun.

In some rivers the mud may last until midsummer, or even later, and fishermen must turn to feeder streams which clear more quickly. The big river's entire schedule may be slowed by a thaw-softened landslide in some unseen mountain gorge, crashing into the river with its tons of silt, broken trees, and stones. For days the river may eat at this new and crumbling obstacle, pouring its dirty flood downstream before dismayed fishermen. Eventually the bulk of the mountain snowpack will melt and even the landslide will be dissolved, altering the river's course, but finally allowing the water to run clean.

Sometime in June—an unreliable period of the river's life—the salmon flies will appear, a breed of insects so large as to appear to be a magnification of other hatches, giant flies to match the big rivers, big fish, and strong tackle.

The "salmon fly," widely recognized on western rivers, is really a large stonefly, as much as 2 inches long, which lays its eggs on the surface. Instead of hatching into winged insects on the surface film as mayfly larvae do, the big nymphs crawl into the open air on stones or bushes before their transformation to large, awkward aerialists. When afloat they bob down the swift rivers, their two pairs of wings folded down along their backs, worthy targets for really large trout as either drowned or living insects. The stonefly, unlike the mayfly, must have swiftly moving water, and is found principally in mountain streams.

The hatch begins in the lower reaches, where temperature rises first occur, and "travels" upward toward the mountains. It is when the bulk of the hatch has passed that some master anglers say chances are best, for trout that have gorged themselves on freshly hatched flies have acquired the habit, and once the hatch has thinned they are looking upward for the easy meals they are ac-

Preceding pages: Aerial coho salmon runs the big rivers, travels far to sea, survives in freshwater lakes, and spawns in mountain brooks.

customed to, which have suddenly become scarce.

In late June and early July the salmon flies are on Montana's Madison, somewhere in the Ennis vicinity. The river is wide, swift, and shallow, going down the valley in a visible slant, making wide turns, and with each underwater boulder showing as a foam-trimmed lump. The water is clear but it moves so swiftly that sight of the stone and gravel bottom is distorted, and the rocks are slick with the living slime that means billions of microscopic organisms near one end of the life chain that supports insects and the trout. The largest of the stoneflies is a vegetarian and its nymphs are often found among plant debris, but other stoneflies prey upon small mayfly nymphs.

It is several miles back to the wooded mountains and most of the snow is gone. The foothills and benchland are mostly tanned by summer sun and dry weather now, an occasional bush or small conifer showing black as the Angus cattle seen on some of the slopes. The fisherman may see a group of antelope, but most of the mule deer are on the cool ridges now. A party of gulls rides above a midstream island of rocks, going up and down in the wind that ever seems to blow across the Madison, sometimes tearing splinters of water from the roaring river and causing the angler to crouch and lean into the blast as well as the current and fire his fly in a tight loop, instinctively ducking his head as the big hook goes by.

Something crawls across my neck and I cringe although I know it is only a giant salmon fly engaged in stubborn reconnaissance for nothing in particular. The river's willows are weighted with the flies and the wind strips them loose and strews them on the water. Before me, one of the floating insects disappears in a short-lived swirl, the disturbance erased instantly by the current, and I feel cautiously for a better stance on the rounded stones, shoved by water, although it is only a little more than knee-deep. The powerful rod responds to the heavy line and pushes my fly into the wind, a great fuzzy thing that will float high in almost anything short of a cataract. Made of squirrel hair, feather, and thread, the big fly, jokingly called a "haystack," seems to live atop the foamy flood, turning a little despite the hampering leader. It has gone slightly upstream and will be picked up somewhere below me for another cast.

I cast and then inch forward a foot and try again, and I have watched the speeding current and bobbing fly for so long that when I look away from the river the whole landscape swims. My back aches a little from the rigid bracing against the river.

I throw the fly at a V of bubbles atop an underwater rock and watch it come down over the mottled bottom, over red, golden, yellow, black bottom rocks, and there is some sort of flash beneath the fly, an obscure change of color that somehow does not fit the bottom pattern, so I try to duplicate the drift and a brown shadow appears, shooting up quickly in two feet of water to erase the big fly and show a broad fin and the edge of a wide, translucent tail.

I set the hook violently against six pounds of leader test and the line sings upstream, throwing a little geyser of spray, and the fish leaps, a long, low leap as if it could not go fast enough beneath the water and preferred to swim in air. I back awkwardly toward shore, my fish working in spurts and pauses against the current, then tiring suddenly and sweeping downstream to hold behind rock after rock with angry head-shaking, four pounds of brown trout aided by tons of swift water, and I stumble along the shore, entangled repeatedly in the willow fringe, to arrive breathless at a bit of quiet water against the land, and there I pump and reel until the fish is at my feet—thick-shouldered and broad-sided, and full of salmon flies. I have not noticed the quick cloud that has formed over the Gravelly Range and is now spattering me with cold rain and a little sleet, but I blow on my ragged haystack fly to straighten the hackles, and lean into the wind and current.

In a week the hatch has gone upstream

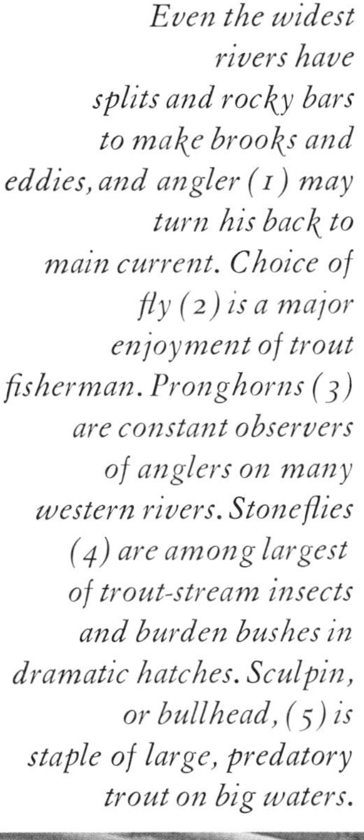

Even the widest rivers have splits and rocky bars to make brooks and eddies, and angler (1) may turn his back to main current. Choice of fly (2) is a major enjoyment of trout fisherman. Pronghorns (3) are constant observers of anglers on many western rivers. Stoneflies (4) are among largest of trout-stream insects and burden bushes in dramatic hatches. Sculpin, or bullhead, (5) is staple of large, predatory trout on big waters.

2

3

4

5

into the mountains, and several weeks later we struggle down the cliffs to the upper Yellowstone River, in Yellowstone National Park, stand on boulders, and cast flies into water that is too swift to wade. It is a hatch of salmon flies, the same kind we met lower down, but now the fish are the Yellowstone cutthroat instead of brown and rainbow trouts. They are olive-sided, with delicate shadings and vivid red slashes at the throat, and they are among the best of table fish, pink-fleshed and firm. A two-pounder is not unusual and we find some of them in the miniature pools of a tiny feeder stream that comes down from the steep forest in a series of falls, and is crosshatched with down timber. We are at the end of the salmon-fly season.

In October, standing in water gradually chilling from the frosty nights of autumn, I fish with other methods for the western trout, but on nearly every willow and on many rough stones are the ghostly shucks of the big nymphs that became stoneflies, now dead for many weeks, and somewhere on the bottom of the rushing river are the beginnings of next year's salmon flies.

Coming from gentle meadow streams, or even from precipitous mountain brooks, a trout fisherman may be awed by big western rivers. The height of the mountain chains produces miles of slopes where rivers still go at trout-stream speeds, even though they are a hundred yards across. In other parts of the country a river of that size would have reached more level ground and would be warm and slow.

So many fine fishermen walk to the brink of a noisy western river, see nothing that matches their experience, and turn away in search of a smaller, more easily read stream, unaware that the same kinds of water can be found in the larger watercourses. Some of the most productive anglers travel the big rivers in boats, doing little of their casting while afloat, but using the craft to travel downstream from one desirable pool to another. There can be miles of classic dry-fly water along the edges of such rivers and in the narrow channels where the river splits, as well as in the very center of the torrent, where some obstruction or particular bottom contour produces a bit of placid flow surrounded by froth and roar.

The rubber boat goes down like a restrained inchworm, flexing over the haystacks in the rapids and sliding over stones in the shallows. The oarsman holds it back against the current to maintain steerage. The johnboat and the McKenzie boat are worked the same way, the heavy McKenzie made for really wild water and carrying a high, sharp stern that can be steered efficiently when held against the current. Canoe and kayak travelers have a completely different system and gain steerageway through their own momentum.

The floating fisherman is almost certain to beach at a spot where a gravel bar cuts nearly across the stream, especially if there is shallow water running over the long obstruction. The depth over the bar may vary from a mere trickle to a foot where a groove breaks through the natural dam. At each spot where a run goes through there is a small stream comparable to a Maine brook or a back-country California creek. The largest fish are seldom found in these spots, but even during a midsummer noon there will be trout in such places, encouraged by the added oxygen found in the riffles.

At the end of the bar, where the main current sweeps through, there is likely to be an eddy, turning away from the heavy water and swinging back below the bar. This is one of the best spots of all for there is a strip between the main current and the sluggish eddy that is fast enough for aeration and carries insects or bait-fish, yet is bordered by sluggish water, slow enough for even a lazy trout. At times there will be schools of small fish in the streak between main current and eddy, turning together as if on invisible threads, and sometimes close enough together to appear as a puff of smoke over the light-colored gravel. They may be juvenile trout, feeding upon microscopic life, and they are fair game for larger fish of their own kind. On the bottom is a quick flash as a sucker shows his side in endless probings. Whitefish may appear anywhere from top to bottom, and often bunch in schools, feeding on small insects. Their rises are hard to distinguish from those of trout and there are likely to be trout among them. Rainbows are likely to be closer to the main stream than brown trout.

For the most part, the trout of the big river have more cosmopolitan tastes than those of the spring creeks or the eastern limestone streams. Unlike the capsule community of the quiet stream, the river has many bottoms, varied currents, and fish foods drawn from a wide area. Its trout are not necessarily better fed but are less choosy of their fare. A fish that pursued a nymph a few minutes ago may now rise happily to a befuddled grasshopper or chase a sculpin. Fly patterns are less exact; often they are old favorites that represent no insect ever seen.

In warm weather at midday the fish are generally most active at the head of the big pool where the current boils. Here there is deep water and well-aerated pockets a little out of the heaviest torrent. As evening arrives fish may go to the tail of the pool where the water runs very slowly and spreads out over a wide gravel bottom, just before hurrying again to other rapids. There a fish may take floating flies, drowned flies, or nymphs. Such feeders are more cautious than when in turbulent currents, for they are easily seen from above. A fisherman may see the fish moving about on evening forays, sometimes rising to floating insects, occasionally showing their tails as they intercept nymphs. His plan is not quite the stealthy approach of the limestone brook but there must be some caution.

The river often splits into several channels, and some of the divisions swing wide into quiet flows. sometimes with grassy, undercut banks and cottonwood shade. Along the banks some grass tips touch the water and an occasional grasshopper miscalculates and falls in, groping fruitlessly at the grass, turning slowly in the current, and finally disappearing in a trout's lazy swirl. Trout live in the undercut, especially brown trout. They will take the grasshopper as a bonus, although they are likely to move to more open water for their main feeding periods. It is a combination of erosion and vegetation that forms their shelter. Shallow roots hold the surface soil and the water cuts beneath it. Eventually, the roots die and the bank crumbles to be cut anew.

The roar of the main stream can still be heard but the quiet run seems a world apart. A trickle of spring water carries bubbles and a little froth that moves slowly away, and if it is very warm a brown trout is likely to lie just below the spring. A pair of resident mallards makes a surprising noise as they jump from the edge of the channel, and the hen quacks wildly as they bore through the cottonwoods. On the noisy river their flight would attract little attention. Here it is a major event that causes an exploring mink to snap to attention and then fade into shoreline willows. A beaver, unwilling to tackle the crashing main stream with his engineering plans, will be more optimistic about a side channel, and leaves dragpaths across the sandy ground where he has hauled his cuttings. He crosses new land, an island that was formed as the river divided.

Side channels, where floods are less overpowering, will have partly submerged trees which provide almost perfect concealment for resting trout. Although those trees have not been swirled away as they would have been in the main river, they can be a sign of more insidious flooding, a constant erosion of softening banks that can eventually lead to broadening, warming, and slowing of the entire river—dangers to its trout. Here in the quiet split of the river the beaver's occasional cutting is much less ominous than the loss of the big cottonwood which gives way as its root structure is laid bare by current. Temporarily, however, the tree is a boon for it leads to a deep hole im-

Firehole River (1) of Yellowstone Park has both hot springs and snow water. Impressive sofa-pillow fly (2) floats beside stonefly that it imitates. Mink (3) patrols driftwood of a shoreline. Party of drifting fishermen (4) slides down broad Yellowstone in wide valley. Hooked trout (5) surfaces when pulled away from bottom growth in slow run.

1

2

3

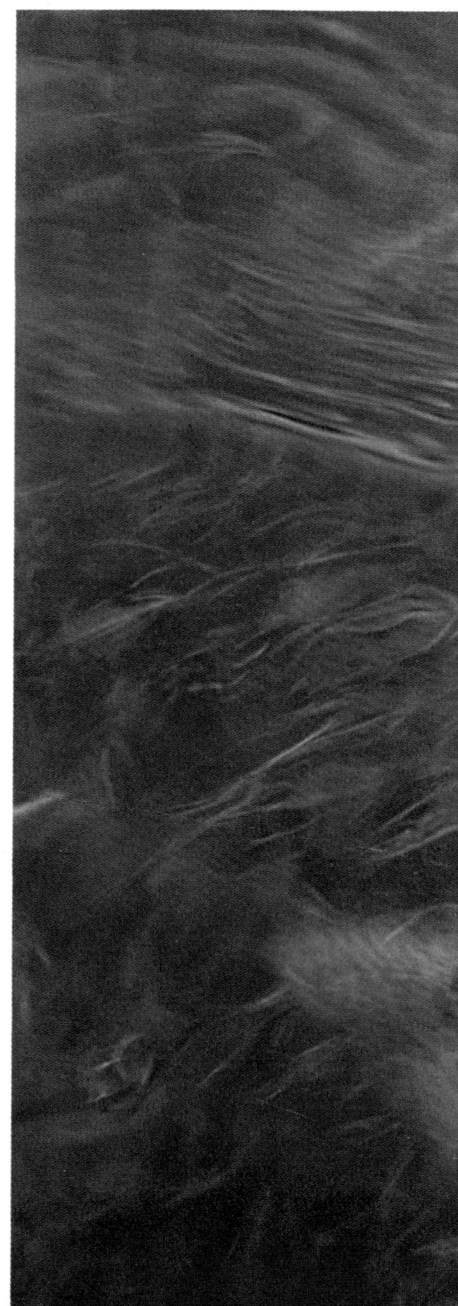

4

5

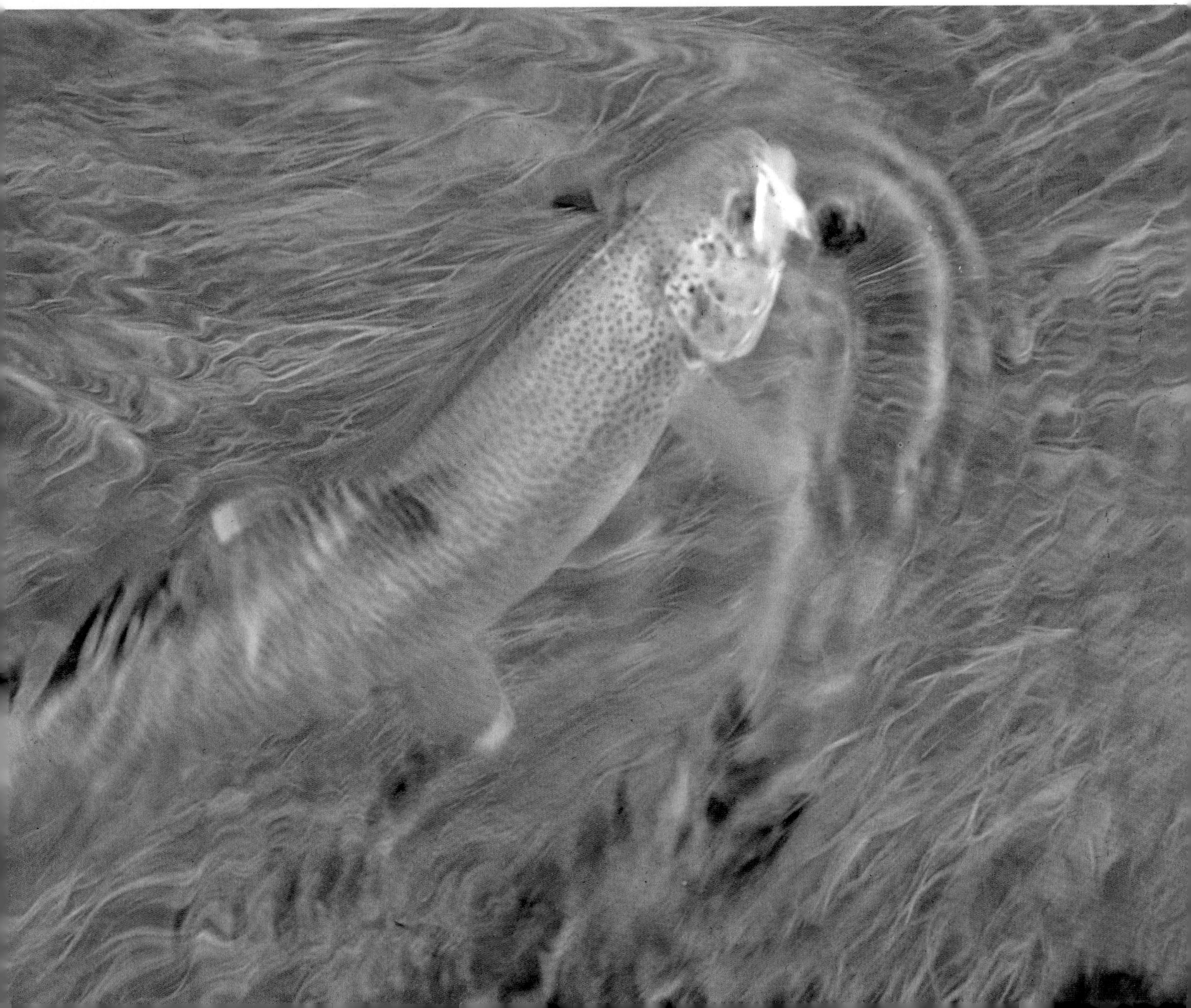

mediately below, a process the biologist recognizes as "current digging."

In October the brown trout have brightened their colors and, unlike the anadromous trouts and salmon, seem bent on feeding heavily in preparation for spawning. The fish are more aggressive than in summer, and the caster who tosses his spoon a little upstream and retrieves it cross-stream and swinging deep over bottom rocks is likely to make his best catches in fall. Even the resident rainbows seem to be feeding heavily, probably in preparation for winter, although they will not spawn until the following spring.

It is not quite the dead drift of the steelhead angler, but the fisherman feels his lure grate on the bottom and bounce in hidden currents. While he may argue about the best color or hammered finish, his favorite spoons are likely to end up with no finish at all, scoured by gravel and thumped by boulders. Generally he fishes the main currents.

The largest trout in the biggest rivers are now thinking of bait-fish rather than insects, and fly tackle is adapted to large streamers with strange names far departed from the traditional fly patterns. Although much trout fishing has deteriorated in recent years, the fly-caught fish have become larger in the big rivers, for the fishermen have adopted the tackle and some of the tactics of the steelhead angler.

The snow is low on the mountains now, and on some days the fringe of ice stays long after noon in the quiet sloughs. Crossing a marshy area on his way to the river, the fisherman is startled

Angler on Alberta river picks his way to shore with Dolly Varden, a predatory, sometimes oceangoing char.

when a Wilson's snipe jumps at his feet, giving a cry that is part cheep and part screech, and flies swiftly down the narrow slough. They have not been there during the summer but have stopped off for a time on their way southward from somewhere near the Arctic Circle.

The occasional pair of mallards that was flushed during summer fishing is now replaced by full-plumaged flocks, some of which clatter from the sloughs, with others making up flights that speed up the river and flare when they see the fisherman, for the gunning season is now open. Busy at his fishing, he may not even notice the fidgety wad of green-winged teal that swoops past him, alights in a shallow backwater, and then rushes off again after a nervous consultation. Occasionally he will hear the musical conversation of southbound snow geese or the far-reaching honk of the Canada.

Now he ignores the little side channels and the small eddy pockets and he wades deep at the head of a long pool and strips heavy sinking line from his big rod. It is backed by monofilament shooting line and he fires his big streamer across the main stream, mends his cast slightly, and then works his line hand as he swings his lure across, a bit downstream. He has cast a hundred feet, and although he cannot see his fly in the boiling race he knows what it does on the retrieve.

As the streamer strikes the water almost at the other bank it lies momentarily crosswise in the upper current, then yields to the pull of the bellying line below it, tugged downward and downstream headfirst. As the line is mended upstream, it darts back to its crosswise position and any fish down-current sees it as a dull silhouette rather than head on. It is but a brief pause in the swift crossing and it drifts down a little more as the angler feeds a few more feet of line, then the fly feels the taut leader and goes down fast to rush across the current and dangle immediately below the fisherman. Here he plays it a little and then strips in, catching loops of loose running line in his mouth, allowing the long coils to twist and swing in the current below his waders.

He feels the gravel wash beneath his feet and the pinch of cold water against the wader legs and he hobbles a little, but still keeps his precarious balance while a groping foot finds a solid niche between two unseen boulders, and he picks up the line to cast again.

The big Loch Leven is a hook-nosed male with orange belly and vivid red spots, and he is almost in the barrel of the current, across and a little downstream from the fisherman, facing upstream and low against the bottom, using a little eddy built by an underwater boulder. He is evil-tempered and always hungry in these prespawning days, and he sees the dark streamer broadside, something that resembles the 4-inch sculpin he took an hour earlier, so he tips his head upward to catch the water's push and swings back sidewise with the streamer.

The big trout drops down with a slow thrust of his tail, keeping a foot from the streamer, a thing he can catch at any time but chooses to inspect closely. A smaller trout would dart over, under, and around it. There are vaguely moving parts to the streamer, hair that hints of fins, and a solid portion that resembles a head, and when the lure leaps with the tug of the downstream line he follows it across the current, sees it make a turn to go upstream again, and seizes it with a twist of his whole body, a solid tug that reaches the fisherman instantly, and whips the already bending rod into a tight arc. It is not the thrilling rise to the floating lure or the gentle tug at a drifting nymph, but a heavy thrust on a tight line. The fight lacks the finesse of the spring creek trout, or even the feeling of expertise when a big dry fly is taken against an undercut bank, but it is a violent tug-of-war in the waist of a long pool.

There is a time, very late in the season, when brown trout will crowd the rivers just above large impoundments while seeking spawning areas. They will spend the rest of the year in the lakes.

1

2

3

4

5

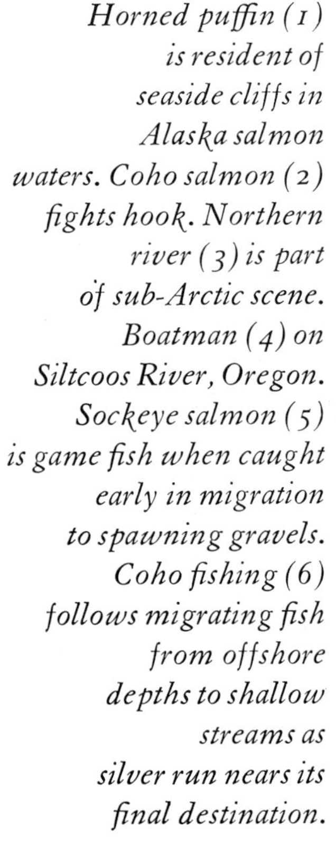

Horned puffin (1) is resident of seaside cliffs in Alaska salmon waters. Coho salmon (2) fights hook. Northern river (3) is part of sub-Arctic scene. Boatman (4) on Siltcoos River, Oregon. Sockeye salmon (5) is game fish when caught early in migration to spawning gravels. Coho fishing (6) follows migrating fish from offshore depths to shallow streams as silver run nears its final destination.

6

1

2

The phenomenon is a miniature version of the steelhead's migrations.

The trout of the eastern slope of the Rockies are blocked from the sea by two thousand miles of rivers, dams, and warm, muddy water, but across the Great Divide are relatives that cruise the North Pacific, climb the coastal rivers, and drive to their freshwater homes to spawn in ancestral gravels. Some of them, the steelhead, the sea-run brown, the sea-run cutthroat, and the oceangoing Dolly Varden, live much as do the trouts of the eastern slope except for their ocean visits (it is believed our inland trouts were simply anadromous fish, landlocked ages ago), but the Pacific salmons have followed another path of evolution to the instincts that make their lives the most dramatic of all.

The Pacific salmon spawns but once, its complex life cycle aimed for that single objective, and the most powerful chinook of the open Pacific uses all of its strength and weight to make its final journey from salt water to the spawning grounds. Its great vitality is measured against the hazardous trip through a polluted estuary, past a swarm of fishing devices, against river currents it may breast for more than two thousand miles, and over fish ladders or cataracts. If the measure balances perfectly, the fish will spawn and die over the spot it has been destined for since it absorbed its yolk sac there as a tiny alevin years before. The fisherman sees the Pacific salmon but intermittently. When trout fishing in salmon rivers he may catch the very small fish before they go to sea. At sea he may troll or drift with bait for the larger fish. In the rivers as the sea-run fish first arrive he may have light-tackle salmon fishing at its best, but farther upstream he is likely to hook dying fish with ragged fins and blotches of gray fungus.

The most sporting Pacific salmons are the chinook (also called spring and king) salmon, and the coho or silver, but there are three others that spawn on American shores—the chum, sockeye,

3

Coho salmon like these (1) are new residents of Michigan waters. California sea lions (2) are hazards to Pacific salmon. Spawning salmon (3) crowd each other in desperate activity as they near end of their mission in shallow upstream pools. All Pacific salmon end yearly spawning runs in death (4), as their eggs begin new generation of fish below covering of coarse gravel.

4

and pink salmon—whose identities are confused by local terms. Japan has the cherry salmon, product of some ancient convulsions of the earth and sea which separated that fish from the others.

The habitat of the Pacific salmon is but a small fraction of what it was before the dams, pollution, and erosion of modern times, and the fate of New England's Atlantic salmon fishery is a somber suggestion of what may be in store. The Alaska coast is least changed, and although commercial fishing from both American and foreign shores has reduced the runs it is still a dramatic tableau of the salmon's life.

A mile from a deep fiord of the Alaska shore, a small creek narrows from a wide, shallow pool where a crowd of pink ("humpback") salmon, some of them tattered and rotting, perform their spawning rituals. The hook-jawed males make violent, snapping charges at each other, and one seems to be the champion although his dorsal fin is only a whitened stub and blotches of remorseless fungus spread along his back.

A few of the fish are trying to get even farther upstream, where passage is blocked by a fallen tree and a tiny waterfall below it. They make futile runs, are swept back on their sides, gulp wildly, right themselves, and try again. The whole stream seems to writhe in the final agonies of the salmons' effort. The most peaceful part of the scene is a single dead salmon, lying flat against the bottom, most of the flesh gone from his bones, and after a few moments of watching the still-living fish, it is natural to wonder if his mission was completed before he found rest.

To most observers it is a somewhat morbid scene, a sort of convulsive festival between life and death, but there are others who view it as a stirring exhibit of nature's process and they are exhilarated by the implacable purpose of the fish. The energy of the humpbacks has lasted barely long enough, and onlookers think of the great chinooks dying two thousands miles up the Yukon.

The chinook runs have ended before the silvers seek spawning territory along the Alaska shore. The silvers, or cohos, have lived in fresh water for a year as youngsters and then spent about two years at sea, a time of rapid growth in fertile waters.

The fresh-run Alaska silvers are often pursued in a drizzling rain, frequently in vertical-sided bays where mountain goats and glaciers can be seen by watchful anglers, and occasional glacial waterfalls make misty white lines among the cliffs. In some spots there are colonies of Arctic terns that fleck entire cliffs, and frantically flying little puffins go in and out of the caves along the great rock faces as our slowly trolling boat swings sharply to avoid the enormous underwater boulders, alternately visible and invisible as the swells come and go with sucking noises, leaving streams of foam about the rock crevices. A distant flash just above the water changes our course, for one jumping salmon can mean an entire school farther down. Some say a jumping silver will not strike. The reason for the occasional display is only to be guessed at, but some believe it is an attempt at breaking up egg or sperm masses for spawning. Others say it is caused by pain from ripening spawn, simple exuberance, or an attempt to get rid of sea lice, small parasites that are quickly lost in fresh water. In any event, one glistening leaper betrays his companions.

The fleets of fishing boats and athletic seals are the first predators to meet the fresh-run silvers. Farther inland they will be awaited by black and brown bears that will chase them in the shallows, and eagles or gulls that will be more patient and find the fish dead or nearly dead. Along the coast there is much other fishing besides the pursuit of salmon. Halibut are enormous; they are mainly fished commercially, but are an attraction to bait-fishing sportsmen also. A visiting bottom angler makes a dainty retrieve when he feels a king crab working his cut sardine, having been told he must land the prize gently as it will not be hooked, but simply hanging on. Then when the catch actually comes aboard he steps back in dismay, faced by what appears to be an immense armored spider, three feet across.

We troll for silvers with lures or sardines and fairly heavy tackle but only a few miles down the coast the methods are different. There we cast flamboyant spoons that come through the slightly milky water with piercing reflections. At another point on the coast the fish seem interested only in bait as they enter a creek that has carried a muddy delta with it.

Wherever we fish for them the silvers act a little differently, mainly because they are in a different stage of their migration, partly because they belong to different waves of migration and may have fed most recently on different fare.

Noting this flexibility of behavior which permits survival, sometimes despite severe changes in the environment, one is reminded again that the trout along the eastern slopes of the Rockies are thought to have been anadromous ages ago. By some gigantic quirk or cataclysm of nature, or perhaps through unimaginably gradual changes, they became landlocked western trout. Some of the salmons, too, can thrive without benefit of oceanic migrations. Man has repeated one of the great and mysterious acts of nature that was performed aeons ago, by transplanting anadromous coho and chinook salmon to the Great Lakes, where they labor up feeder streams to spawn after using the lakes as they use the salt Pacific. Under these new conditions, the cohos have become established.

They are adaptable fish and have produced a valued sport fishery in the Great Lakes, where they wax fat on alewives. When lamprey eels destroyed the lake-trout fishery, there seemed little hope for the deep lake waters. Then, with lampreys under control by the mid-sixties, the cohos were imported and consumed alewives by the ton to make unheard-of weight increases, while ridding the lakes of the alewives that had been dying in stinking windrows on the beaches. Then came some apprehension that there would not be enough alewives for the exploding coho population. The cohos have been maintained by artificial means, for although the lake waters nourish them to great size, spawning facilities are largely unsatisfactory. Few feeder streams have suitable gravel.

Residents of the Lake Michigan area, where coho fishing is at its best, have accepted the immigrant salmon with an enthusiasm they have never shown for any other kind of fishing, and boats suitable for deepwater coho angling (and some decidedly unsuitable) have been built and bought by the thousand.

After the coho came an introduction of the largest of the Pacific salmon tribes. The chinook now adds still more to the Great Lakes fishing, an influx of new fish to counter the staggering depredations of pollution.

When the silvers come into the Alaska fiords they are chromed slashers, and when one takes our spoon near Valdez it whistles the line across the surface, splitting the slight chop with its back and fins, then jumps in a shallow plunge to circle the boat as the angler cranks furiously. In some rivers and along some coasts the silver strikes steelhead flies or takes streamers cast into the moving schools. And on one coast the broiled salmon steaks are as good as any seafood ever tasted.

But the salmon are changing as they come ashore, and we wade a winding Kenai stream, flicking a tiny lure against undercut banks and across gravel runs. We catch an occasional humpbacked salmon, already dull-colored and soft, and then the coho strikes, swirling up from near the bottom. The fish fights hard but does not jump, and when it is landed its fins show golden borders.

We broil that fish over a campfire at the base of a great mountain and it is very good, but it is not quite so firm as the fish from the bay, and though the fish of the creek have not been there very long they are changing rapidly in the way that all Pacific salmon change as they near their goal of death.

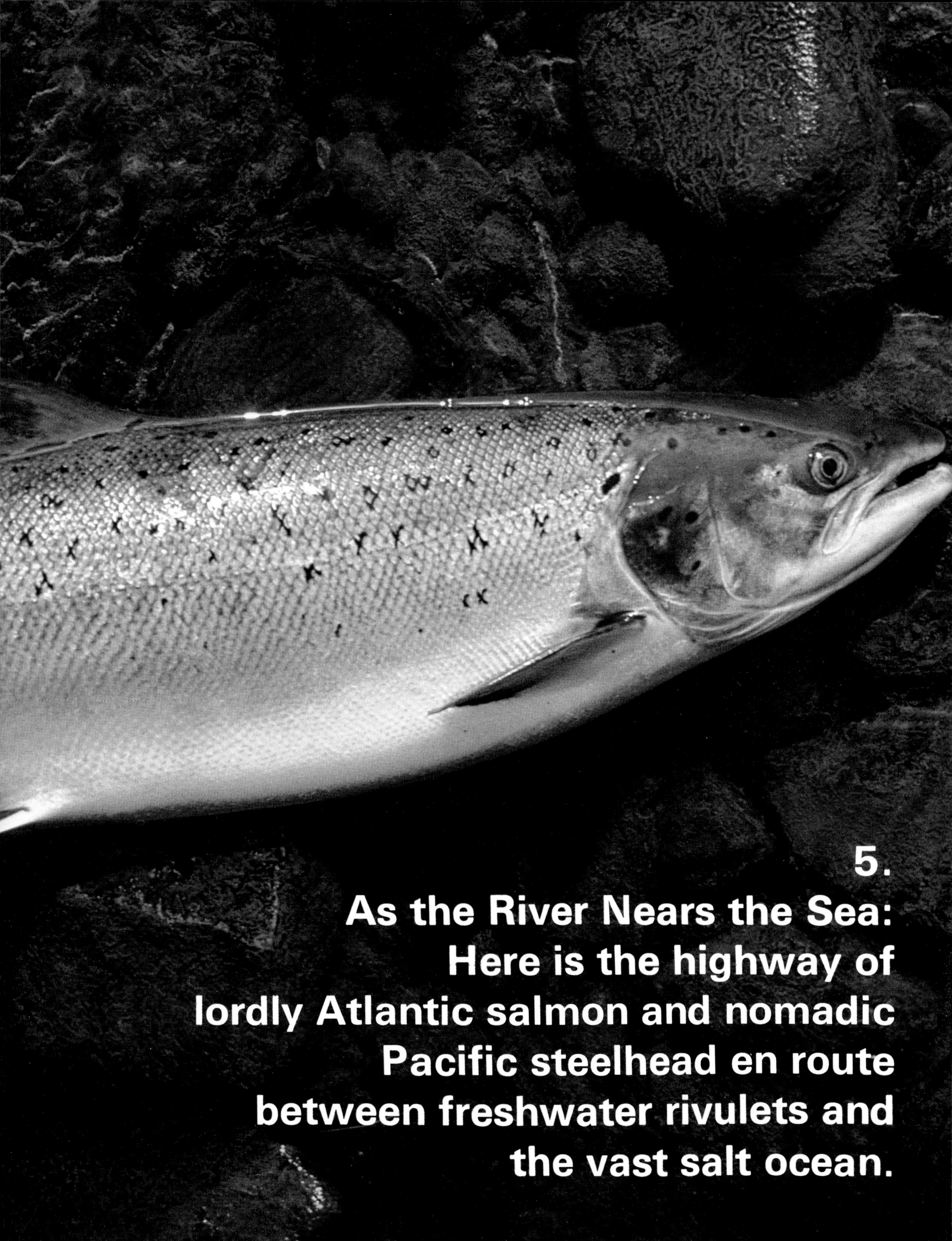

5.
As the River Nears the Sea:

Here is the highway of lordly Atlantic salmon and nomadic Pacific steelhead en route between freshwater rivulets and the vast salt ocean.

 The salmon has not moved much for several hours. It is barely visible, a faint shadow on the mottled bottom gravel, an indistinct section of slightly curved outline. It can be seen only when the gently writhing current moves in a certain way.

It is late summer and the river is too low and warm for salmon fishing. Earlier in the season it was too high and cold, but when the right level was reached this salmon had moved in and upstream as one of a loose school of fish. They had come with the spawning urge, weeks before their spawning time, and had progressed from pool to pool in intermittent travel, becoming somewhat scattered as they moved. When heat and low water came they ceased their restless movement and settled into holding pools to await the rains that might not come until fall.

The fish has been cast over many times and many natural flies have drifted past it, some of them sitting upright on the surface and some of them drowned and suspended near the bottom. The salmon does not feed seriously on its spawning journey but sometimes takes the fly for unknown reasons, a quirk of fish nature no one explains, a gesture of anger, habit, or impulse, unreliable enough under ideal conditions, seemingly unlikely now in the slow, warming river. There are more than one hundred salmon rivers in Newfoundland and they are among the most productive in the world, yet even here the wrong conditions can mean fruitless days of angling effort.

When it is alarmed the salmon is less likely to flee than the trout, more likely to drop slightly lower against the bottom. When it is interested in something carried by the current it tilts upward very slightly and its fins move a little faster. Today this happens after the fish has seen a hundred casts. On another cast the fisherman succeeds. After the salmon has shattered the river, flashed high in the air against a dark green background of conifers, and is landed on a gravel bar, the fisherman studies the graceful shape and the small, angry head, and is awed that he has caught this gleaming thing come back to its river of birth from far and unknown places.

On one day there may be no fish in the known lies, in the deep eddies, the barely visible depressions in shallow runs, or the tails of the most productive pools. The next day a crowd of salmon may appear in gently moving shallows under a midday sun but ignore the fly—and the fisherman, too, unless he moves closer than ten feet. Then the fish may turn slowly, one at a time, and drop fifty feet downstream, to return in twos and threes when the danger has disappeared. At such times there are many reasons given for the fish failing to strike, yet when one of them does rise to the fly there is no explanation.

For hours fish may lie like sunken logs in a great muttering salmon river, ignoring fluttering live flies as well as ornate and fanciful artificials. And then when a narrow twist of summer breeze flirts a high fir branch and needles and particles of bark shower onto the smooth surface of the pool, there is a wide boil, and a salmon rises to take some shapeless speck of debris.

In early season, when the salmon rivers are high, the wet flies are fairly large, although still a slight temptation for so big a fish. In high water the river is likely to be discolored, even muddy, and anglers feel that smaller offerings will not be noticed. The heavy flow makes it easy for fish to enter the estuaries and these new arrivals are careless of heavy leaders. Some of the smaller rivers are nearly blocked by bars during drought, but fish come through when rain or melting snow builds the head of water. Then, as the water clears and falls, the effective flies become more and more sparse and are shown on progressively finer leaders to increasingly cautious fish. Visibility has increased a hundred-fold and coarse tackle is seen in all its crudity. At the same time the lessened flow eliminates holding areas used when water is high. The fish are concentrated, however difficult they may be to catch. While the mature salmon can see the fisherman more plainly, the parr is easily sighted

Preceding pages: King of game fish, Atlantic salmon fights for survival against efficient commercial fishing methods, dwindling of habitat, and pollution.

by the heron, kingfisher, and merganser.

There is intense effort to interpret the salmon's motivation and anticipate its responses. Some salmon will take a fly in a broadside drift, which enables them to inspect it in detail; others may be attracted by a brief and incomplete view of the fly. Still others will chase a fast-swinging fly, the very act of pursuit lulling caution and stimulating the feeding instinct, which has been quiescent since the fish entered fresh water. There is even a theory that a salmon's temper may change in rhythm and that the fly can be presented repeatedly in such a way that a motionless fish will accept it simply because it returns in cadence. The salmon is a deliberate taker even though he is addicted to playful gestures at the fly at times when he will not strike.

When the salmon enters fresh water its stomach and digestive apparatus become largely inoperative, incapable of utilizing solid food, but it may be that the fish takes quantities of insects at times, ejecting the crushed bodies and retaining the juices. The stomach often contains what may be insect juices, and mature salmon sometimes rise regularly like trout, taking surface flies or nymphs. Sometimes their mouths contain quantities of insects although few find their way to the stomach. Bits of wood or a winged maple seed may also be taken.

It was perhaps inevitable that the Atlantic salmon should be one of the first large fishes to be approached with ultralight fly gear. The very proficient caster who has studied the fish can often succeed with equipment more often associated with fingerling trout. To such a contest he brings not only his restrained skills, but the practical knowledge that the Atlantic salmon, like other fishes, is incapable of the profound thought and scheming that is romantically ascribed to him by thoughtful and scheming fishermen. He knows that the fish is likely to respond in proportion to tackle pressure: with smashing fury against force and with puzzled uncertainty against light and pliable restraint. With all of its tremendous power the stream salmon cannot swim for long periods without resting, and it will tire quickly against a light pull, simply because it cannot acquire enough oxygen to keep driving.

So the tiny rod casts the tiny fly on the thread-like leader, and when the fish takes and is hooked he is almost, but not quite, allowed complete freedom. He may leap to escape the hook, although the impediment is so intangible he may return to his lie, driving forth again when the gentle strain makes him unsteady in his delicate state of balance and flotation. It may take a long while, but gradually the fish is tired and finally he is landed gently, perhaps somewhat mesmerized by the steady persuasion of tackle he could have broken at any time by simply swimming away.

It is the same gentle persuasion with which an experienced angler can slide his hands beneath a tired fish and scoop it to shore, a fish that would thrash violently if struck by a hurried landing net or an awkwardly applied gaff, or with which a large and nearly fresh fish is sometimes led to beach or net without ever having been truly aroused.

While other fish have a variety of local names in America, the terms for Atlantic salmon are from the Anglo-Saxon and are rigidly unchanged: "alevin" for freshly hatched fry, "parr" for young salmon that have never been to sea, "smolt" for those about to take their first ocean tour, "grilse" for fish that have returned to their home streams after one year at sea, and "kelt" for the spawned-out fish or black salmon.

All of the anadromous salmon (some are landlocked) pose immensely complicated management problems. They are born in cold streams amid the hazards of logging and pulpwood cutting, migrate through polluted lower rivers, and meet the most advanced methods of commercial fishing on the high seas, then return through the same gantlet of dangers to the original spawning gravels. The United States salmon fishery, having been wantonly destroyed, is now being brought

Icelandic salmon, cast to (1) by Roderick Haig-Brown, live in windswept rivers flowing through treeless landscapes, are still plentiful though small. Salmon often hold at shallow tail of pool (4) and are approached from below. Careful knot (2) holds elaborate fly such as those in this box of traditional patterns (5). Netting fish (3) is tense moment.

4

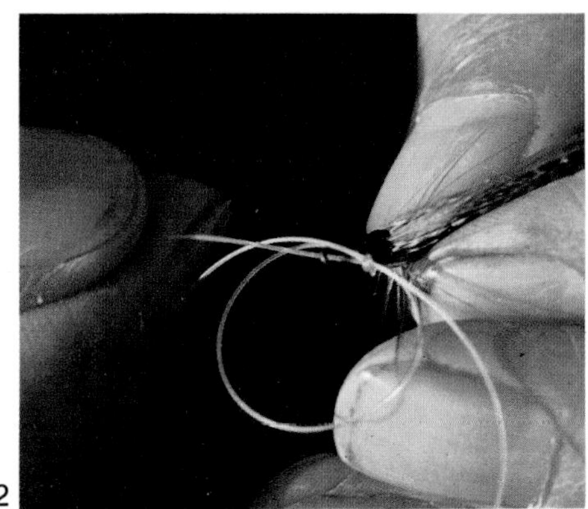
2

5

3

back with token runs in New England. Canada retains some excellent fishing, although the runs have weakened or failed in many rivers.

Man's hard-earned knowledge of salmon is a questionable prize, for systems of catching fish commercially have kept pace with those of management. It is known now that many American fish travel to the Greenland fishing grounds where they are targets for any high-seas fishermen, and European crews without salmon rivers in their homelands can prey on fish from America and the British Isles. Most of Europe has long since lost all salmon angling, although the Norwegian rivers and the Baltic coasts have exceptional fish. The British Isles still have fishing, and in Iceland salmon are plentiful if small.

Until recently the largest commercial salmon catches were made at the mouths of native rivers. Although such fishing may greatly reduce the population, it can be regulated and the results readily learned. It is the high-seas fishery, now guided by electronic fish-finding gear and aided by improved nets and craft, that endangers the salmon. Fish caught near river mouths are nearly always in their home territory, but a large share of the fish from a given Canadian river can be netted a thousand miles from their spawning grounds by fishermen who have no idea where they came from. There are great oceanic staging areas where salmon from many points seem to group before dispersing to their native rivers, and it is here that they are most vulnerable.

Most controversial of the high-seas fishing is in the vicinity of Greenland and the Faroe Islands. In the late sixties the commercial catch there suddenly became many times what it had been before, and the Danes, who control Greenland and its salmon rivers, were leaders in the disastrous harvest. It was a matter of locating the concentration of fish, which had probably been there all along, and which may have been enlarged through some change of migration routes. When diplomatic conferences failed to help, conservation groups in America and Britain advocated boycott of Danish products.

Which fish should serve the commercial fishery and which should be left for the sportsman is a subject of debate. Nets with large mesh allow the grilse to escape. Some consider the larger salmon more valuable, believing the tendency to stay long at sea is hereditary. Grilse, it may be, carry the instinct of one-year return, and their progeny will be a strain of small salmon. Netting regulations are relatively easy to enforce at river mouths. On the high seas rules are a different matter. Rod and line catches are generally discounted but the nearer the fish are to their redds the more valuable the individual salmon becomes.

Salmon runs are irregular. Sea-run fish may be halted by low water at the river's mouth, or they may stop when faced by a river that is too cold. If the stream is too warm they may dally in the lower stretches but hurry onward with the first cooling rain. For that matter, rain is known to be a salmon stimulant, whether near the estuary or far up the river. Little smolts respond to rain by hurrying their migration, shoals of them leaving an estuary overnight.

Each salmon river has a schedule of runs but the run is more dependent upon water conditions than upon calendar dates. One river, its lower stretches slow-moving and open to the sun, may warm early in the spring. Nearby, a snow-frosted river that goes through deep channels and shaded canyons and does not warm until late in the season will have a late run of fish.

Just off the estuaries salmon may be seen moving near the sea's surface, invariably heading toward the rivers, although once they reach the tidal section of river current they may go in and out with the tide, awaiting proper conditions for the continued migration. Even just outside the fresh water they may feed heavily; the fast will commence when they enter the river.

When the water's flow and temperature are right the fish begin the last phase of their pilgrim-

Glassy pool tumbles into broken water on Nova Scotia salmon river. Fish often hold just above and below rapids.

1

2

3

Parr (1) bears bright colors before beginning journey to sea. Grilse and salmon (2) lie thick in a shallow hold of Newfoundland river. Mergansers (3), swift underwater predators, are enemies of young salmon. One salmon netted (4), Newfoundland fishermen prepare to continue a downstream journey by canoe and will stop to cast again at next good pool. Fishing low, clear water, caster (5) works slow current in lower reaches of a Newfoundland river near tide line.

age. When they first enter some rivers they are willing to strike freely; on other rivers the first fish of the run are invariably seen many miles upstream. Those that have come fresh from the sea seem to retain a trace of their ocean-feeding gluttony; those that have been a long while in the river are less susceptible to food temptations, but when they do strike they do so more in the fashion of the parr that rise to flies in the shallows, returning to the habits of their youth.

Fish entering a river early will spawn at about the same time as the last fish to arrive; the early fish are thus a long way from being mature spawners. The late arrivals have more fully developed roe. The early fish dally and rest for long periods at a time. The late fish move rapidly toward their beds.

Some rivers are predominantly grilse streams, most of the returning fish having spent only a year at sea. Other runs are of predominantly older and larger fish, but in some sections, where the sea-run salmon have limited food, even the older fish are small in size. A four-pound fish may be a grilse in one river and a mature salmon in another. Long ocean migrations may mean that there is little food near the home river, but there are many salmon that never go great distances from the stream's mouth.

Once the upriver trip is begun, travel is mostly at night. The holds that seem to be selected at random may be located where daylight catches moving fish, and the first fish that settle in a pool act as decoys for those coming later, thus establishing a lie for the season, one that may not be used the following year. Fish that have entered a pool the night before are likely to be restless during morning hours, cruising about the area until midday when they usually settle down to wait for evening. If they are about to move again that night there is renewed activity in the evening.

But evening activity is hard to interpret for it is a natural time for stream fish to feed. Simple preparation for a night's travel brings about fish

Above: Atlantic salmon surfaces in Nova Scotia's St. Marys River as fisherman leads him to landing. Opposite: Guide heats kettle by Harrys River in Newfoundland during summer low water. Foreground fish is grilse from nearby riffle.

movement, little groups of salmon stirring about a pool, although evidently with their attention on other things and unlikely to take a fly. Rolling salmon may be going through the motions of feeding, or actually taking flies and nymphs. The free leapers, those that rend the wilderness stillness with mighty silver flashes and booming plunges, may have no interest in taking any sort of food. They may, however, give away the location of their fellows.

Groups of fish may stay for days or even weeks in a given pool, becoming less and less likely to take living or artificial flies as time goes on. Individuals may retain their positions in the holding formations, and a fish that rises or moves to inspect a drifting object will often return to a precise spot in the resting pattern. Some of the surface rises are playful and deliberately misguided, yet there appear to be accidental misses when the fish rises to the reflection of a fly rather than to the fly itself. The salmon is actually out of practice in its fly taking, being less deft than when it was a greedily feeding parr, and now more accustomed to subsurface feeding at sea.

Activities of holding salmon seem to be contagious and the mood of an entire shoal of fish may change within a few minutes. At such times silent loafers suddenly begin to move and to take flies they have ignored for days. The active period may cease as suddenly as it began and the fish again become oblong shadows on the bottom. Such periods of activity may have obvious causes—a moose slashing through the shallow tail of a pool, or stones deliberately thrown. The fish seem alarmed and disturbed for a while, then they return restlessly to their hold and lie ready to strike.

Immediately below a dam of falls, fish may stir constantly but ignore the fly, evidently preoccupied with their serious problem of ascension and gathering their strength for the assault. It is here that they produce their most dramatic leaps and make what appear to be reckless jumps but which are actually carefully gauged attempts. As a vertical or nearly vertical fall of water plunges into the pool it rebounds again in an upward thrust, and the fish begin their leaps by going up with the rebounding water, coming out of the foam from near the bottom to sail far up the cataract, swimming furiously as they re-enter the slanting torrent, using all the power pent up in their months of preparation. The accessibility of such an obstacle may depend upon the thrust of water from its base, a thrust that has been gauged by enlightened engineering in the case of some man-made dams.

Salmon hold in spots where the current is exactly to their liking, places trout usually ignore, and their instinct for safety leads them to choose open water, the result of experience at sea where no undercut bank or drowned treetop offers sanctuary from pursuit. Even in daylight, salmon sometimes rest at the lower lip of a pool, facing the deeper water, and a rise or fall in the river's level brings an immediate adjustment in location of the lie.

Underwater ledges make breaks in the current that enable the fish to find water moving at a rate to their liking. Areas near midstream boulders, where the main flow splits into streaks of varying speed, are attractive. A group of salmon may lie in such a spot, somewhat scattered but with fish holding to a place where the current is acceptable. If the current is not strong enough to please the fish they cruise upstream ponds and lakes as they cruised the quiet bays before entering the river. They are most likely to be found at inlets or outflows of lakes.

The silvery fresh-run fish darken as they go farther upstream, changing color to fit their surroundings; lighter gray in clear streams, brownish in muddy water. They leap occasionally, even after their fresh-run sea lice have been left behind, jumping in exuberance or in an effort to separate or pack the spawn, or possibly in a preparatory flexing for difficult passages of the stream.

The salmon lies which show so plainly at low water are carefully remembered by the expert,

Campbell River, British Columbia, one of the better-known Pacific-salmon streams. Mountain slopes indicate deep water and steep bottoms.

Winter steelhead from Clackamas River, Oregon. Boat is designed for fast-water rowing. Casting tackle is preferred gear for winter floods.

for they may still be productive during a near-flood. He knows that the most likely ones are near difficult passages of the stream. Fish will rest immediately below the wild torrents in preparation for the assault. Once a smashing rapid has been scaled, they rest again in the first suitable water above. He knows the resting water must move and that the fish seek a suitable flow, moving nearer to rapids in low water.

Salmon are most likely to strike when found in swift and shallow water, and are extremely difficult to attract from deep, slow pools. Current obstructions that break the flow are likely to concentrate the fish. But the mature salmon's defense is speed and agility, and it wants open water when frightened. It may appear unafraid when approached from the shallows but will flee when its access to deep water is threatened.

More than a million years ago the waters of the Atlantic and Pacific were joined over what is now land and ice across northern North America. When the land rose, Atlantic and Pacific salmons were separated and continued separate evolutions. The Pacific salmons spawn only once and die afterward; the Atlantic salmon may spawn several times.

But *Salmo salar,* the Atlantic fish, has a close relative with very similar habits on the Pacific side. This is the steelhead, aristocrat of the Pacific sports fishery, an anadromous fish that may spawn more than once, and one which can be fished by the most sporting methods. Landlocked Atlantic salmon and ouananiche (a very similar fish) have their counterpart in the rainbow trout. There are theories that all of the trouts were historically anadromous, but became landlocked through geological changes, and the idea is borne out by the abbreviated migrations of inland fish.

Both Atlantic and Pacific salmons return to their native streams after swimming thousands of miles at sea. It may be that the final choice is made through scent, or perhaps the home stream's location is found by sensing the relative amount of dissolved oxygen in the water at various places. Still, some fish wait at a river's mouth for mud or sand banks that close the stream temporarily to be washed out. Is there enough seepage for a salmon to make a determination by scent or taste?

Most fish unerringly seek the home stream, even though it is a shallow creek hundreds of miles from salt water, even though the homeward journey negotiates a series of tributaries from a large river that has almost endlessly diluted the discharge of the little creek. But there must be some errant spawners as well, or new ranges would never be established.

At very low water some rivers are not deep enough to accept migrations and a throng of fish will mill about the estuaries awaiting a freshet before continuing their spawning run. Not only are these restless crowds especially vulnerable to nets, but they may be attacked by needle-toothed seals and agile porpoises. At an earlier phase, the same salmon, less than 6 inches long, waited on the other side of the tide line; then the hazards were cormorants, gulls, herons, and kingfishers.

Regardless of the lower river's character, the spawning grounds upstream must fulfill certain requirements. The spawning bottom, or redd, is preferably gravel, usually coarse. The ripe female scoops out a wide depression in the bottom, using her tail and side for digging. As she discharges her eggs, preferably in rock crevices, they are fertilized by a male immediately alongside. She then covers the eggs and may immediately build another redd, spawning several times. Each new redd is built upstream, so that materials loosened by the digging may add to the covering of previous nests.

The eggs may be dislodged by current before they are properly covered and they attract darting forays by parr or other small fish. If properly and loosely buried in the gravel they are usually safe from larger predators but may suffer from fungus. Too much silt can cut off the oxygen supply, or actually prevent the fry from escaping the miniature labyrinth of loosely packed gravel.

When spawning grounds are severely limited and thus abnormally crowded, the redds of one fish may be destroyed by a later arrival which cuts out one nest to substitute its own. A ten-pound female may be expected to lay seven thousand or more eggs, and if one or two salmon mature from this number to return to the spawning grounds in the following years, it has been a successful hatch.

Eggs are laid in the fall and will hatch the following spring if they escape the hazards of siltation, flooding, and insect predators. Newly hatched fry—alevin—hardly more than mobile yolk sacs with eyes and tails, leave the gravel sanctuary as their yolk sacs are consumed, and grow rapidly into fully equipped fish with dark parr markings. As parr, Atlantic salmon may live for as long as three or four years before entering the sea. Short growing seasons in the far northern rivers cause a long premigratory career, but British parr usually stay in the rivers only one or two years.

At first the little salmon feed on almost microscopic water life, then they begin to take insects and tiny fish. In both Pacific and Atlantic streams innumerable parr are often caught, violent little fellows who leap destructively on carefully dressed dry flies and turn them into soggy wrecks, or who wrestle with wet flies.

The parr live a tenuous existence. To their inexperienced eyes, the motionless legs of a heron can pass for willow stems. Mink, otter, ospreys, and mergansers take their toll, and the belted kingfisher, striking from its high perch like a decorated spearhead, can go some distance under water with a stiletto beak that grasps as well as pierces. Most of the parr lost to such predators are caught in the shallows, where at times schools of them can be seen in only 3 inches of water, hard to distinguish from other small fish.

Just before entering salt water, parr become smolts, losing their dark markings and acquiring hints of the silver sheen they will bear during their ocean lives. Pacific and Atlantic salmon have similar juvenile careers.

While the eggs are hatching and agile parr begin their careers, spawned-out Atlantic salmon, or kelts, weakened, emaciated, and darkened, undertake the difficult task of simple survival. A large percentage never reaches the sea again, being unable to resist the attacks of eels. Many are ice-locked in upriver pools and attempt their return to salt water the following spring. They are discolored fish, still in various stages of exhaustion. In some areas, kelt fishing is allowed and some kelts are game fish. Others are too weakened to afford sport and too badly deteriorated to be desirable as food. But the Atlantic salmon that again feels the salt in its gills begins a rejuvenation process and a new growth. The rare fish which survives spawning two or more times becomes a giant.

At sea, the Atlantic salmon feeds on herring, capelin, and many other small fishes, and especially on shrimp-like crustaceans. Adult fish and grilse that return to rivers for the spawning season vary greatly in size from river to river, generally due to the quantity and quality of food available in their ocean ranges. Icelandic fish are notably small. Some of the short and steep Norwegian rivers carry huge fish, and there was at least one Scottish salmon reputed to have weighed more than one hundred pounds.

At sea, with cold depths and usually plentiful food, growth is exceptionally fast. After a year of ocean gluttony a grilse will weigh from one and a half to nine pounds. It is difficult to follow the course of salmon at sea, but it is known that they feed at varying depths, often as great shoals of fish, and appear to take occasional rest periods. Tagging experiments show they may move in a single direction more than thirty miles a day. Some go more than two thousand miles from their home rivers. Feeding diversions undoubtedly greatly increase the actual distance covered. Seagoing salmon seldom appear on the surface, and even as smolts they go very deep, for smolts have been found in the stomachs of codfish, which are almost exclusively bottom-dwellers.

September steelhead (below) from Kispiox River, British Columbia, home of many record fish. Bottom: Steelheading on Deschutes River.

Most fishermen think of the steelhead as an errant rainbow trout which left fresh water to go to sea in some evolutionary coincidence, but the biologist feels that these trout, the closest relatives of the Atlantic salmon, were historically anadromous and that some became landlocked to produce nonmigratory rainbows. The rainbow and the steelhead are the same fish, although the sea instinct is handed down in some, while others, sometimes in the same waters, are stay-at-homes. Rainbow trout of the Great Lakes migrate up rivers and tributary creeks and are locally called steelhead. The largest rainbows reach maturity in deep lakes or at sea. In the lakes they usually run deep, although sometimes near the surface in spring or fall. Sea migrations are made by brown trout and cutthroat trout on many coasts. The Dolly Varden and brook trouts also are seagoing, but technically these two small trouts are classed as chars.

It is the steelhead that makes the more predictable migrations, coming fresh from the sea in silver and then regaining his vivid red stripe in fresh water, while retaining the metallic head that gave the sea-run fish its name.

At one time steelhead ran the Pacific rivers as far as southern California, but coastal developments and damming have stemmed the flow in many areas. Some of the California runs have stopped completely. The steelhead spawns in late winter or spring, often coming home early and living in home waters for many months before spawning. Those that enter the streams early are called summer steelhead, and the migrants of mid-fall or later are called winter steelhead; nevertheless, the spawning time is likely to be about the same for all.

Opposite: Steelhead fishermen cross fast water with fish landed from midstream bar. Left: Big fall steelhead was caught by author on fly in Kispiox River. Kispiox shares contest wins with Babine River, also of Skeena watershed.

The fighting qualities of the steelhead can vary greatly. Fresh-run fish, their crimson fresh-water stripes almost invisible against their ocean silver, enter the river mouths with the full vigor of their prespawning condition, strike with the ferocity of ocean fish, and leap to startling heights. In very short rivers their violence may last through the whole run to the spawning ground, but on a journey of hundreds of miles the fish lose some of their power and begin darkening to match the resident rainbows. Near spawning grounds, the steelhead may be sluggish compared to his fresh-run condition, although as he rests from his labors he can regain power, and a dark steelhead is not necessarily an easy catch.

The steelhead is often a wide ranger at sea, sometimes going more than twenty-five hundred miles from its river, and staying at sea for two or three years. Although the fish can survive for months without eating prior to spawning, the steelhead's fasting is less determined than that of the Atlantic salmon, and steelhead sometimes take food a long way from the salt water where they make their major growth. Their stomachs often contain stonefly, mayfly, or caddisfly nymphs, and they are known to take surface flies. Steelhead which return early to the stream, as in the case of "summer fish," are much less prone to fasting and match the resident rainbows in feeding habits. Steelhead enter coastal rivers in every month of the year, although each stream has its prime times for fishing.

Along the mountainous coast of the Northwest, the steelhead and the resident rainbow are less sharply separated than are migratory Atlantic salmon and landlocked fish. While there is an instinct to migrate in all rainbows the distances traveled are set both by geography and some invisible hereditary tendency in the physiology of the individual fish. The rainbow is more tolerant of high temperatures than any other trout, but pollution and dams have blocked the southernmost runs and nearly all of the American steelhead live their lives from northern California northward. For the steelhead, Alaska is still a frontier which has had limited fishing pressure, while the Pacific salmon is more closely followed.

There is a pattern to the steelhead's selection of spawning gravels. The favored place is at the lower end of a pool, generally in brisk and shallow water where the bottom is scoured and without mud or vegetation. This same location is sought by resident rainbows with no avenue to the sea, but they have adapted so well to less ideal conditions that the rainbow is probably the most widely distributed trout of all. In American rivers that flow to the east the rainbows introduced many generations ago will seek the same type of spawning ground, but have been able to make do with less ideal bottoms. In some midwestern rivers where propagation is impossible due to warm and vacillating river conditions the planted rainbows will, nevertheless, rival Pacific steelhead in size, adapting to local foods in plump, red-sided prosperity.

Widely different migration timetables and ranges have made the steelhead less vulnerable than the Atlantic salmon as far as natural or commercial catastrophes are concerned. Although certain runs are fairly predictable, there is an almost continual movement of rainbow trout in some coastal rivers and some individual fish are hard to classify as resident rainbows or true steelhead.

An adult steelhead is less distant from his youth than the returning Atlantic salmon. The salmon may revert to parr-like fly taking, but he is at ease in open water, even with a fisherman nearby. The steelhead is frightened almost as easily as a resident trout. An alarmed Atlantic salmon may simply settle closer to the bottom while the steelhead characteristically darts away.

The Atlantic salmon is noted for his slow rise, a deliberate take of the fly that is the undoing of experienced trout fishermen. In some waters the steelhead is a fast striker. On the Trinity River of California the battle is joined almost before the angler learns what has happened, the fly being taken in a furious flash and the fish continuing away at top speed. Even when it misses a floating target the steelhead has a habit of hurrying to a hiding place immediately afterward as if startled by its own rashness and fearful that some waiting predator has seen it.

Once they have spawned, the steelhead appear as exhausted as do the doomed Pacific salmon but they tend to recuperate in fresh water more than the Atlantic salmon do. The eastern kelts drift to the sea in emaciated fatigue, sometimes so weakened that they are prey for eels or otters. Immediately after spawning, the steelhead is as vulnerable as the Atlantic kelt although much of its vigor returns before it reaches the sea.

Some steelhead turn into their rivers as early as midsummer, hardly noticed in streams that also hold Pacific salmon, and they fight the same battles to reach their homes. In midwinter, when herring gulls, sleepy bears, and bald eagles have eaten most of the remains of the chinooks, sockeyes, and other salmon, steelhead may still be working upstream, passing over the new generation of salmon eggs. They pass through mature forests and often enter brushy brooks for their spawning, fish too large to have been developed by their home waters with its limited forage, bringing the sea's bounty to the back country.

The high stream provides a thoroughfare for land creatures as well as the steelhead. The snow beside it carries the trails of deer, elk, moose, and often puma, which use its banks as an easy way beneath the cliffs and slanted mountainsides. It will probably be spring when the steelhead go down again, riding cold snow water that is clear at the beginning, then is sullied by eroding banks

1

2

3

4

Steelhead fights fly on North Umpqua, Oregon (1). In shallows (2) angler works a heavy run. Fish on log has come hundred miles from sea. Ruffed grouse (3) are thick on many steelie rivers. Alaskan brown bear (4) is regular guest on rivers.

and the pollutants of the lower sections, then reaches the brackish segment where man's rubbish goes in and out with the tide. Here the steelhead feel the salt again and begin their rejuvenation.

Most of the flies used to catch the steelhead are suggested by its diet, dark nymph-like creations that resemble the immature insects of the fish's early life, and colorful designs, often pink or orange, that resemble the stray salmon eggs that steelhead take. Summer steelhead are likely to take floating flies when found in clear water, but winter fish may come from turgid floods where even wet flies must give way to lures or bait.

Salmon eggs, fished in clusters on or very near the bottom in winter, are perhaps the most deadly steelhead bait of all and many lures and flies are made to imitate them. It must have been the salmon eggs that inspired the bobber type of lure, bringing forth a new form of fishing, best executed with a long and light-actioned casting rod.

Most steelhead flies are designed to ride the current near the bottom on sinking lines, simple ties that often are lost among bottom rubble and bear little resemblance to the traditional masterpieces made for the Atlantic salmon, for the steelhead is a later comer, first recognized as proud game hundreds of years after European noblemen enshrined the salmon.

Certain waters, as is well known, produce races of big fish. A small river can have twenty-pounders while a larger watercourse a few miles away in the same watershed system holds fish little more than half that size. Size evidently is hereditary, for growth is acquired at sea; river forage does not have much effect.

Two British Columbia rivers produce especially huge steelhead, consistently so much larger than any others that serious record hunters hardly consider other streams. These are the Babine and the Kispiox, both part of the Skeena River system. It is largely wilderness, a land of heavy rainfall and deep winter snows, and the Skeena is a frightening river to many, subject to booming muddy floods that roll eighty-foot trees into driftwood and smash through cliffed canyons to spread into broad, silted flats. The two most famous steelhead rivers enter the system more than a hundred miles from salt water. There are other excellent steelie streams of the Skeena watershed, but the strains of fish are smaller and they do not often produce contest winners.

The main Kispiox runs come in fall after most of the salmon are dead, their carcasses grounded on gravel and sand bars. Like many steelhead rivers, the short Kispiox is a little murky at best and capable of turning to a chocolate flood in minutes, subsiding almost as fast. By the time the fall runs are under way there is snow on upstream mountains and a warm day will melt enough to make the river too high and muddy, a matter of slight degrees of opacity and a few inches of depth.

The Kispiox valley is brushy and the river is willow-trimmed. Crowding the banks are coverts holding an incredible number of ruffed grouse, locally called "willow grouse." A local farmer has given up growing oats, for his crop was partly eaten and partly crushed by playful black bears. A fisherman skirting the field is amazed at the destruction, the well-fed bruins evidently having indulged in wrestling matches after their dinner.

Bears feast on the salmon carcasses that drift ashore. Bear hunters thus have an excellent area to hunt, but bear meat fattened on decayed salmon is not gourmet's fare. It is believed the giant brown bears of the Alaska coast outgrew inland grizzlies because of a salmon diet. Bears are sometimes able to catch migrating salmon in river shallows, engaging in clownish antics as they endeavor to capture large fish with mouth and paws while fumbling through heavy current and over slippery rocks.

Kingfishers, nearly always residents of salmon and steelhead streams, appear occasionally. Mergansers bob to the surface with perpetually surprised looks, or buzz the surface at power-on speed. Both are hazards to rainbow fry. There are mountain goats on nearby precipices, but the snowfall is evidently too heavy for the mountain sheep found in adjoining watersheds.

On the shallow riffles is an occasional labored and erratic wake, invariably pointed upstream, usually made by a laggard and faltering salmon, its last reserves of strength expended in uncertain efforts, about to fail its life mission in the last few miles. Sometimes the wakes are steelhead, usually going more steadily. In September come chill rain and days when line freezes in the guides and must be cleared by immersion in river water. Even so, there are fishermen who stay into October and even to November.

Long pools with medium water speed are often the most reliable holds of all, although the exact spot is chosen because of bottom conformations unseen from above the surface. The steelhead that moves on upstream may be replaced by another fish of similar size almost immediately and the same spot is often occupied by such fish year after year, barring natural current changes. On the Kispiox, as on many such streams, the holding areas are called "drifts" and have names, often taken from anglers who have caught big fish there.

The Kispiox and Babine are not noted dry-fly waters. The sinking line is cast across river, a little upstream if the run is swift, a little downstream if it is a slow drift. An upstream cast allows the fly to sink before it feels the line and is pushed upward by current. Most fishermen prefer to feel the bottom as the heavy line and the fly on its short leader move downstream, telling their progress in infinitesimal tremors of the delicate rod tip and hesitant vibrations of the line in the stripping hand. Some anglers work the fly in a gentle retrieve; others swear by the dead drift.

The fly simply stops and the fisherman strikes automatically as he strikes at dozens of rocks each day. And once he has struck he holds his curved rod hard, eyes glued to the tip for a telltale twitch. After a thousand casts and a hundred strikes the tip does move from a leisurely pull, the shifting of a heavy fish suddenly annoyed by the thing it has just taken. Now the fisherman pulls back with a quick look at his reel to be sure there is no tangle, anticipating a run that finally starts slowly but is irresistible, stopping after fifty feet of line has left the spool in a steady buzz. There is a pause, the fish holding steady after moving upstream. Near the bottom the steelhead is quiet behind a boulder under four feet of heavy current. The fisherman, a little fearful of what is to follow but knowing a resting fish will not tire, gives a series of sharp jerks. At first there are several vicious tugs, the fish really aroused now and shaking its head against the pull, finally aware of where the trouble comes from. Its head is tipped downward behind the boulder, resisting the slightly upward pull of the persistent leader, and now it twists and tugs heavily and its tail throws up a broad splash, plainly audible over other river sounds.

A moment later the big fish drives swiftly upstream into a slanting trough of rapids and jumps clear in a shining curve, still heading upstream, then swings about in the slightly slower water below the rapids and repeats the upstream leap, showing a hint of pink stripe, and again drops slowly downstream to take up a sullenly tugging position behind another underwater rock.

Finally, after another rush at the boiling head of the pool, the fish tires and begins to drift downstream with weakened pulls, the leaping over. The nearly dead weight of a twenty-pound fish in heavy current may be the hardest test of an angler's gear. It is then the fisherman applies all that his tackle will stand, bringing the fish head-first toward a pocket of dead water against a small sandy beach.

Like the Atlantic-salmon fisherman, the steelheader expects only one or, at most, a few fish and takes long journeys and violent weather as part of his game. His fish quickly builds its own traditions, a purposeful traveler between sea and mountain torrents.

6.
Cool-water Habitats:

Pike—and possibly muskie—hover in sun-blotched weed beds. Lake trout dwell in the chill depths. Grayling enjoy the river's shallow riffles.

 Pikes lurk and sulk—villains of sport fishing, regarded in the same way as the great barracuda of salt water which they resemble. The pike's evil look and occasional great size have caused it to be associated with ancient superstitions, some of which persisted despite the refutation of scientific fact. When it "appeared" in Old World ponds without having been introduced it was believed to have hatched from sections of water weeds exposed to strong sunlight. People thought it could live more than two hundred years, although fifteen years is a more realistic estimate of the life span. Parts of the pike were thought to have magical healing powers and pike bones were worn as protection from witchcraft. Some American Indians and early white settlers believed the pike would attack humans.

The name pike has been loosely associated with a variety of toothed fishes such as the walleye, which is in fact a perch. The name has been given to almost any long-bodied fish of similar appearance that incurs the fisherman's displeasure, whether toothed or not. The squawfish has been called a pike, although it is only a large member of the minnow family. The northern pike itself is sometimes called a "snake" by fishermen who feel its correct name is not derogatory enough. However all of the true pikes strike artificial lures and most of them jump freely and fight well when hooked, thus satisfying the chief requirements of a game fish.

The evil demeanor of the fish is impressed upon the youngster who fishes for bluegills in a Michigan pond. He hooks his quarry and brings it thrashing to the surface only to have it disappear with an explosion and a blur of sharp teeth and maniacally staring eyes. Or, almost as startling is the sight of a big, motionless pike, glaring grimly at his angleworm. Perhaps his awe is justified, for the fish he instinctively draws back from is capable of capturing wild ducks and of launching suicidal attacks on outboard-motor propellers. Whatever else may be said of him, the pike is a colorful performer, a sneak attacker, and as coarse a feeder as the grayling is dainty.

Half a century ago there was an extended argument among fishermen, some of whom felt the muskellunge was simply a great northern pike with coloration adapted to specific habitats. All pikes do have very similar silhouettes, but there are several different fish, the muskellunge being the largest of all. The northern pike is a cold-water resident with a range that reaches the Arctic Circle. The muskie lives farther south and will tolerate warmer water. The smaller eastern chain pickerel, the grass pickerel, and the redfin pickerel are widely scattered, some of them as far south as Florida.

The pike has been introduced over much of the northern United States. Its original range was the Northeast and the northern states of the Midwest, and it did not appear on the Pacific Coast. It is widely distributed in Europe and Asia, plentiful in Canada and Alaska. There is a theory that when Asia and Alaska were joined at what is now the Bering Strait the oriental pike migrated through fresh or brackish marshes to establish itself in North America. Although tolerant of brackish conditions the pike is primarily a freshwater resident; another theory holds that it crossed in a blanket of fresh water that may have covered the salt sea due to melting ice (the fresh water, being lighter, would have stayed on top).

In the same latitudes northern pike spawn earlier than muskellunge, generally beginning migrations to suitable shallows shortly after ice-out. Spring and fall are the best times for northern-pike fishing unless the angler is far enough north for cold surface water to continue through the summer. They are not deepwater fish in the sense that the lake trout are, but they will move from more active feeding grounds when the water temperature reaches the mid-sixties and may descend to near the 100-foot mark in search of a proper temperature. Such fish are caught by deep trolling or bait fishing, although more sporting pike angling is at the appropriate temperature in less than ten feet

Preceding pages: Stern glare and sharp teeth have made northern pike object of superstition, but it is respected as a ready-striking cool-water game fish.

of water. Although smaller fish tend to move considerably, some of the largest pikes take up permanent residence and are almost as territorial as the large muskies, many of which have acquired individual names and reputations through months or years of angler frustration. Generally creatures of weed beds, the pikes, including the muskies, have some distinctive feeding habits and the fisherman takes advantage of them by observing the designs of northern lakes.

A typical pike lake will have a weed line around it, running close to a natural drop-off. Often there is a band of relatively open water between the shore and the weeds. Pikes are stalkers rather than chasers and they use weeds for concealment, lying hidden within the growth and facing the edge where bait-fish are likely to be moving. So, when there is a band of weeds around a lake, there may be pike facing both the shore and the deep water.

Lying shallow in a northern lake the pike is truly camouflaged by its mottled colors. The green back mingles with the green of the weed bed and the lighter oval spots match the blotched light that comes from above through weed tips, bubbles, floating seeds, and breaks in the surface film made by the weed stems. The pike is nosed to the edge of the weeds and shows a form of concentration seldom seen in fish. Its only motion is the curling fin ends and the slow action of the gills and mouth. The fish's belly matches the background of sandy bottom and stems so well that it seems to shade into them without a break. When the bluegills first appear there is no visible tension in the killer.

The bluegills are about 4 inches long, not too large even for a small pike whose duck-like mouth is lined with sharp teeth. A bluegill cannot escape, even if barely nipped, a form of entrapment that sometimes makes the pike's feeding a prolonged procedure, since the prey must be held and juggled into a swallowing position. The bluegills are in the open water between the weeds and the shore and one of them fins slowly to the surface to examine flotsam that might be a dead insect. The bluegill then heads downward with a flick of its tail and rejoins the others, moving ever so slightly toward the pike's ambush.

A pike often strikes like a snake, its long body curving into a spring that snaps outward from concealment, perhaps thrusting against water growth for added impetus. Now, as the bluegills come a little closer, there is a barely perceptible change of position as the pike seems to gather for the rush.

The strike comes with so much force that there is a surface boil a foot above the scene. The weeds bend and whip with the water's explosion and the bluegills scatter, some of them disappearing into the foliage where the pike has been hiding, some of them rushing for the shoreline. But the little pike does not have his prey; he has himself become prey. He is crosswise in the grim mouth of a much larger pike that shakes its victim roughly and slides back toward the weeds to maneuver, swallow, and digest its meal. Cannibalism is a way of life for pike, which are marauders with a great appetite for any potential food that appears to be alive. The way in which the little pike was captured is not unusual, for the species has a reputation for such extreme concentration upon its prey that when stalking it is almost oblivious to danger. It is the same weakness that causes a fish to strike within the very shadow of a boat once it has chosen to take the lure.

The angler wades the shoreline of the lake, casting toward the inside border of the weeds. He throws his flashing spoon into the edge and retrieves it rapidly. Where it is possible he makes a raking cast, pulling the lure almost parallel to the edge so that it will pass near the head of any watchful pike concealed in the weeds. Some fish strike at the border of the weeds, some trail it almost to the angler's feet before striking, and some follow with a series of swirls and disappear without touching the spoon. One fish pursues it almost to the rod tip and then stops suddenly as the lure is picked up

1

2

3

4

Muskie water (1) has vegetation for hiding predator in ambush, often weedy shelf dropping to considerable depth. Pike are found in wooded lakes (2) shared with bass and trout. Little pike (3) shows ferocious nature against big plug intended for his elders. Moose (4) leaves water in headlong flight for wooded shore.

Leaping muskie is often climax of weeks of fishing and the muskie angler must be a patient seeker for a single large fish.

for another cast. When the fisherman sees the quarry lying there he makes a very short cast which splashes the lure within inches of the fish's head. The strike comes instantly, as if the fish had wanted the spoon all along and had been unable to catch it.

In that particular lake however, most of the larger fish are facing the deep center, lying on the offshore side of the weed line, and as evening approaches the caster moves along that stretch in a canoe. Thus he takes larger fish; only the smaller ones had been willing to strike during the bright heat of the day.

In heavily fished lakes the pike can be difficult, for the ready strikers are quickly skimmed from the population. In such areas the fish may be extremely obstinate and appear to be feeding for fairly long periods. There are wilderness lakes, on the other hand, with consistently cold water and pike near the surface whenever the ice is out. These are highly reliable strikers. This is the sort of lake patronized by bush pilots who are prepared to guarantee fish for their customers.

To reach one such lake the fisherman must travel a long slough ridged with abandoned beaver dams and made up of several slow-moving channels, only inches deep in places and hidden by rushes and sedge. The slough extends for a quarter of a mile before developing into a deep and steep-banked lake, fringed by dead conifers that have skidded down the banks and are decomposing slowly, most of their limbs gone and only jagged stubs trimming the mossy trunks. To navigate the slough the fisherman must drag or carry his inflated boat part of the time. He moves small fish and frogs as he goes and there is an occasional ripple made by a larger fish. A moose has left tracks over much of the boggy area. As the angler nears the lake the beast, roused from a noonday nap, peers over some low alders, then turns away and disappears, probably to lie down again in a better hiding place. There are caribou tracks where the solid ground gives way to bog and tussocks.

As the slough enters the lake there is a narrow stretch of open water only two feet deep with an unstable bottom of detritus almost in suspension. The small oars stir the bottom slightly as the fisherman navigates very cautiously to avoid startling the fish. As the little channel widens to enter the lake he notices a slow wake approaching which stops thirty feet away. Two other wakes appear and subside where the first disappeared, and their makers, heavy northern pike intrigued by the unfamiliar boat, lie motionless, like logs, halfway between air and bottom. The fisherman casts his spoon at the spot and the largest of the fish slashes at it, catches it in his undershot jaw, and stirs a ball of mud and decaying plant matter as he tries to escape. He makes a shaking half-jump with his twisting dragon's head a foot above the surface and slides through a foamy splash, gill covers flared sharply showing the red gills themselves. On his next leap he gains enough speed to clear the water completely and comes down twisting and writhing and rattling the offending spoon. He appears to tire and turns half on his mottled side; but when he is at the boat's beam he begins the thrashing fight again. The fisherman pulls him against the gunwale, works the hooks loose with pliers, and releases the fish. It moves away slowly, no longer showing fear. Wilderness fish have been known to seize the lure a second time, immediately after receiving their freedom from a first encounter.

The other two pike have shown only academic interest in the troubles of their associate and they have moved slowly away from the muddy area to stare at the boat from clear water. When the fisherman casts toward them, the next largest fish strikes, maintaining seniority in the order of attack, and when that one is landed the fisherman looks about for the third fish, finally locates it, and has no difficulty in catching it on the same lure. It is such performances that give the northern pike a low standing with many erudite anglers, yet there are times when more sophisticated pike are all but impossible to take.

Most big pike such as this one come from remote places and are found after long and difficult travel, usually by canoe.

Probably because of its durability, the metal spoon has been used more than any other artificial lure in fishing for pikes, whose needle teeth are very destructive to plastic or wood. The large streamer fly is extremely effective for northern pike, especially when retrieved rapidly, but that fishing method has made a slow start, for those traveling in pike country have generally carried only light fly tackle for trout and heavy casting or spinning gear for pike. The pike streamer is large and requires a sturdy rod. Floating fly-rod lures will take pike, but most of them are too fragile for more than one or two fish. Streamers do not last either.

Large pike have few things to fear except fishermen and even larger pike, but the juvenile is in the same position as any other tiny fish in clear water when the loon is hunting, and the eerily musical cries of the little pike's enemy float across the backwoods lakes all through the fishing season. The common loon is a master of aquatic travel, although it can move on land only by a flopping crawl or a series of awkward leaps. It stays submerged for long periods, swimming at great speed, propelled by both its webbed feet and its adaptable wings. Many loon dives are charted after a leisurely surface inspection, the floating bird putting its head under water to look about and then diving when a target is presented. Sometimes the bird simply swims down, sinking with hardly a ripple. The calls of loon have been mistaken for those of madmen and bull elk, and their half-running, half-flying dashes across the lakes have caused serious fishermen to neglect their lures for the moment. Some of the surface sprints appear to be family races. Some are designed to distract enemies from the loon's nest, built at the very edge of the water so that the bird can be quickly launched in flight. In late evening a loon leaves the darkening lake by a takeoff run, a gradual ascent on short wings, and possibly a circle to gain altitude before pointing for some other lake. And though the loon's belly may be full of little fish, the large pike will have his day if newly hatched little loons should try their webbed feet under his cold appraisal as he lurks in ambush.

Although they may spend hot weather in gloomy depths, pike are dependent upon shallow spawning areas, and the requirements for the spawning areas are rather exacting. The spawning itself is a rather inexact process: The eggs are scattered freely, generally in marshy shallows. The best lakes have such quiet shallows, or are near them. A fairly long migration is often required for the fish to reach an ideal spawning location, and the search begins shortly after the ice goes out. Residents of open rivers are more likely to be wanderers than those living on the edges of acceptable spawning grounds. Some of the best pike fishing is in the sluggish backwaters of large, cold rivers where purposeful wakes and booming strikes move the weeds along the boggy shores. Evening is a time of pike movement in most waters, and the pike spawning runs are most active then. In summer a far northern river and lake system can accommodate pike in the shallows, lake trout in the deepest and cleanest lake sectors, grayling on the shallow riffles and bars, and the inconnu, or sheefish, as a migrant, usually caught in backwaters just off the main current.

There is a common belief that pike and muskies shed their teeth during midsummer and thus decline to strike, but high water temperature is a more likely reason for this. Teeth lost accidentally are replaced, and where a new tooth is about to appear the jaw is reddened, which leads to the tooth-shedding and sore-mouth theory.

The sheefish, prized as a fighter and a popular food fish among Eskimos, is a long traveler, swimming perhaps a thousand miles up a Canadian or Alaskan river, making the trip during summer in preparation for fall spawning. It is a large-scaled predator and classified as a whitefish. It lives to more than twenty years of age and may weigh over fifty pounds.

While the pike sulks in bog-bordered backwaters and beside rotting logs, the lake trouts hold

1

Big lake trout (1) live in deep, cold water but may be on surface at ice-out. Muskie water (2) can be misty-silent with promise of violent strikes from weedy nooks. Angler (3) plays leaping muskie near stumps of drowned trees. Frog (4) lives dangerously near any species of pike family. Heavy-headed caribou (5) travels springy tundra. Pike (6) has met defeat.

3

2

4

5

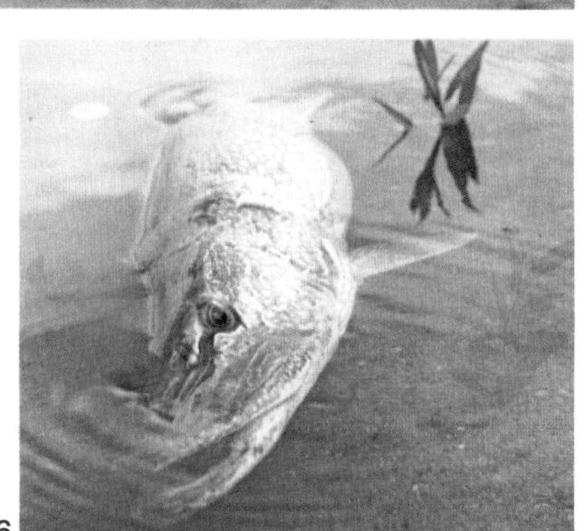

6

1

2

Hungry pike (1), called "snake" by its detractors, takes crushing grip on plug. Muskie (2) has nearly same silhouette but grows larger and has added allure of scarcity. In Yukon lake (3) northern pike shakes a spoon. He was one of several fish that waited their turn at lure in weedy cove near Alaska Highway. Inflated boat was packed to site.

to the cold, clear areas of water in the same latitudes, and the same lake often accommodates both fishes with little overlap. The lake trout, or mackinaw, is a char, a resident of water with scanty life. It demands a chill temperature intolerable to most freshwater fishes, and it is only in cool weather or in the northern parts of its range that it moves in the shallows. As northern ice goes out, the bank fisherman works from a steep shore, where gravel is mixed with stone, and casts far out. His shining lure twinkles as it begins its descent, then disappears in darkness, finally reaching the clean, uptilted bottom. The retrieve brings it up the slope to the fisherman's feet. At such times the lake trout follow shallower reefs and points, but as the long days of sun heat the surface they continually go deeper until only a wire line or heavy weights will reach the mackinaw's level, which may be hundreds of feet down. Here the strike is a remote thing. The play is to bring the fish up from the pressures of its depth, rather than to hold it in horizontal runs; as it nears the surface it is often more dead weight than game fish. But at ice-out, or in the constantly chilled waters of the Far North, the fisherman prospects for the proper depth with his casting tackle and then hooks a fish that sweeps and dives with slab-sided power. Once he has established the trout's cruising depth he has moved a long way toward continuing success.

The largest of the trouts has the simplest existence. Temperature is the key to the lake trouts' welfare and they seek it between 40 and 45 degrees. In such cold waters the food chain is short. In many lakes the lake trout feeds on small ciscos, a bait-fish

3

that lives on plankton or small minnows. At times the big trout live with alewives, another forage fish, and yellow perch are sometimes available. Many lake-trout lakes also contain smallmouth bass, but their paths seldom cross, for the bass wants much warmer water.

The chief enemies of the lake trout in the Great Lakes have been the sea lamprey and pollution. The former is largely under control at present, the latter not at all. In the Great Lakes the laker's popularity has suffered through the infusion of the more prolific Pacific salmon species.

More glamorous than the northern pike, larger, and with tolerance for warmer waters, the muskellunge is perhaps the goal of more unsuccessful fishing trips than any other American fish. The true muskie fisherman expends many hours per strike, often many days, and frequently fishes for known individuals. Nowhere are trophy muskies plentiful, and a population of one per surface acre would mean a good lake indeed. The large muskie, with his assassin's glare, is strongly territorial, is left alone by lesser fish, and with age his craftiness begins to control his unrestricted gluttony. So he examines monstrous baits with caution and often becomes a local fable among guides and anglers alike.

Muskie coloration varies with location and bottom tints, but the "tiger" pattern of shaded vertical stripes is ideal for the fish's habit of hiding in rooted weeds with their upright shadows. The stripes tend to fade away on the edges and the fish becomes a hazy part of its environment. The large fish literally takes on some of its surroundings;

1

3

Muskie (1) jumps in typical twisting style. Green heron (2) makes off with sunfish gathered with lightning thrust from low shoreline perch. Probing obstacles and water growth, anglers cover muskie water (3), which is likely to border fertile marsh. Floating pads are muskie shade. Walleyed pike (4) is really a perch, but it has teeth and other traits of its namesake. Eastern chain pickerel (5) are smaller editions of toothy muskie and widely distributed pike.

4

5

water growth begins on the broad back as the giant becomes more and more sedentary. So, in the case of the muskellunge, the term "mossback" is appropriate.

Persistent trophy seekers will go so far as to chart the locations of large fish in miles of muskellunge lakes, and sometimes fish for only a short while at each known residence on a day's fishing, hurrying on to try for another giant if the first does not respond. Because the fish is experienced and may have broken tackle on earlier occasions it is likely to follow baits cautiously for some distance from its ambush. The muskie fisherman is seldom devoted to ultralight tackle. Strikes come seldom and he is prepared to make few concessions to a trophy once it is hooked. The outsized plugs require powerful equipment. A large sucker is the traditional natural bait for muskie, trolled or cast. Most specialists prefer cloudy, windy days. Although the muskie is best known as a lake fish, some of the largest specimens are found in the St. Lawrence River, where trolling has killed many record individuals.

The cruel image of the muskie, like that of the pike, is enhanced by the villain's practice of maiming prey and carrying it crosswise in the mouth for long periods. It may be a method of rendering the victim incapable of escape, but it appears to be sadistic.

The muskellunge is found across much of Canada, lives over a wide range in Minnesota and Wisconsin, and is even found in some of the impoundments of the South. It can be distinguished from the northern pike by the number of tiny holes, or mandibular pores, along the ventral margin of the lower jaw. The pike has no more than five on each side, the muskie has six or more. The muskellunge differs from other pikes by lacking scales on the lower half of the cheek and gill cover. There have been breeding crosses between pikes and muskies.

There are smaller editions of the pike. The eastern chain pickerel, for instance, has wide distribution. Where the muskie may be large at thirty pounds, the northern pike over twenty pounds is big, and a chain pickerel of more than five pounds is a trophy. Pickerel are year-round strikers and are valued by icefishermen.

Some of the largest pickerel are found in areas where they are not highly regarded, and very large ones are caught far south of the range of northern pike and muskies. Some of the trophies come from the pickerelweed and pondweed flats of southern lakes and backwaters. They are found as far south as southern Florida and are scattered from New England to Texas, but they are most plentiful in the Northeast. Even more than the other pikes, the pickerel is a weed dweller with a mouth almost completely filled with slender, sharp teeth, and an appetite proportionately as large as that of its great relatives. In its preferred waters it slashes viciously at frogs, minnows, and other pickerel, but can go for long periods without feeding.

If not truly a panfish, the pickerel is a fellow resident of panfish waters in the East and has prospered in the weedy edges of hundreds of ancient millponds, which become more attractive as they age and fill with sediment and weeds. But pickerel live in large lakes, too, sharing the more southerly habitat with largemouth bass. When found in weedy bass lakes they will sometimes be in that marginal water which appears too thickly grown to accommodate bass. In these large lakes they tend to colonize certain points and coves, while seldom appearing in other waters that look about the same. Fast-moving lures will attract them from thick weeds, and the noisy surface spinner is among the more successful attractors, drawing attention when sputtered through the greenery, or better yet, retrieved lengthwise along the weed-bed's edge in the same plan that attracts the border-hidden pike or muskellunge.

The pickerel's home waters are peaceful, pleasantly noisy with the calls of red-winged blackbirds by day and vibrating with the sounds of frogs and limpkin at night. Now and then a blackbird will flutter a little on its cattail perch as a menacing pickerel bulges beneath it. The frogs are pickerel fare, sometimes caught where the fish is flopping as much as swimming in matted grass or elodea. Where the minnows are thick in the shallows the pickerel competes with white ibis, blue heron, and green heron, sometimes so close to land that it swims away from a raccoon's busy wading.

The true panfish of the pikes are the grass and redfin pickerels, small fish that seldom grow larger than a foot long. Both grass and redfin varieties live in the eastern half of the United States and are only slightly different, the grass pickerel appearing in the Mississippi drainage, while the redfin is a resident of the Atlantic watershed. In waters where both northern pike and grass pickerel are found the spawning times are about the same and the spawning territories coincide. Thus it is possible that the young of the grass pickerel may divert some hungry perch from the offspring of the larger fish. At the same time young pickerel are likely to compete with little northern pike for small crustaceans, insects, and algae.

The little pickerel shun wide open stretches and fit their slim bodies to narrow gaps in swamp vegetation where current is very slow or nonexistent, leading to unusual fishing methods. Along some grass and brush-choked creeks, fishermen walk gingerly with a light cane pole and short line, using nothing but a little strip of white cloth as a lure. When the briskly dapped rag is taken in a rush the angler simply lifts the fish out. He uses no hook and the squirming prize is held only by its tiny teeth impaling the cloth.

Walleyes and saugers are members of the perch family, although often grouped with the pikes because of their toothy mouths. The walleye grows much larger than the sauger and both have been taken through commercial fishing in some of the large northern lakes, although they are protected for the sports fisherman in most of their range. They are basic fishes for many of the large impoundments of central and southern United States, although they were primarily considered a northern fish before those constructions.

Both spawn in the fall over shallow gravel and rubble, but at other times both are primarily deepwater fish, taking live bait and artificial lures. In some of the large impoundments most of them are taken through slow and fairly deep trolling off the rocky points and along the steep bars. Both fish have an aversion to small waters and efforts at planting them in narrow lakes or streams have been unproductive, although the biological reasons are obscure.

Many of the finest walleye and sauger catches have been made within sight of the great concrete walls of the impoundments, and the heavy jig, worked on the bottom and immediately beneath a drifting boat, has been a productive method. Foul weather has long been associated with such fishing for the glassy-eyed fish, both above and below the dams.

In the man-made turmoil below the spillways, the walleyes and sauger appear in schooling runs, their upstream travel blocked by the concrete cliff, and they take bait or lure far down in the chilly turbulence, usually accepting it with a light, turning strike. Once they are hooked they carry on a dogged and twisting fight, less spectacular than many fishes, but they are prized as gourmet material and remain one of the most valued fish of all.

The waters of the pikes and the big-toothed perches bridge the gap between the cold trout waters and the warmer more sluggish watercourses that please the largemouth bass. The pikes have a niche in both worlds, neighbors of the lake trout on the one hand and near to the smallmouth bass on the other. The muskellunge and the northern pike have added drama to angling and no fishes have stirred more folklore or contributed more to the mystery of inland waters. They are cold-water fishes, but some of the rivers they inhabit widen into warm-water fisheries in their lower reaches, and the pikes and big perches are part of the transition.

7.
Bass Country:
Increasingly it is the man-made impoundment, where smallmouth prowl the twilit bottom and largemouth cruise the warmer levels above.

In nature's scheme the home of the smallmouth bass falls somewhere between the colder flows of the trout stream and the sluggish rivers and warmer waters of largemouth habitat. To some extent he adapts to both environments, a violent bronze surprise for both trout and largemouth anglers in those marginal waters where either trout or largemouth methods may attract him.

One part of the smallmouth's world, the streams of the mountain valleys, has shrunk because of dams and pollution, curses sometimes escaped by trout brooks that are too far up the slopes to be affected. But the smallmouth has taken up housekeeping in the reservoirs, and it is in the impoundments that he has reached his largest known size, becoming a deep-bodied bottom-prowler, striking slow-going baits in the perpetual twilight—and if the glancing surface lunges are missing, there is another kind of thrill in the durable resistance of a broad side turned against deep water in downward thrusts.

Streams which become overfertile or polluted are likely to purify themselves when harmful practices are stopped; this rarely happens with lakes. The smallmouth stream, generally swifter than largemouth rivers, can live on the very verge of industrialization; some of the loneliest fishing in America can be found only a few miles above the eastern cities in small watercourses of the wooded hills, in streams well-filled with smallmouth bass but forgotten by sportsmen who prefer either some species of larger fish or the accepted glamour of trout.

And there are many sectors of the Northeast where the smallmouth bass—all bass for that matter—has never been accepted as a game fish by a citizenry brought up on trout and salmon. It is a traditional dislike, a custom in thinking, going back a hundred years to the time when bass lovers were spreading their fish by means of wooden buckets in wooden railway cars pulled by wood-burning locomotives. Angling has its own caste system, both in fish and fishermen, and in those days it was an active question whether any black bass introduction was wise. History proved that some of the first plantings were in error, for the smallmouth is capable of taking over from trout and salmon in marginal waters. It is a blow to trout men to find that biologists list the bass as a more advanced and resourceful species than their favorites. Evolution has simply moved farther for the bass. At any rate, large lakes cannot be changed once productive plantings are made and some New England salmon lakes were permanently transformed to bass waters.

The smallmouth can compete with the largemouth in many places but gives way on some muddy bottoms—waters where experts say the smallmouth could live well if relieved of the largemouth's efficient competition. At the other end of its habitat, the smallmouth can crowd the trout as long as the water is not too swift; trout can live in torrents that are too much for bass. The brown trout, tolerant of temperatures and turbidity, is the nearest neighbor to the bronzeback on one side. Between the largemouth and the smallmouth is the spotted, or Kentucky, bass, more addicted to swift streams than the largemouth and said to be more tolerant of turbidity than either of the better-known fishes. The spotted bass is restricted to an area in the southeastern quarter of the contiguous states and in many respects is an intermediate between the other basses.

There is little difference between the silhouettes of large- and smallmouth bass except for the dorsal fin. In the largemouth it is deeply notched, almost two separate members; in the smallmouth the notch is very shallow, the forward spiny portion attached to the soft rear part, almost from top to bottom. This feature itself can give an illusion of greater body depth when the fins are extended. The spotted bass is more like the smallmouth in fin design, as well as in size of mouth.

The mouth of the smallmouth bass does not reach past the eye. In the largemouth it commonly extends well past. Colors are generally dif-

Preceding pages: Gentle paddle and careful cast bring fishermen to America's favorite fish, largemouth bass, pugnacious citizen of varied waters.

ferent, although there is striking similarity in some waters. Usually, the smallmouth is mainly bronze, the belly often having a muddy look, and the markings on the upper parts are uneven dark blotches. The largemouth has a more distinct lateral line of ragged dark areas, giving him the local name of "lineside," and is likely to appear greenish, less of an olive shade. Smallmouths generally have reddish eyes which may gleam like wet rubies.

The smallmouth is usually a harder fighter, although he may not give a good account of himself if the temperatures and waters are better suited to the largemouth. Along the edges of deep water the largemouth may jump more, simply because it works to the shallows when hooked, while the smallmouth may dive until the rod tip bows under. The smallmouth is at its splashy best in streams, where a jump can develop into a bent-tailed skitter on the surface, the head pointed straight up.

For spawning the smallmouth chooses gravel bottom in clean water and, as with the largemouth, it is the male that prepares the nest and herds the female to it, possibly with competition from other males. After the young hatch, in a few days (the exact time is dependent upon water temperature), they are guarded briefly by the male, which then becomes impatient and may scatter them with cannibalistic charges of his own. Although less dependent upon gravel, the largemouth has a similar routine, generally in somewhat warmer waters, and often with dramatic harassment from panfish predators.

One largemouth nest is almost white on the sand bottom, lighter than any of its surroundings, and located in an open space between thick patches of eelgrass and pickerelweed. The underwater eelgrass waves gently when wind pushes up waves, or as a boat passes, and it barely reaches the surface where it is industriously nibbled by coot, so that some of the tips are ragged. It is fertile water, a million particles of plant and animal life are suspended near the nest and give off tiny glints of light when the sun strikes at just the right angle.

The male fish sees almost completely around his guarded perimeter. He is suspended a few inches above the nest and the shadow he makes is more visible than the fish himself, a crisp black outline on the white sand of the bed. The fish is almost motionless, but the translucent tail weaves in smooth undulations, making minute adjustments in balance. The bass weighs less than two pounds, yet he commands a difficult situation and will do so for several days.

Several feet away a 5-inch bluegill moves restlessly, barely visible against a sun-blotched backdrop of grass, the dark gill spot its most prominent marking. It fins slowly toward the nest and makes a little false start at higher speed.

The male bass darts at the tormentor and the bluegill disappears in the grass. The bass makes a turn too quick to be seen clearly and spurts back to his bed. As he left several other bluegills appeared and rushed at the nest, but now they scatter and the bass stops almost as if jerked by a string, settling again to his precious eggs for the thousandth time. The game will continue until the spawn hatches and for some days afterward. If the male bass loses a few eggs to the ravenous bluegills, he will save many, and the predatory panfish will be the prey on another day as the bass grow to full size.

Water insects, crayfish, and other underwater residents also will consume bass eggs, but if only one or two of the thousands in the nest become mature bass the hatch will have succeeded.

Like other small fry, very small bass feed on tiny crustaceans and other minute creatures, but when they near catchable size the bass, especially the smallmouth, turn to foods strikingly similar to those of catchable trout. A stream fisherman, unable to catch larger bass, may turn through boredom to trout flies and fish them dry in the edges of fast runs. The rise may be like a trout's; the fish will be a 6-inch bass. In another era, true dry-fly fishing for smallmouth bass was widely

Left: Smallmouth water overlaps largemouth habitat in slow streams where a veteran can name the spot where each will live. Smallmouth (1) and largemouth (4) differ in preferences but act much the same when found together. Silent canoe (3) has long been choice for smallmouth. Raccoon (2) is nocturnal prowler of shoreline where frog (5) may be victim of either coon or fish.

3

1

4

2

5

practiced. It was before the advent of the cruder but more efficient bass bug and came about evidently as an offshoot of trout angling, so even the wet flies used were established trout patterns, simply tied in larger sizes. The classic dry fly works better for smallmouth than for largemouth, the latter desiring more action in the deception.

Smallmouth bass, wedded to rocky bottom more than their cousins, are adept in pursuing nymphs along the river floor, sometimes rooting almost like grazing carp, but with a different objective. The hellgrammite, larva of the dobsonfly, a primitive creature that eventually becomes an insect with a wingspread of 5 inches, has long been a favorite bait of anglers who usually fish it with a bobber on a light leader. The thing is 3 or more inches long, with busy pincers and a hard shell that makes for durability on a hook. Although artificial nymphs tied to represent the hellgrammite can be successful with smallmouths, most flyfishermen use bugs or streamers.

The crayfish, found nearly everywhere the smallmouth lives, is probably the fish's first choice in foods, especially in the softshell stages. A slow crawler on the bottom but a swift backward sculler, the crayfish hides either in rock crevices or holes in mudbanks and bottoms. Its growth comes with a series of shell changes, a hard one abandoned while a soft one forms. There are innumerable species of crayfish and all of them seem to appeal to bass. Sometimes crayfish and hellgrammites are caught together by bait fishermen using nets stretched downstream from where they overturn bottom rocks, although youngsters are likely to scorn such mechanization and catch their crayfish by hand in the shallows.

The smallmouth-bass stream has quick-changing moods which produce eager strikers at times, fish that change to suspicious shadows in low water. Usually, the best smallmouth-stream fishing occurs when high water is first clearing and subsiding in the cool weather of spring or fall. The water is not too transparent and the better fish will take larger lures cast to the banks. Cool spring or fall was the chosen time of the traditional float trip in the Ozark Mountains of Missouri and Arkansas on such rivers as the White, Buffalo, Current, and James, as well as on dozens of lesser-known streams.

Most of the old float rivers are finished now, only crooked grooves on the bottoms of the impoundments that engulfed them, and fiberglass cruisers and water-skiers skim the surface many feet above. On the streams that are left, aluminum and fiberglass have largely replaced the pine johnboats that ran a full eighteen or twenty feet long and came over the shoals (no hill-country guide would call them "rapids") with measured thumps. The guide wore bib overalls and ran his boat with a hand-hewn paddle, seated on a gunny sack that held his spare clothes, and his hat was often the black felt of the mountaineer. If he had to go upstream he might pole with the handle of his sucker gig.

The float trip could last half a day or two weeks, going downstream as the river wound, the parties camping on gravel bars, and when the trip ended the dull red boats went back to the starting points by rail or truck.

Today most float trips occur on waters where big rainbow trout have been planted, but where—in the chill discharge from impoundment spillways—they seldom reproduce. This may have appeal for some, but it is not the float of the die-hard smallmouth men who drifted the misty rivers between the hills for some forty years. Old books about smallmouth will mention the names of the guides, men like Charley Barnes, who may have been the most famous of them all, and who showed me how to trotline for channel catfish when the James River was just right.

When the river is going down it is the shoreline that produces. The really good fishing may last only a very few days while what was high and muddy becomes low and clear. As the water level falls the fish change habits, daytime feeding is likely to slacken, and the gentle eddies just below the fast water hold bass that watch for upstream food and enjoy the extra oxygen that comes from boiling currents, which is especially important to them in warm weather. But the bass cares less for the really quick current; out in the fast runs he will find a spot immediately below a boulder in nearly dead water. The cushion above the rock, although slower than the tilted rapids, is still too swift to please him for long. He may lie quietly against the deeper banks, especially those with roots and undercuts where the pool's current slows a little and there are quiet pockets.

When the water clears, the big plugs that attracted him a few days before are no longer valid; it is a time for light terminal tackle, little spinner-and-fly combinations on delicate spinning rods, and fly presentations that originated with trout tackle. The small bug against the undercut banks could be a terrestrial, a fallen cricket or grasshopper, and should be worked gently, for the low-water bass is seldom activated by mighty pops or gurgles. For that matter, the smallmouth, with all his mad rushes, is not so vulnerable to big noise as the largemouth. In the edge of the heavy run at the pool's head, the small lure should drift down, then turn slowly into the eddies. For the most part, the shallow tail waters are not occupied until dusk.

In the widened tail of a river pool the fish has changed from a reckless charger to a craven sneak who darts away at the shadow of a bird and slides toward deep water when a heavy lure or line falls nearby. There a fisherman can employ his trout tactics with long leaders or light line but it is unnecessary to cover the shallow flat thoroughly, for the fish can see the lure from far away. At evening, the fisherman wades cautiously on the edge of the shallow part, looking for telltale wakes, and perhaps seeing crayfish and minnows streaking away from his feet or disappearing in tiny mud clouds as they slip into hiding in large gravel or beside larger stones. Bullfrogs may take to the deep water or try to hide near the shore, and the tail of a pool is an ideal spot for a raccoon to start his evening rounds. A hound's voice carries briefly from a darkening hollow.

The small lure is cast well out and left for a long while with minor twitchings, for repeated casts are likely to frighten the fish. If the bass strikes in such a place he is likely to come as a dark streak and be gone before he knows he has made a mistake.

In New England lake waters the smallmouth-bass season opens around June 1, about the time when the spawning begins in average years. In Maine there will be a period when only single-hooked flies or lures are permitted, bait fishing being allowed later on. The map of Maine is flecked with lakes and chains of lakes. Some are tied together by brooks or rivers and shallow until they become great bogs in some sections, wide flats where a moose may travel in splay-toed nonchalance although a man will curse and flounder. But it is the granite shorelines and islands that the visiting fisherman remembers best, granite in chunks and shelves and submerged heaps. On sunny days the boulder-heaped edges stand out with sharp shadows and miniature caves. On rainy days they are misty gray, with an occasional pine standing black in a spot which the wind has cleared momentarily.

A great blue heron, silent watcher for movements in the water, is part of an involved chain of events affecting the bass. He will spear a fingerling, meanwhile releasing eggs of the yellow grub from his throat into the water. The larval grubs enter snails; another generation leaves the snail and attaches to the bass. They are harmless to the fisherman but unpleasant to his sight. A heron strikes a bass and the grub comes with it, lodging in the bird's throat to begin another cycle.

In early June, New England water temperatures near the lake shorelines are likely to be very close to what bass prefer. Spawning beds

1

2

3

4

Granite lakes of Maine (1) are smallmouth meccas, but where bass has displaced trout it is not always welcome. Teal (2) are swift visitors of bass fishermen and often nest near smallmouth water. Smallmouth lake has rocky islands (3) and deep holes for resting in summer. Bull moose (4) will be seen near some New England lakes and many in Canada. A Maine bronzeback (5).

5

Pickerel, landlocked salmon, and smallmouth bass may be found in same waters although often at different depths. And at some times of year all can be caught on same tackle.

may be some distance offshore, possibly as deep as twenty feet, and the larger fish are generally some little way out, whether spawning or not. The angler prospects at varying depths, near but not quite against the bank. He finds very small bass in plain sight, sliding in small schools past rock faces or lying almost stationary in crevices between boulders.

Above-water granite boulders are mottled gray except where covered by moss. Submerged rocks appear brown or tan from the surface; many of them are covered by minute growth, a thick coat of living brown slime. When the fisherman can see them well ahead of the drifting boat they are indistinct light areas, and he is careful to cast near each boulder, knowing it provides shade and hiding. He is attentive to underwater ridges and can guess where they are by watching the conformation of the dry land. Ridges may be close enough to the surface to be called shoals or bars, and are especially good during or after high winds. The bar breaks up the wave action, keeping the leeward shallows calmer and collecting considerable food for smallmouths lying on the downwind side. If he has been catching fish along the shore, a fisherman often tries to intercept an underwater ridge at the same depth.

The fishing is likely to be easier if there is a little surface ripple to conceal the fisherman and if all lures or flies are worked slowly, especially the floating deer-hair "powderpuffs," sometimes shaped to resemble frogs or mice, and in several colors. On a dull day in Maine color seems to make no difference and neither does shape, but the angler recalls summer fishing on a Michigan lake when late-evening smallmouths came with a rush to a white deer-hair floater and ignored the browns, grays, and bright colors. Perception is there, even though selectivity seldom is.

The lure is twitched only a little unless the fish, from some mystic bass perversity, prefers a gurgle. To keep the floater quiet, the fisherman coats it with line dressing. If he leaves the waterproofing off, the bristling hair collects water, sinks slightly, and gives off plops and gurgles as he works it. In any event, the smallmouth lure need not retain the airy high-floating dryness of the trout fly, but it is likely to be somewhat more dainty than largemouth choices.

The smallmouth will watch the surface thing for a long while, perhaps as long as half a minute, and then come up in a charging sweep, sometimes from almost directly beneath, actually going half out of the water with his own momentum. From the side he is likely to show his dorsal fin in a more deliberate take. Almost invariably, he goes down when the hook is set, then comes up to jump, and starts for the bottom again. The jump may be an effort at throwing the lure, the fish's head going almost straight up and the entire body shaking and falling back tail first, for a lure is obviously easier to shake in the air than in the water. The smallmouth also has a clean, trout-like leap, going back headfirst as if he had been launched into the air by simply darting too close to the surface; and he is capable of a brief tailwalk.

As weather becomes warmer, the surface striking will be less reliable and most likely to occur at night, dawn, and dusk. The smallmouth deep-troller in New England, who frequently uses streamer flies, may encounter landlocked salmon or brook trout, fish that had already retired to deeper water by the time spring surface activity began for smallmouths. In a southern impoundment he may collect walleye with the same trolling methods used for bass.

Even after New England's surface waters are warm enough for good bass fishing there will be an occasional gleaming turn of a landlocked salmon, temporarily strayed from more ideal depths. A pickerel may come from a fallen treetop or a narrow cove of spike rush, and the smaller lures will take both white and yellow perch. The yellow perch is food for the smallmouth but the white perch is a direct competitor, highly regarded

Largemouth bass (opposite), gills agape, tries violent leap to shake hook. Walleye (below) is favored table fish and has fared well in deep reservoirs and cold discharges of dam spillways.

because of its value as a food fish. In some areas, for some unknown reason, the white perch is seldom eaten by the bass and is prone to crowding. Perch are largely dusk and nighttime feeders, and so are underharvested by anglers.

Smallmouth bass, needing cool water, have prospered in the deeper lakes. Before impoundments were constructed they were not well known in southern lakes, most of which were shallow and weedy with little choice of temperature during hot weather. Deep northern glacial lakes tend to have a formal sequence of water movements throughout the year, events that, once understood, are the key to much good fishing that might otherwise be missed. The principles of thermal stratification, governing certain physical qualities of water, are valuable to fishermen pursuing any of the trouts, especially lake trout and landlocked salmon, as well as smallmouth bass, the pikes, and the deep-going walleye or perch.

The seasonal shifts of lake water, or "turnovers," are based on water density, which changes with temperature. Water is heaviest at 39.2 degrees Fahrenheit. This is its "turning point": The colder or warmer it becomes relative to this temperature, the lighter its weight. Ice is lighter than liquid water and floats. Warm water is lighter than cold water and stays on a lake surface in warm weather. Thus there is a formal programming of what occurs in a deep lake in moderate

A slowly-worked popping bug with busy rubber legs is leading fly-rod tempter of black bass when fish are near the surface.

 or cool climates. In warmer climates the program of stratification is less pronounced or lacking because of milder seasonal changes, but it is still important to fish location.

In winter, if the surface freezes, the water immediately below the ice is very near 32 degrees and becomes warmer the deeper it is tested, until a temperature at or near 39.2 degrees is reached. That will be the temperature at the bottom. However, although all resident game fish may prefer the warmer bottom water, their depth may be restricted by lack of oxygen, a frequent condition in deep areas that are stagnated during winter conditions. Some of the deepwater fish, such as lake trout, can live in areas with a relative minimum of oxygen. A smallmouth bass, restricted to chill upper levels by a need for oxygen, will not be very active.

"Winter-kill" is usually a result of lasting snow that covers the ice and blocks sunlight, halting photosynthesis and the production of oxygen. "Cold-kill" is another matter—simply the death of fishes that cannot withstand low temperature.

When spring comes and the ice melts there will be a period when the lake "mixes." The sun warms the surface to the temperature of the deeper waters, usually near 39 degrees Fahrenheit, and assisted by the mixing action of wind the entire lake becomes about the same temperature. This is the "spring overturn" and the brief time for surface fishing for lake trout and landlocked salmon in a temperate climate. In the Far North a few lakes may retain that condition through the short summer. Such water is too cold for good smallmouth fishing.

As warm weather progresses, the surface water becomes warmer, finally becoming too warm for most of the game fish present. The deeper the angler works his lures, the cooler and heavier the water he fishes, until he may again find the temperature approaching 39.2 near the bottom of a deep lake in a temperate climate. Somewhere between the surface and the bottom, of course, is a combination of food, oxygen, and temperature that will best satisfy the fish he is after. Generally, this occurs near the thermocline, a stratum of water where the change from surface warmth to the cold of the depths takes place. (The terminology of stratification includes "epilimnion," referring to the layer of water above the thermocline, and the "hypolimnion," referring to that below.) The thermocline usually has a satisfactory oxygen supply—if shallow enough for good acceptance of light—and an abundance of aquatic life. In fall, when the surface waters cool to that of the bottom temperature, there is a turnover before freezing, a time when the lake is again the same temperature throughout.

The depth of the upper level of the thermocline changes with the amount of surface disturbance due to wind, heat, and the eutrophic state of the lake, but it can be located by use of a thermometer. It is likely to be somewhere between ten and thirty feet down, yet may be more than twice that. To check the depth his lure is working, a fisherman often trolls near enough to the shore for his lure to hang up, and from immediately above the hangup he can make an accurate measurement of depth. After considerable checking he can adapt his trolling speed and line length to the desired depth.

The clear-cut conditions hinted at by thermal stratification are complicated by the variety of sources of lake water. Spring-fed lakes have a special factor, since spring water has a relatively constant temperature through the seasons, and bass may spend both winter and summer in the same general area because of attractive temperatures. In shallow lakes with subsurface seeps and springs, some fishermen locate cool and productive summer spots by wading, or even swimming, or using thermometers extensively. The location of proper temperature is complicated by the need for oxygen. Turbulent waters that enter smallmouth lakes may collect fish at the stream mouths, even when more attractive temperatures are found

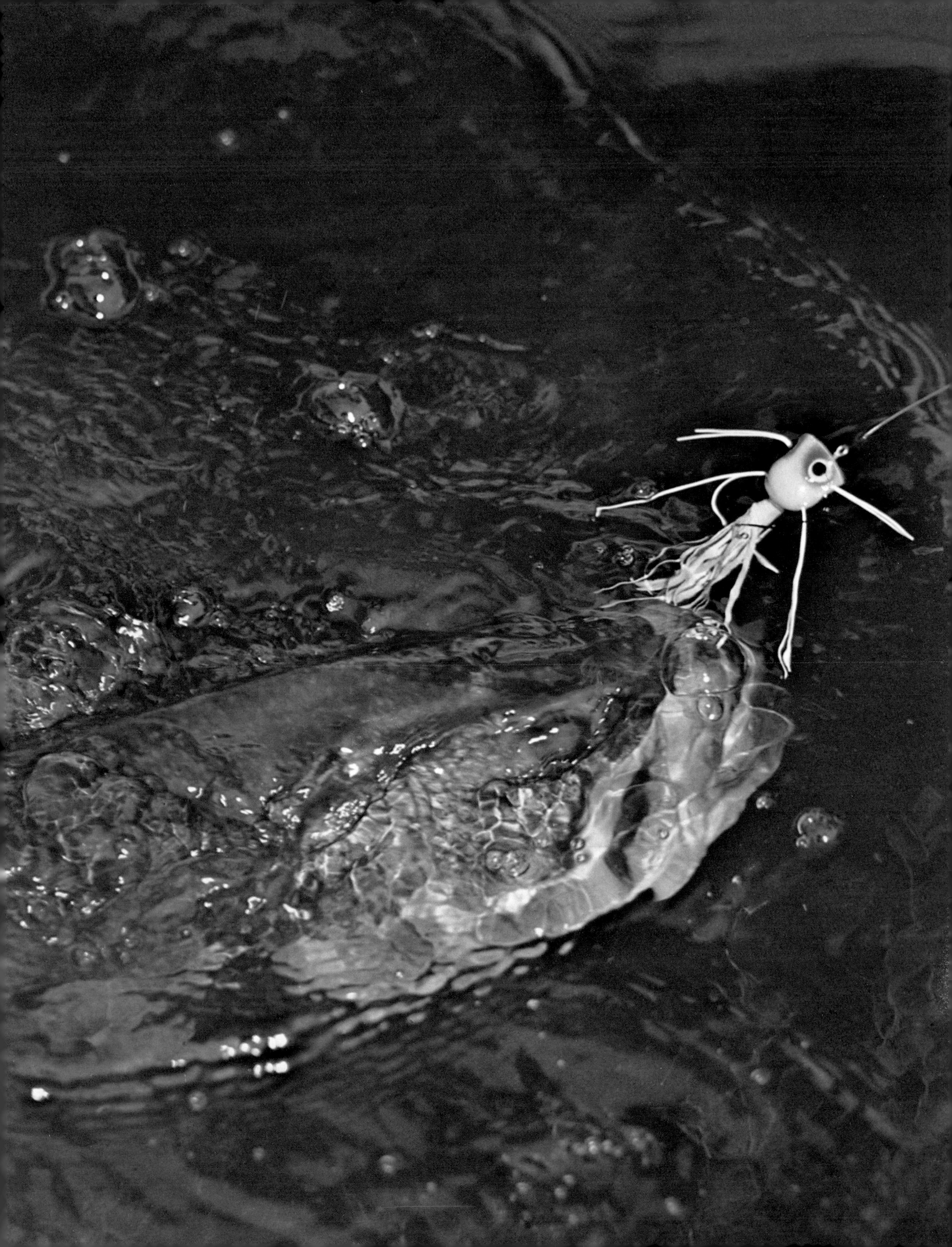

Fisherman (top) leaves his boat to work beds of grass and weeds on shallow lake. Leaping bass distorts a reflected image of reeds.

elsewhere. The temperature desires of fishes are extremely helpful to know, but unqualified statements about them are dangerous.

Even in southern waters, where fish are traditionally very sensitive to cold, there have been cases of largemouth bass striking a lure in 46-degree water. Smallmouth are known to feed at temperatures as low as 40 degrees, but they seek water in the upper 60's if it is available with food and oxygen. When surface temperatures approach 80 degrees the smallmouth will generally seek deep water, although feeding in shallows at night. Depending upon latitude, largemouths generally prefer temperatures between 65 and 75 degrees, although they are more tolerant of high temperatures, less of low temperatures, than smallmouths. Observers have set the ideal smallmouth temperature at 67 degrees.

Largemouth bass are established in all of the United States except Alaska and there may be isolated colonies in southern Alaska, unmarked on the biologist's map. The fish is at home across much of southern Canada, widening its range by casual introduction, as well as through the planned operations of ichthyologists. At first the largemouth was an easterner. Now it is a western fish as well, adapting quickly to slow streams and natural lakes, and more especially to the giant impoundments where the trouts seek great depth in warm weather, leaving the upper levels of steeply sloping bottom to the bass.

When the big Florida bass, finally accepted as a subspecies, was introduced to a similar latitude in California it prospered and retained its size. Now California challenges Florida as a big-bass state. The size of the mature bass is partly a product of temperature and the length of the growing season, and partly genetic. Although the northern fish are smaller than those of the South, the largest fish of all seem to be in a belt somewhat north of Florida's southern tip. Accounts of giant bass in Cuba are poorly documented, but if record-size fish do live there it upsets one theory—that growth can be too rapid in a very warm climate, leading to a relatively short life and less size in mature fish.

A tagged bass occasionally develops wanderlust that takes him twenty miles in a few days, but bass travels are generally very limited, hardly far enough to be called migrations, and the largemouth's spawning grounds may be in the same area the fish has occupied throughout its life. The days immediately preceding spawning are some of the most productive for fishermen, for both male and female bass are then feeding busily in preparation for bedding and are especially susceptible to some of the more flamboyant lures that represent nothing in particular yet trigger response by producing glitter, wrigglings, and colors associated with many bass foods.

Reports that the fish are "on the spawning flats" are often accepted as describing a fairly permanent condition when actually, during the early stages of the reproductive program, the fish may occupy the bedding area for a few hours and then be gone for days. Fish that seem to crowd the flat may disappear abruptly with a temperature or barometer change.

The busiest spawning season varies with the latitude from February to July. The fish require temperatures compatible with the areas, northern bass being active through colder weather, although water temperature in the upper 60's will fill requirements anywhere. If prespawning conditions change drastically for the worse and remain bad throughout the season, neither sex will perform its spawning duty and the roe-laden female will eventually absorb her eggs into her body system.

Freshly hatched bass are minute creatures, milling in a dark, swarm-like school and hard to tell from many other kinds of fry. Small bass absorb the remains of their yolk sacks, assume a somewhat slenderized silhouette of their elders, and begin their feeding on tiny water creatures. By the time they are 6 inches long they are taking good-sized insects and tiny minnows. Many bass of that size are caught on baits or flies intended for

Mixed bag of eastern chain pickerel and largemouth bass is caught by fisherman using inflated float to carry him through deep weed bed.

bluegills or other small sunfish. (The black bass is a sunfish himself, true bass being of another classification entirely.)

Even when only 6 inches long the bass has a distinctive dark tail that sets it apart from most other fishes, and the irregular dark line along the largemouth's side is most distinct in younger fish. At 6 or 8 inches, bass commonly appear in twos or threes. This practice often continues until a fish is large enough to prey on other bass; then it becomes a solitary. The true trophy bass are large females.

Not generally considered a school fish, the largemouth bass will nevertheless congregate in true schools for feeding purposes, and will rest near the bottom in looser associations. Bar bass, also commonly called school bass or jump bass, make noisy attacks on schooled bait in certain impoundments and rivers. Usually it is the smaller fish that cut up the frantic shad or menhaden, the really big fish being unable to compete in agility and speed, and thus inclined to lie deep and wait for crippled bait-fish or unwary small bass.

On lakes the bait schools will flee under attack, and casters are frequently forced to follow the striking fish that come up in frothing fury for a few moments, then disappear completely to relocate the bait again, perhaps more than a hundred yards away.

On some southern rivers the "schooling grounds" are more or less stationary, the same spots being used year after year. Current is essential, and bottom formation is the basis for most such feeding. Often the key is a submerged bar below which the bass can lie and over which the bait must come on its way downstream—or sometimes upstream—the route somewhat compressed by the abrupt shallowing of the flow. The juncture of two streams, usually a small creek feeding a river, may cause schools of bait to form route patterns in the resultant eddies, and here the bass will gather for the kill. Fishermen anchored within casting range watch closely for surface activity, which may last only seconds during each individual rally. The first sign may be a single jumping bait, followed by a single fish, then a flurry of strikes, perhaps over a large area. The casting lures usually match the size of the bait and must be fired accurately, especially if only a few fish are up, the ideal situation being a lure that drops between a charging bass and its fleeing quarry.

River schoolers usually come up repeatedly in about the same area, so the fisherman's skiff remains at anchor. Once a school of bait has been scattered the bass settle to the bottom and wait for another. It was many years before fishermen learned to catch the bottom fish, but that has now become one of the more effective methods, the anglers using a bottom lure after learning where the congregation of bass is holding between rallies. Although schooling bass, both top and bottom, occasionally strike almost anything offered, they can sometimes show a selectivity rivaling that of the most civilized brown trout. The bass fisherman uses a vast assortment of lures, dramatically successful models suddenly falling into disfavor, sometimes to return again, but often to lie neglected in tackle trays after their brief fame is ended.

Live bait is sometimes drifted successfully over schooling bass in the rivers. Sometimes an artificial "school" is contrived by anglers who net large quantities of the bait-fish, often menhaden, and chum with them over a "schooling ground" in the same deception practiced by the fly caster for trout or salmon who builds his own "hatch" by continued presentations. If surface striking begins, the fishermen either resort to artificials or simply insert hooks in some of the bait.

Although the pressures of development and pollution have damaged or ruined bass fishing in many rivers and lakes, it is probable there are more fish than ever the country over, man-made impoundments providing thousands of square miles of warm-water habitat and bringing new forms of fishing—methods more refined than any dreamed of, even in 1945. The new systems, most

Shoreline casting for bass is
a sport for late evening
or early morning when fish move
to shallows to feed,
seeking debris and emergent weeds.

of which are aimed at black bass, may be regarded as somewhat less sporting by veterans but they are productive.

The history of an impoundment can be forecast by biologists. First comes the gradual flooding of new areas, rich in mineral nutrients for algae and bacteria. The result is quick-growing small predators and active bass with almost unlimited food supply and little competition, fish that cruise the streets and alleys of submerged towns and may follow the depths of old watercourses that are slowed by the downstream dam. Thousands of small bass are found on the constantly changing shorelines where a fisherman may look down upon the tops of conifers or hardwoods, still green although completely submerged. It may take a long while for an impoundment to fill and as the waterline rises the bass become larger. There are mobile bass fishermen who watch the progress of a distant reservoir, and are ready to take advantage of its first few years of peak productivity.

When California's Lake Shasta was new I patrolled the coves, casting plugs against banks where mountain vegetation was being submerged. As yet, no water plants could be seen there. The water, cool and clear from the arrested rivers, and originating from melted snows in high country, was inching its way up the mountain canyons, stopped by a dam that also halted the Pacific salmon milling in the fast water below it. Along the wilderness banks were bands of mule deer, gradually displaced from their canyon homes.

Generally the fish were almost on the edge, but now and then one would shoot upward from blue depths, a fast-growing blob that would suddenly take on a bass's form and crack a surface lure in a shower of water. Standing on a cliff, I watched another angler and the cruising bass he cast to, although the fish were invisible to him.

When Lake Mohave grew across the Nevada desert I first fished the sheer rock bluffs for bass, intrigued by the dark caves, newly flooded and high above what had once been a dusty valley floor. I caught bass, and there was an occasional rainbow trout when the lure went deep, but my best bass fishing came when I drifted across cactus flats where a bass could come from the shade of a submerged prickly pear in shallow water. Newly submerged land of almost any kind has an abundance of bass food.

Biologists have learned that the excellent fishing on a new impoundment is of limited duration, being followed usually by a slack period and then by slow improvement as the impoundment begins to become a stabilized biological community. At the time I fished Lake Taneycomo in southern Missouri, the falloff in fishing on the fast-aging lake was not understood. Much later, with the Tennessee Valley Authority lakes, came the same lake-aging problems on an immense scale and knowledge increased rapidly.

By geological standards a lake of any kind is an ephemeral thing, whether caused by a volcano, gouged by a glacier, or formed by a dammed river. From its birth the lake begins to fill from its watershed. Its shallows become marsh, then solid earth, and the bottom rises from siltation and from the decay of plant and vegetable matter. On a rocky mountainside, the process may be one of uncounted centuries. A farm pond that collects the erosion of cultivated land can fill in a few years, or even from a single flood. A large impoundment may not fill rapidly, but its bottom is soon transformed from the food-rich, freshly flooded terrain as currents are halted, bottom structure crumbles, and erosion spills into the deep water. There will be some degree of fish stunting or change in species populations; poor angling results. Then there is a gradual improvement as natural aquatic vegetation flourishes, affording cover for bait. As the bait-fish prosper, so do the carnivorous game fish.

At first, water fluctuation was believed to be detrimental to fish populations, but the "drawdown," a process of lowering and then refilling easily controlled lakes, has helped to restore good fishing in many instances. Slow-moving or sta-

2

4

3

Quiet country ponds (1) furnish easy sport in rural communities. In some cases fisherman stands on neatly mowed grass. Rod held high, fisherman plays lily-pad bass (2). Eelgrass (3) is difficult for lure but good for bass in prespawning feeding binge. Crayfish (4) is staple of both large and smallmouth bass and subject of many lure imitations. Giant Florida bass (5) comes from warm shallow lakes with continuous growing season.

5

 tionary bodies of water collect pollutants that may be oxidized or "broken down" by exposure to sunlight for a considerable period. The drawdown is now an accepted instrument of fish management. Resident fish are confined to smaller areas while the drawdown is executed, returning to "new" borders when the lake is refilled.

Historically, the largemouth black bass was fished primarily on shoreline and against cover, but when deep impoundments came into use a new school of bass fishermen appeared. One of their first practices, a technique known to lake-trout fishermen for many years, was to probe the bottom, though sometimes quite close to shore. The deep impoundment bank, much steeper than that of most natural largemouth lakes, gives the fisherman an opportunity for quick prospecting since he can cast out from shore, allow a lure to sink, and bring it up the sloping bottom to the depth where fish are to be found.

The dedicated impoundment fishermen employ detailed maps, usually made before the impoundment was filled, with careful attention to old river beds, highways, railways, and even buildings. With due attention to water temperatures, they probe with electronic depthfinders for submerged ridges or mounds, knowing that bass are likely to congregate where any obstacle occurs and often prefer one that is a considerable distance from the busy shoreline. Even without a map or fathometer, an observant fisherman can see shoreline shapes that indicate the presence of underwater ridges, channels, or drop-offs. Deep trolling at high speeds with heavy tackle often locates congregations of bass which can then be fished with more sporting equipment.

When careful fishermen found that bass spend most of their time away from the shorelines they adopted some completely new lures. Bottom and near-bottom bass fishing is best done with lures that work slowly and can be kept well down during most of the retrieve. The fishermen used live minnows and lizards, but they also adopted a vast variety of soft plastic things that resembled eels, worms, or small snakes. Many of the creatures represented are not common bass food (a biologist who has dissected thousands of bass stomachs says he has found only three snakes), but the qualities of the soft plastic lures were the same as those of a variety of bass prey and the soft lures—usually worked gently—are among the most effective of all attractors.

A natural or artificial lake may lose its good bass fishing through normal aging, or through a hastened process spurred by pollution of many kinds. Nutrients, essential in moderation to fish life, may outgrow their ecological function and disappear. Pollutants may indirectly bring about excessive growth of water organisms which, in breaking down, use up oxygen needed by game fish, silt the bottom, or become toxic, as in the case of some blue-green algae. Excess of "bloom" on any lake is an indication of this process of overfertilization. "Pollution" can be relative; a polluted body of water may not lose all of its bass, yet with a gradual deterioration of game fish there is a corresponding increase of rough fish, such as carp, bullheads, gar, or grindle—fish that require less oxygen than bass and contribute to a crowded condition while consuming much of what oxygen remains. An overfertile lake may actually produce increased amounts of fish as it ages. Fish quality is debased, however, and the lower orders of aquatic life thrive. The carp, an import from Europe deplored as trash by most sportsmen, is the best subject for fish farming if production weight per acre is the objective.

Fish deaths from extremes in overfertilization come in a sinisterly dramatic form, the execution occurring most often in the dead of night. During a sunny day, prospering organisms suspended in water produce and give off oxygen. But the process reverses when light is gone; then the crowded community absorbs oxygen at a rapid rate, accelerated by high temperatures. So, on a dark and quiet night, with no wind to mix in oxygen from the warm air, the vital supply dwindles and some

Flyfisherman casts for bass on Lake Taneycomo in southern Missouri, one of earliest of the large midwestern impoundments.

time before dawn the game fish suffocate, feebly gulping a liquid that means death instead of life. A series of cloudy days may intensify the condition.

A quiet body of water receiving large quantities of nutrients, supporting a large biological community, and aging rapidly, is termed eutrophic by biologists. One that receives small quantities of nutrients, such as a cold mountain lake, is termed oligotrophic. It is usually more stable in its oxygenic conditions and generally host to small numbers of fish, such as lake trout, noted for survival in deep, clear water.

In addition to the problems of suspended matter, any surplus of dead materials is likely to settle to the bottom, forming a sludge that is incompletely decayed and arrested in its decomposition by lack of oxygen. Such a deposit may be prevalent in slowly moving or stationary waters; it makes bass spawning unsuccessful and can build up to great depths unless flushed out by moving water. It is an accelerating factor in aging. Such a condition exists in waters where chemicals have been employed to kill certain organisms, without truly destroying large quantities of plant life.

Although considered a hardy and prolific fish, the largemouth prospers in a zone of delicate balance, sometimes in danger from overcrowding by its own race or by the panfishes. The bass is able to survive predation by the pikes or other large fish, but it plays a losing role in the intensely eutrophic lake, where a few exceptionally large and hard-to-catch predator fish may flourish, but where slumping catches are the rule and where very few of the in-between sizes that make up most bass fishing are available.

If aging time cannot be set for most man-made lakes, at least the order of events is predictable, as much for the giant canyon reservoir thrusting forth its marching lines of skeletal steel towers, as for the farm pond only a cast across.

In the Midwest a boy and a lake were born about the same time. The lake was a mile long and resulted from damming a small creek that was only a series of small pools in midsummer. Before the creek was dammed, the small pools held a few bullheads, pumpkinseed sunfish, green sunfish, and an occasional small bass. The creek ran through some natural prairie with cultivated ground set back from it. There was no terracing in those days and the farmland was beginning to erode, so that after hard rains the creek bed was a wide flat of silt and sand in some places.

The dam was built for two purposes: to provide a railroad grade across the creek and to hold water for a tank that serviced steam locomotives. When the boy first fished there he used a cane pole and worms, and sat on the edge of the grade. At that time there were hardly any visible water plants, although grass and weeds grew a little higher next to the edges of the lake because of the steady supply of moisture. When the shallow-set bobber went down the boy usually found he had a green sunfish, which he called a "black perch," but if he set his float so that the worm barely cleared the bottom the taker was likely to be a bullhead. The sunfish took the cork down with a series of hard jerks; the bullheads simply moved off slowly, their bites hard to distinguish from those of an occasional snapping turtle.

When the boy began to fish for bass he was fourteen years old. He had missed the fertile bass period that occurred three or four years after the lake was first built because he had no proper tackle, and now the lake was lined by patches of willows. For some time there had been a fringe of cattails, high on the list of pioneering plants of aging shorelines, and some bulrushes. At the edges were scattered plots of pickerelweed and there was a little coontail moss at the shallow end.

The boy fished from a leaking old rowboat that had been dragged to the lake on a buggy chassis and was left for anyone who wanted to use it, hidden in a little channel that ended at the base of some cottonwoods. He used a hollow steel rod with glass guides and bait-casting reel without a level-winding mechanism. The silk line was dried carefully after every use and the lure was a large plug, jointed in the middle and designed to run a foot under the surface. The procedure was to move along the shoreline very slowly and cast as close to the willows as possible. The big bass struck at the edge of some coontail moss, and the boy, seeing it was the largest fish he had ever hooked, fought his excitement grimly, forcing himself to give a little line, the spool making a few turns under his thumb.

When the bass jumped it was the gaping-mouthed surface lunge of a heavy fish. Strands of moss flowed from the first two feet of line, and when the boy had seized his catch by the lower lip it hardly flopped on the boat bottom. The time was October, when the water was cool enough for bass to strike at midday, though too cold for wading comfortably in tennis shoes and overalls. A squad of green-winged teal hissed by as the boy played his fish, forgetting the shotgun in the boat beside him.

Ten years later, when he hurried out from town after work, he usually fished in late evening during warm weather. The sport was likely to be best when great sections of the evening sky were taken up by boiling heaps of thunderheads, sometimes with lightning reflecting from deep in the cottony masses that changed to gray-blue at the bases. Hundreds of crows passed on their route to roosts in a nearby tree farm. There was a sound of cicadas from the cottonwoods, and frogs croaked tentatively and then began their evening din in unison. It was even better when a light breeze riffled the water out near the edges of water growth where bladderwort and pondweed reinforced the coontail moss.

The bass, which had spent the hot day in deeper water or completely within the vegetation, were moving near the surface, now and then striking a frog or dragonfly. The fisherman found that he had to wade through considerable muck near the shore before he reached solid bottom. In some spots bubbles of smelly gas were released from the bottom as he laboriously slogged along, though once he cleared the shoreline mud he waded coolly and comfortably in water well above his waist. He held the heavy bamboo fly rod high to keep his elbows clear and made short casts with the cork-bodied bug. He let it lie for several seconds, twitched it ever so slightly, repeated the small movement several times, and then popped it loudly. If there was no response, he picked it up and moved a step or two. The strikes might come loudly and without warning, but often there was a perceptible bulge or moving V of wake before the fish took. The lake was becoming difficult to fish by other means; vegetation was appearing in areas that before had been clear.

When he managed to reach the lake early, he often fished for bluegills near some dead trees at the shallow end, using small, dark trout flies twitched gently near the shallow bottom. The bluegills took viciously and then swung in underwater circles on their sides, often giving the impression of much larger fish for a few moments before the big rod brought them up. Often it was hard to remove the little flies; the fish could swallow them almost as quickly as the fisherman could set the hook.

Larger bluegills were active on the surface later in the evening, although by that time the fisherman was using large bass bugs and the bluegill strikes generally meant no more than sucking plops. Occasionally a green sunfish would get its big mouth around the lure with a sound that tricked the angler into thinking he had a bass, and he would involuntarily skitter the little fish over the surface as he set the hook.

Sometimes the striking bass gouged into cover almost instantly and it was necessary to wade to them in order to land them at all. As night came on, the fly line made silver streaks of moonlight on the surface. If the bug were cast into a cattail shadow its noises seemed remote and a strike was a startling occurrence. True bats squeaked overhead and bullbats seemed to make special dives toward the fisherman out of curiosity. When the fisherman crossed a part of the lake to his car he had to swim a little in the deepest parts, his flies stuck in a wet hat and the rod held awkwardly horizontal to the water.

He often thought of the lake after he moved to the city.

He was middle-aged when he came back to a lake that no longer had a purpose. Although the railroad spur was still used, there had been no steam locomotives for several years and what had once been a well-used road to the lake shore was now grown up with weeds. Not much fishing was being done. The fisherman found it almost impossible to get through the boggy bank; it seemed to extend much farther into the water than he remembered. Where he waded the bottom was generally soft and sludgy, although there were some firm places, probably where high-water currents had cleared a path on the bottom.

The surface was mainly a tangled mat with patches of muskrat grass but there were open pockets where it was possible to fish a bug. There were some lily pads with small openings about them and he caught a small bass in one of those spots. In some areas the water was strangely roiled, as if something might be working on the bottom, although he could not see the carp there. He put the conditions down to a series of droughts and thought the lake needed cleaning out. He found that he could wade over near the railroad grade in spots where he had never been able to touch bottom before. For the first time he noticed that almost all of the nearby land was cultivated, and when he talked to the farmers he was amazed at the yield from what had once been only fair farmland. Pesticides and specialized fertilizers, some of which drained into the lake, had done what no amount of back-breaking labor had accomplished when he had cultivated corn with a team of mules many years ago.

He came back to the little lake as an old man, but it was much smaller and covered with a heavy green scum. Several miles up the little creek they had built a new impoundment, especially for recreation, and bass fishing was quite good there.

8.
The Modest Homes of the Panfishes:

For bluegills, weed beds in warm shallows. For green sunfish, a midwestern farm creek. For bullheads, mud. For yellow perch, a cool, deep lake.

Even during high water the southern river runs slow and murky with the stains of vegetation. When the water level is low and there is an up-stream wind the river sometimes stops completely or flows backward for a time despite the contributions of a number of cool springs. Much of the river is lined by timbered swamp which accepts overflow easily. The tall cypress have shawls of Spanish moss and stand at the very edge of the water, while oaks occupy the higher ground. In the swampy sections there are water hickory, red maple, and water elm, and the shore is crowded with willows. The river has only a slight gradient and spreads loosely over a wide area of wooded backwaters. Some of the side channels return to the main stream after wandering for miles through chains of mud lakes, and they have their own tributary creeks and backwater.

It is late evening when the bluegills begin to appear in a slow channel. During the day they have stayed fairly deep. Some of them have been in the coves where lily pads provided shade and protection. Some have moved along the drop-off a few feet out from shore in the main river or in the deeper side channels. None of them has traveled very far. The drop-off is a miniature of that in large lakes, an edge of the shoreline shallows where earth and detritus have been washed in from the solid land. As evening approaches, some bluegills will move to the very edge of the land itself, in water only a few inches deep.

Natural erosion and the sweep of powerboat wakes have cut at the river banks until the wide-spread roots of large trees have been laid almost bare. High wind has finally uprooted some of the trees and they have fallen shoreward, their branches forming tangles that even raccoons find difficult to negotiate. Each uprooting has torn a deep segment from the bank. Considerable soil clings to the broken roots and makes a vertical wall of earth on the land side of the pocket. There are bluegills at the base of the roots, well out of the current. There is another bluegill thoroughfare where a strand of water lilies grows parallel to the river's course but at some distance from the bank. Here again the fish have a pond-like habitat with the deep-going lily-pad stems for protection.

In the side channel there are fewer overturned trees because there is less boat traffic and a more gentle current. In some spots the trees interlace overhead, and there are sunken logs and snags over much of the bottom. Now that evening is coming on, the wading birds have begun to move toward their roosts and a pair of wood ducks flutter down through the trees, squealing at each other, to alight in the middle of the run. Five minutes later they have disappeared, having walked out on the land for their evening feeding in the swamp. They have spent most of the day in a nearby lake.

It is the very young bluegills that come up first, where a carpet of duckweed has caught against a fallen limb along the bank. The duckweed is simply a small, rounded, flat leaf with a tiny dangling root system, and the smallest bluegills make sucking noises as they feed on minute larvae among the roots. The fish are invisible but sections of the duckweed bob gently with their efforts. A little later there is a swell among the lily pads in a cove and the louder plop that the fisherman has been waiting for.

The lure is a brown sponge-rubber spider with white rubber legs, made to float on the surface film. The angler casts it only a short distance with his light fly rod and it lands on a lily pad, causing the plant to quiver slightly in the still water, making barely perceptible waves. When the lure is pulled from the bonnet it strikes water with a light spat as if a tiny frog or burly insect had misjudged its route from pad to pad. The spider lies almost still but the rubber legs, folded back as the retrieve began, now straighten with little twitches and stir the water slightly. The bluegill has watched the quivering lily pad and now he sweeps upward and seizes the spider, showing his dorsal fin and back above the water. As the rod tip goes up and the

Preceding pages: Best known of America's panfish, the bluegill—shown here as mature "copperhead"—is caught on fly-rod popper with teasing rubber legs.

little hook is set, the fish dives for the bottom and the cluster of green bonnet stems, but is held so tightly that it must turn; it lies almost flat on its broad side and swims in swift circles, headed downward yet pulled steadily upward. The use of its broad side against the leader's pull has gained the bluegill a reputation as one of the hardest fighting of all fish, a small edition of the stubborn resistance offered by the jack crevalle and the mighty permit of salt water. On the surface, the big bluegill splashes helplessly, and as the angler lifts it into the little boat there is a wide swirl where the fish surfaced, a swirl made by a largemouth bass or bowfin, barely cheated of a meal, for the bluegill is seldom the master of its habitat and is prey as well as predator.

Not all of the bluegills take the rubber spider so briskly. Some of them, hardly large enough to engulf the hook, tug energetically at the sprawling rubber legs. Occasionally there is a mass attack by several bluegills, a tactic that can result in the dismemberment of a live grasshopper or cricket. Once a pair of nibbling, sucking little fish leaves hurriedly when a bow wave indicates a bigger fish on the way. Occasionally the strike comes from a small bass, but larger bass seldom bother with rubber spiders.

It is almost dark when the angler ends his day. The frogs are calling and the barred owls argue in the swamp; the wood ducks have left for their roosting pond.

The bluegill is designed for casual navigation in vertical forests of rooted underwater plants. Its body is a finned disk that slips between the stems effortlessly, leaving pursuers helplessly entangled. The deep body is built for short turns in still water, not for contact with fast currents where the trout's bullet form is at its best. The bluegill usually prefers weedy growth but takes up warm-weather residence in almost any kind of shade, preferably with escape cover nearby. Large individuals frequently live around boat houses and docks, often becoming so familiar with man's devices that they are not easily caught. Bluegills are not travelers. They stay close to a chosen territory until weather or the spawning urge causes them to move. In cold weather they find deep weed beds; on sunny days they shift to fast-warming shallows. They seek water above 70 degrees. In all, their living requirements almost duplicate those of the largemouth black bass, but they are even more prolific reproducers than the bass. Fish managers have concluded that the hook and line are no hazard to bluegill populations, and in some areas an unlimited harvest is encouraged. Removal of bluegills is desirable to avoid stunting, since a single nest may contain more than fifty thousand eggs deposited by more than one female. Most bag limits are merely a gesture to retain the spirit of conservation and prevent commercialization.

The bluegill is one of the true sunfishes and lives over almost all of the contiguous states, generally preferring lakes and slow rivers, being less of a creek fish than some of its relatives. A long, drawn-out spawning period can begin any time from March in the South to June in the North. Nesting is done in colonies, the beds sometimes so close together that guarding males face each other almost nose to nose. The male builds the nest, clearing off a basin with his tail and body, preferably on a clear bottom of sand and gravel. One or more females will lay their eggs in the nest and the male stands guard for the several days necessary for hatching; then, after a short guardianship, he drives the fry away. The small bluegills eat plankton and small crustaceans and larger ones will take small minnows. A small mouth, however, makes the bluegill ill-adapted to catching other fish. The larger fish eat nymphs and larvae, as well as worms and adult insects. May-fly hatches will cause bluegills to cover a pond's surface with feeding dimples.

The lily-pad bed is often a complete warm-weather habitat for bluegills. The vertical stems form perfect escape avenues for the compressed shape of the fish, and a variety of insects lives in the pads themselves. One perfect bluegill bait is

1

Bluegills, bass, and warmouth perch lie against this cypress strand (1) in southern swamp. Wood ducks (2) have come back from scarcity and are common sight about cypress clumps and along oak ridges where they look for acorns. Duckweed (3) carpets fishy pond and blocks passage of a bass plug. Bluegills and hyacinths (5) go together in many southern rivers where evening feeding can be located by gentle plops of greenery. Small, mirrored pools make panfish habitat, and quiet approach is best for these anglers (4). Ever present is snapping turtle (6) and his great appetite.

2

3

5

4

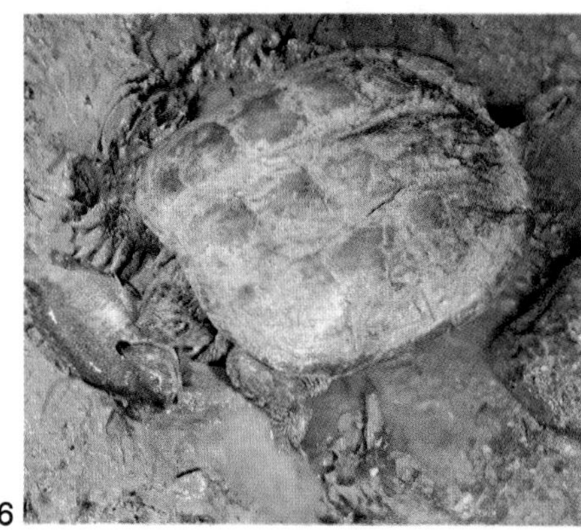
6

the bonnet worm, or "water caterpillar," which will be transformed to a moth as an adult. The worms attack pads at the leaf end of the stems and infested pads turn yellowish before dying. The worms themselves are found within the stems above the water line and are attractive to a variety of panfish.

Except when audibly feeding on the surface, the bluegill's depth is the angler's most difficult puzzle and fish of different sizes are often grouped as to underwater level. It is perhaps the most popular fish in America, caught most often on bait, yet taken also by a variety of small lures. The most productive period is usually at spawning time, when drifting fishermen peer for the light spots that indicate clean-swept beds on the bottom. The good bluegill lake is probably eutrophic and produces several times as much weight of fish per acre as does the cold-water trout lake.

Ice fishing for bluegills is successful once the proper depth is found and gleaming attractors accompanied by small baits are best. As its metabolism slows in winter the bluegill takes smaller meals. The icefisherman prospects carefully for both location and depth, sometimes searching for fish with an electronic fathometer. Winter bluegills are likely to be found in lethargic schools. Although growth is generally most rapid in warm climates the adult size will depend upon competition and the food supply, and a bluegill of more than a pound is a large one. In the southern United States the bluegill is often called bream, although that name is used freely to cover some of its sunfish relatives as well.

The hardy bluegill may be America's favorite fish, but there are other species that thrive in waters which even the bluegill would find untenable. The green sunfish is a midwesterner and a westerner, and it lives in some farm creeks that have only puddles in late summer. There are sometimes a few largemouth bass there to add an incentive for the fisherman.

One such creek is bordered by farmland: wheat, oats, soybeans, corn, and pasture. There is only a narrow strip of brush and trees along the watercourse. Willows hem the creek's edge, and patches of blackberry and gooseberry bushes furnish hiding, with ready access to farm crops, for innumerable cottontail rabbits. At dawn the partly dry watercourse is followed by coyotes as they return from their night's travel, staying close to brushy hiding spots rather than crossing clean farmland. It is truly a wet-weather creek, set largely in a dark soil, and it turns to chocolate with a heavy rain. Now it is only a series of seemingly dead pools, some of them rock-bottomed and thus resistant to seepage. While some of the deeper pools have sections of clay bank, the creek's long habits of erosion continue; even though the surrounding farmland has been terraced in recent years. Only in a few natural depressions where limestone holds the line against yearly floods does the creek stabilize itself. The best fishing is in these permanent holes.

There are some shady parts of the creek, strands of elm trees with bulky old crow's-nests in their high branches. There are other nests, great bundles of freshly cut green material, mostly leaves, occupied by fox squirrels. They come to the creek often, leaving rabbit-like tracks on the mudbanks. Local hunters recognize the difference immediately: The squirrel has a wider stance than the rabbit and articulated toe marks. There is one small cluster of oaks, and a few black-walnut trees are not far away—enough to provision the squirrels in normal years. When there is a bad nut year they may feed in winter on Osage oranges.

The fisherman sets up a continual shower of grasshoppers as he nears the creek, occasionally brushing a cocklebur or sunflower. He reaches one of the best pools in late afternoon. It is only thirty feet across and twice as long, with rock bottom and a high bank on one side. It is late enough in the day for the high bank to be shaded by some elms. There is a scum of algae and a fringe of sedge against that shore, and an enormous bullfrog sits on a wet and muddy ledge. The fisherman casts a floating deer-hair bug to the shady spot and

Wind-blown tree tears loose section of river shoreline and makes indentation to gather tiny minnows, errant insects, and hungry bluegills.

1

Long-eared sunfish (1) came from Ozark stream shared with many other panfish and smallmouth bass. Bullfrog (3) opens evening feeding period with his deep bass, and cottontail (2) appears as panfish begin to strike. Bullhead (4) is hardy bottom fish which can survive in wet mud during drought.

3

2

brings a loud, plopping strike. His lure is large enough for bass, but it is a green sunfish that takes. It darts about helplessly, for it had followed the shade too far from the thick cover it used during the heat of the day. After the green sunfish is landed, the angler tries a few more times and attracts only some very tiny fish, too small to be hooked, so he wades on through the warm water and walks toward another pool, staying in the dry creek bed to avoid head-high sunflowers and higher willows.

As a boy, thirty years before, the fisherman had fished the creek in somewhat similar fashion. Then he used a light cane pole with a few feet of green line, a bottle-cork bobber, and earthworms. He waded barefoot and expertly flipped the worm and bobber to the best spots along the shore. He caught green sunfish and a few pumpkinseed sunfish, and then he changed his tactics and fished the pool again. This second time he was very careful of the length of line below his bobber. He used a small sinker and quietly tried the depth until he was sure the sinker barely touched bottom in a muddy part of the pool. Then he shortened his line so that the baited hook was just above the bottom. This time he waited several minutes, for a bullhead catfish moves slowly and is attracted by scent. When the bullhead took the worm there was no violent bobbing of the bottle cork. It simply moved away in a gentle swaying motion to match the slow strokes of the bullhead's tail on the bottom, and the boy set the hook briskly and swung the bullhead to the bank.

The bullhead, or horned pout, is one of the hardiest of panfish, with a body flattened to fit the bottom and fierce spines in dorsal and pectoral fins. It swims with a wide, weaving motion of the entire body. Although the tiny eyes are inferior, the bullhead uses its fleshy barbels, or whiskers, as feelers and has a keen sense of smell. It feeds upon both animal and vegetable matter, and is sometimes indicted as a scavenger. There are three common bullheads—black, brown, and yellow—but they have almost exactly the same habits. The black bullhead, smallest of the three, has the most tenacity.

Near the creek where the boy waded years ago and the man had waded today there is a feeder stream with a mud bottom. It originates at the edge of a cultivated field where it is fed by an old tile line put in before contour farming came to the region. Long before the main stream stopped flowing in dry midsummer, the feeder creek was only a series of pools, lined by scrubby willows that did little to break the sun. The bank is undercut where it is held by sod and there are continual cave-ins of the dark loam. After the drought was well under way, only one pool remained in the creek. It was no more than ten feet wide and becoming shallower as evaporation and thirsty plants drew off its remaining water. The oxygen began to disappear and the few crowded fish that were left had little to eat except a few mud-dwelling larvae and an occasional grasshopper that fell from the crackling dry bluegrass.

Earlier in the season, there were pumpkinseed sunfish and some small green sunfish in the pool, residents which had worked their way up from the larger creek. When the water became only a puddle the sunfish died and crows found them at the muddy edges. Later, oxygen became so scarce that the bullheads moved along with their mouths at the surface to draw air from above the water, their mouths and gills working rapidly. Even that failed as the last of the water disappeared, leaving only mortar-like mud. The bullheads flop-

Sportiest of catfish is channel cat (2), which sometimes strikes artificial baits. Yellow perch (1) is northern favorite. White perch (3) share stringer with the more glamorous landlocked salmon and will sometimes take same lures in New England lakes and slow streams.

1

2

3

ped about seemingly in their death throes, but gradually they worked their way down into the mud until they disappeared. Above them the sun baked a dry and crackling crust, but below it the dormant bullheads waited for rain. If it came in a muddy rush they would revive, and begin searching for food in the opaque flood. Bullhead fishing is at its best at night or when the water is very muddy.

Bullhead eggs are laid in some convenient depression, and the male will guard the nest, keeping eggs clean by tail sweeping or washing them in his mouth. When the young are first hatched into a wriggling cluster of miniature catfish they are sometimes protected by a mud screen thrown up by the male. Later, as the young bullheads roam about in their ball-shaped schools, they become feeding targets for largemouth bass. The bass, attacking sometimes in small wolf-pack groups, thin the prolific bullheads and serve as a principal biological control to maintain the community balance.

Catfish are a homely change of pace for serious fishermen, their capture requiring special kinds of study. The bullhead is least prized because it is the smallest; the highest-ranking catfish is the channel cat, which is a bit more streamlined and prefers cleaner water. Sometimes the forktailed channel cat lies in clear and fairly swift streams, feeding mostly at night, and the fisherman sets bank lines—using odorous baits—fastened to a springy willow that will hold a large fish under constant tension. The bank line is placed where the scent from the bait is carried into a likely downstream pool; the fish follow the scent trail at night.

The trotline fisherman tries to find catfish routes, knowing they travel the bottom on well-established trails marked by some unknown means. In a strange river the trotliner first strings his lines at right angles across the stream, and thus finds what course the moving fish are taking. When a few nights of fishing have located a fish route, he puts his line parallel to the bank on the catfish trail itself. It is coarse fishing, but many a black-bass camp dines on catfish.

There are several panfishes much like the bluegill in performance and appearance, each with slightly different traits. Some of them are highly localized and appear to be recent crosses of better-known species. Others are almost as wide-ranging as the bluegill. The redear sunfish, or shellcracker, is of less sporting value because it stays deep and feeds primarily on snails and other shelled creatures. The pumpkinseed, orange-spotted, long-eared, yellow-breasted, and spotted sunfishes have habits similar to the bluegill's.

The warmouth bass, or warmouth perch, has a large mouth, similar to that of the green sunfish, and is capable of taking the rather large lures intended for largemouth bass. It is somewhat less of a fighter than the bluegill, its body shaped much like the bass, but with a less-developed tail. The vast number of local names for panfish is confusing and the warmouth is sometimes called goggle-eye, a name more commonly associated with the rock bass. The true rock bass lives in stone outcroppings and bottom rubble, often duplicating the smallmouth bass in residence and habits, and is caught by bass anglers who use lures of modest size.

The yellow perch, a true member of the perch family, is one of the deeper-running panfish, a standby in the northern United States and a frequent target of icefishermen. As is sometimes true on a lesser scale with sunfish, large perch are often found deeper than small ones. Yellow perch, like their relative the walleye, prefer cool, deep lakes, and are not as insistent upon thick vegetation as most of the sunfishes. In hot weather they will be as deep as fifty feet, nearly always near the bottom, but depth preference sometimes gives way to the necessity for a proper oxygen supply, and the fish move upward along a deep shore. Yellow perch are not good surface feeders. In early spring when the lake is well mixed they can be caught rather shallow with artificial lures, but they have none of the bluegill's love for things that ride in the surface film, and the best lures resemble minnows rather than insects. Some authorities believe the perch is almost entirely a daytime feeder and that they rest on bottom after dark. Although somewhat separated at night, they again form feeding schools with daylight.

While many weed-dwelling fish prefer to find open sand or gravel for spawning, the yellow perch lives on the open gravel and goes to weeds or brush for egg-laying. The female strings a gelatinous rope of eggs about the vegetation where they are immediately fertilized by male fish. The spawning often results in droves of small fish which will crowd a lake in spite of the introduction of predators. When a lake has once been overcrowded, fish managers resort to mechanical or chemical destruction of the undersized fish, and then start over with what they hope will be a balance of predators.

The yellow perch is distinguished by a slightly humped back and a rather long body, with dark vertical bands against yellow. The fins are reddish or dull orange. The white perch is an entirely different fish, a member of the sea-bass family and strongly resembling the striped bass in smaller sizes. It can adapt to brackish water and is one of the stronger of the panfish. Where it lives with bass it strikes the same lures and, although it does not jump when hooked, the rest of its fight is much like that of the bass. It is a difficult fish to catch at times, spawns carelessly in feeder streams—with males and females scattering millions of eggs and a corresponding amount of milt in a communal effort—and it lives to old age. Some individuals have lived as long as twelve years. It is so prolific that hook-and-line fishing, even netting, cannot curb a white-perch population when it is enjoying otherwise ideal conditions.

The white perch is a school fish, and finding the school can be difficult. When fly fishing in boulder water the fisherman will sometimes find

Resemblances between rock bass (top) and black crappie (below) include willingness of both to respond to fly or lure.

1

2

3

4

Black crappie (1) takes tiny light-tackle jigs and lies deep in submerged brushpiles and log jams. White crappie (2) has similar habits and sometimes the same range. Pie-billed grebe (3) is sleek and impudent diver and silent companion of fisherman on panfish waters. Bittern (4) appears as swatch of weed. Fisherman's intrusion brings loud complaint from Florida grackle (5). Evening's low sun (6) lights operations of drifting casters.

5

6

white perch moving on very shallow shelves in broad daylight, somewhat nearer shore than the smallmouth bass, but generally the fish are rather deep in the daytime. It is in the late evening calm, when a hatch of insects brings them into the shallows, that the perch are at their best, taking small spinners or flies. Appearances on some shallow spots become so predictable that good fishermen will meet the perch there each evening after spending the day in pursuit of larger game.

The crappies run larger than most of the other panfish, and there are two kinds: black and white. The blacks prefer a more solid bottom; the whites will live over soft mud. The white crappie is barred, the black crappie has uneven dark blotches. White or black, the crappie is a creature of brushpiles, fallen trees, and brushy banks. Some of the best crappie fishing is on slow-moving rivers, and some of the most sporting angling is had with small spinning lures, especially jigs, in white or yellow. Traditionally, the crappie is fished with small minnows and such bait is reliable, although the artificial lures may be more productive much of the time.

Crappie populations are prone to cyclic fluctuations. The white crappie, especially, is likely to overpopulate, but the supply may be governed by the "dominant brood" condition. The dominant brood appears in a good year for the hatch and then controls the population in subsequent years, being so plentiful that it thins its own progeny. This continues until the dominating age group itself begins to die off.

Crappie fishing is a quiet sport. In spring, before spawning time and when the water is cool, the fish are around the river brushpiles and the angler works his little jig delicately. The boat glides down the sluggish current, almost against the brush and fallen trees of the shoreline, and the jig, constructed for operation from nearly straight above, probes the smallest crannies. So slowly does the boat arrive that sunning turtles remain on their perches until it is almost opposite them. On shore the bittern stands stiffly, his vertical streaks of dark feathers mingling with the pattern of cattails and pondweeds. There is a moment when he crouches ever so slightly in preparation for flight, but he decides to stay hidden and the boat, steered gently by a paddle, slides on past.

The air is still enough that the woodpeckers seem to be riddling the forest with their blows, and a flock of grackles is heard overhead with their distinctive wing swishing. A gray squirrel retires silently from an overhanging limb and observes intently from nearer the tree trunk. At the center of the creeping river a grebe bobs up to watch and then dives. The fisherman does not see him come up again, although he does so against the bank, appearing so close to the boat that he puts only his wet head above the surface and holds it still in a little strand of pondweed. A whitetail deer fades into the forest.

The fisherman flips his little jig almost to the bank and feels his monofilament line go slack as the lure touches bottom. He tightens a little, brings the jig off the bottom, and lets it drop back. He is feeling for the drop-off he knows is there. On the next lift the jig goes deeper and is worked toward the boat in a series of short hops that stirs tiny puffs of mud from the bottom ten feet down. The slow current swings a little at a brushpile. On the upstream side of the obstruction is a collection of leaves and grass, caught in the fine branches. Here the cast is made just below the brush, where a small eddy turns gently over several feet of water, and as the jig drops in gently there is a tiny shower of minnows frightened by the intrusion. But the crappies are farther down, where the jig is probing. It strikes the bottom and is picked up once, lowered again, and picked up a second time. After the second lift it does not reach the bottom and the line is slack; it moves a little, and the fisherman sets his small hook with his light line, hardly more than the gentle lift he used to maneuver his lure.

At first the resistance is steady, the hook

catching in a corner of the papery mouth, and then the big crappie turns partly on its side and with the line stretched across its humped back it drives strongly toward the brushpile, as the little rod bows against the two-pound line. Now the hooked fish is followed by other crappies interested in the thing the hooked fish has in its mouth. As the fish is pulled in a ragged circle toward the boat, one of the pursuers goes clear to the surface, showing its speckled side as it turns. The fisherman gently nets his fish. He picks up his paddle, goes slightly upstream without commotion, and slides his anchor overboard, so that the boat will stay in a good casting position for the eddy. He is sure he has located a school of fish. He begins the procedure again, and after he has caught another fish he changes from a white jig to a yellow one and hooks a third. Now he hangs up in the brush and recovers his lure only after considerable tugging, and when he casts again there is no response. He lifts his anchor and moves on down the river, looking for deep holes against the outer bends, for brushpiles near the deep banks, and for patches of water lilies growing in deep water.

When it is the crappies' spawning time he fishes shallower spots, sometimes finding his fish in quiet backwaters, where the nests are made near rooted growth. And when summer weather scatters his quarry he does most of his fishing in the evenings, sometimes finding the fish willing to strike on top, especially at little run-ins where food is carried from tiny creeks or swampy areas. He may catch bass at the same time, and if the bluegills are unable to take his large bugs he will change to something smaller.

It is on the big southern and midwestern reservoirs that the crappie is often king, especially the white crappie. Here during the early spring, when the large spawning schools form and move into shallow water, the fishing is at its best. The fisherman slowly trolls his tandem rig of jigs, dressed in bucktail or marabou, moving erratically through the stump-choked coves and along ragged shorelines that were once part of the eastern deciduous forest. Now the sunken forest turns slowly to more typical lake bottom as the trees decay and erosion softens the contours with earth from the high ground.

In such fishing, strikes come as gentle tugs and when one or two fish are caught the boat is circled in hope that a school has been located. As other anglers recognize the circling pattern, they join it in an orderly procession which may continue for a long while, for the feeding crappie is extremely cooperative.

Later in the year the same fishermen return to their reservoir at night, equipped with gasoline lanterns and fine-meshed dip nets. Their objective is the threadfin shad first, and the crappie next. They anchor the boat in some thirty feet of water, usually over a previously located sunken tree. When the lighted lantern has attracted the threadfin shad (a small plant-feeding species), they capture a quantity with the net, attach them to small hooks, and do their crappie fishing just above the submerged treetop.

When the fisherman uses artificial lures for crappies, his fish will average less than a pound and they will take an eighth-ounce jig on two-pound line. At another time, the same fisherman fishes a four-ounce jig in much the same way in two hundred feet of water, but then the objective is an ocean fish on a reef twenty miles from shore. And when the fisherman catches his bluegills on the tiny rubber spider, his angling is a miniaturization of what he does when he throws a great popping bug against a coastal wind above cruising striped bass that weigh more than twenty pounds.

Panfish are only the beginning of sport fishing, a quiet beginning offering more satisfaction than excitement, but requiring many of the skills that apply in all fishing. A famous angler comes home from abroad, where he has won an international casting tournament and fished for giant Atlantic salmon, and then he goes bluegill fishing in a quiet pond.

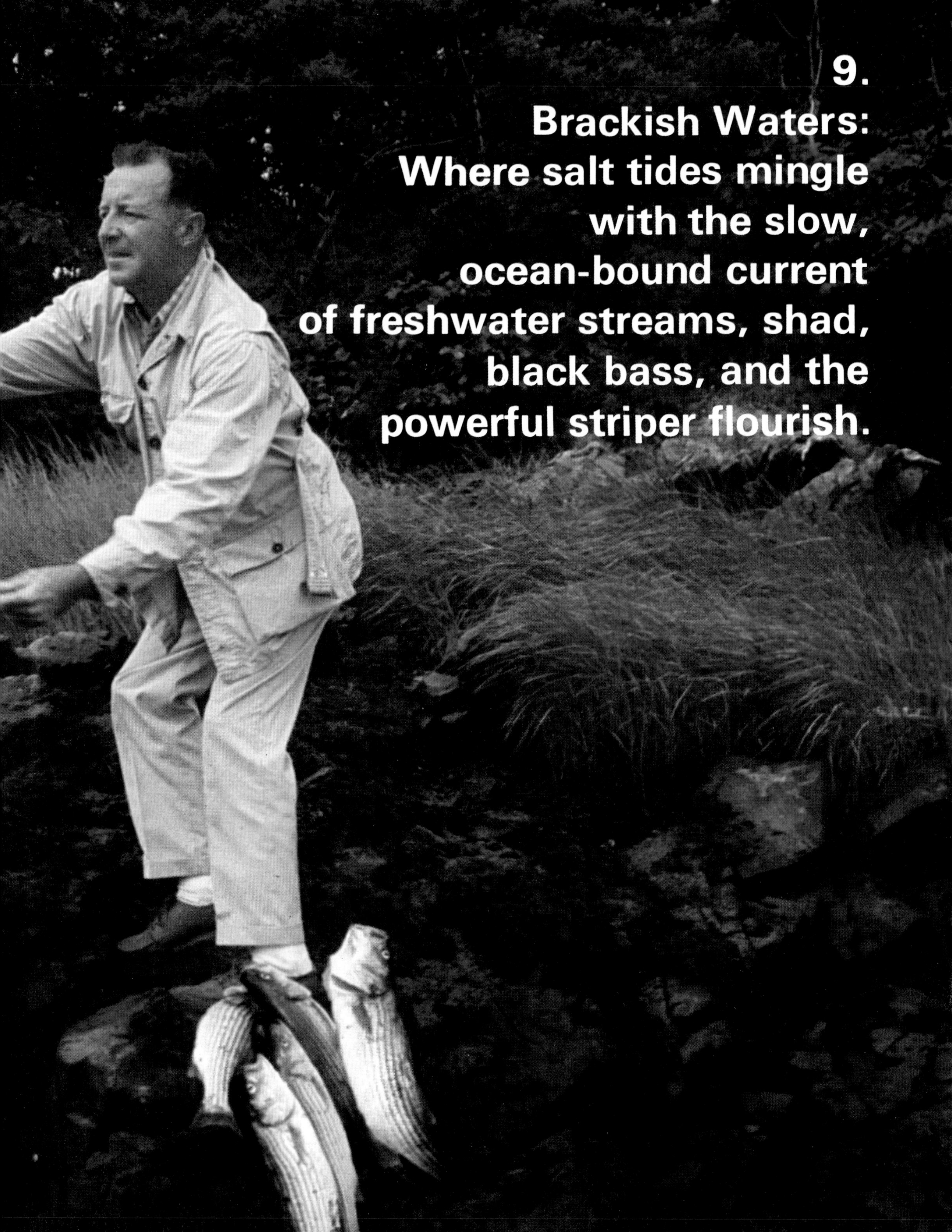

9. Brackish Waters: Where salt tides mingle with the slow, ocean-bound current of freshwater streams, shad, black bass, and the powerful striper flourish.

There had been good rainfall for three years and the river of grass flowed steadily—across the true Everglades of sawgrass, cattails, palm and cypress hammocks, and occasional patches of open water. It is an immense delta, sloping with such a slight gradient that the current is not apparent to the casual observer. Run-off is so slow that there is no noticeable siltation and the water is clear, unlike the burdened yellow flood of the Mississippi. In some parts of the Everglades, which cover most of southern Florida, the slope is only an inch to the mile and when the water becomes quite shallow its progress can be completely blocked by vegetation. Arriving to pursue his sport in this rich and varied habitat, the angler feels keen anticipation.

Historically, the Everglades have flooded regularly from hurricane deluges and normally wet seasons; in time of drought the bogs burn with dirty smoke clouds that stain the spring thunderheads. Formerly, when it was very dry, water was held only in a few low sloughs and in the alligator pits. Alligators are a basic factor of the Everglades ecology, digging holes to hold water and building great heaps of mud and vegetation to use as nests. Later the old nests become small islands with their own plants, possibly the beginning of true hammocks. The cattail is likely to appear early as a pioneer plant on an unused mound.

In happy times between flood and choking fire, black bass, bluegills, pickerel, and warmouth perch thrive in the deeper water; the canals nurture a population of catfish more prosperous than the scattered few of the natural Everglades. The higher ground supports whitetail deer and innumerable raccoons and bobcats. Especially in winter, there are egrets, herons, bitterns, limpkins, and storks present in thousands. They scatter widely during the day and in the evening organize into flocks that beat for their hammock roosts in the pink light of the sunset.

When high water comes, most of the deer die, the fawns and small adults going first, a natural culling process that helps to evolve the tough, leggy survivors, capable of competing with swamp buggies, airboats, and hunting hounds.

During high water the largemouth bass disperse over the entire Everglades, going wherever the sawgrass is thin enough to be penetrated. They increase in size very rapidly because of an endless growing season, but usually do not acquire quite the girth of fish from slightly farther north, a puzzle to fish management experts. One popular theory is that the endless hiding places make bait catching too active for corpulent largemouths. Natives call most of them "rattlesnake bass" because of their bold, dark markings against lighter scales. Where the open Everglades give way to the black waters of cypress stands, the bass have a much darker color: black backs and dark olive sides, with the characteristic mottled pattern almost completely invisible.

If the water level were constant the deer would overpopulate the hammocks and the bass would crowd the waters; both species would suffer eventually, starvation bringing death to the deer and stunting or worse to the bass. But nature seldom works that way.

The water goes down, the bog burns, and the Everglades fish concentrate in shrinking pools, use up their oxygen, and die in great belly-up windrows of stench, while the earnest nature lovers who abhorred the death of the deer during high water now fear that the fish population is doomed. Observers wrote of the same things sixty years ago. The long-term cycle of want and plenty has served nature but is unsatisfactory to the sportsman who is unwilling to wait two or three years for a new crop of fish or game.

Man, in endeavoring to control the hurricane floods that wiped out farms, homes, and settlers many years ago, has built a series of dams, gates, and locks to moderate the ups and downs of Everglades water flow, and has incidentally developed the largest black bass preserve in the world.

Preceding pages: Striped bass may be caught from rocky shores of fresh water, or from booming surf of salt—it is many things to many fishermen.

When the levees were built to control the water excesses, canals were dug parallel to them, creating deep water where bass could live as the Glades level went down. They still die during drought, but a larger breeding population is retained.

Ideally, the flood-control program holds water to nourish the great brackish sea-life incubator of the eastern Gulf of Mexico, but prevents disastrous flooding with straight canals that carry the surplus quickly to sea, bypassing the traditional water routes. It is a moderating influence on both flood and drought but it is not perfect, for the porous earth beneath the river of grass takes a great toll of stored water, and thousands of wells near the coastal developments suck millions of gallons, adding to saltwater intrusion. At any rate, the conservation areas, actually impoundments that may be only inches deep, have provided an unusual bass fishery.

These are mainly shallow-water fish in times of normal weather, and the expert may prefer to wade for them. For miles the depth may vary only a few inches and the bottom is likely to be hard and sandy. The fisherman gets to his area by skiff or airboat, the former operating satisfactorily in the canals, the latter needed for sawgrass or cattails and capable of putting him where he can spend days alone, disturbed only by Miami's jet airplanes and a few irate Everglades birds.

Some of the best fishing is in water approximately waist-deep where the dense sawgrass gives way to spike rush, bladderwort, and pondweed sparse enough for use of lures or flies, and the fisherman wades relaxed, although his feet cautiously feel their way for possible burn holes or alligator excavations left over from times of drought.

In that latitude, bass are likely to spawn in February, one of the best times for the larger fish, but the fishing may be good at any time if the water level holds. Working his way slowly with casting lure or weedless popping bug, a fisherman gives special attention to occasional patches of lily pads which afford solid shade, even at noonday. Where very heavy sawgrass borders more open water, the bass are likely to cruise the edge, reassured by the dense cover yet able to move out swiftly in feeding forays.

Our angler uses a wiggling surface lure with a busy spinner at the nose and a pork frog bringing up the rear, a horrendous device in the eyes of a fly purist, though bearing only one weedless hook and handicapped in its busy maneuvers by constant contact with stalks of grass and bonnet leaves. Its chuckling spinner makes a ragged wake on the surface and draws bright-eyed attention from a boat-tailed grackle atop a swaying cattail stem. When the strike comes, it is a swirl and a chopping sound, and the angler sets hard, hoping to force a huge hook past the resistance of a wire weedguard and possibly a few blades of grass. He continues his reaction with rapid reeling and violent pumping, knowing the fish will roll into a bundle of soaked grass if given a moment's chance.

If the fish is large, the fisherman may be unable to keep it coming toward him. It may go down to the bottom and become a solid weight, aided by the hanks of vegetation it has caught with the line. If he cannot bring it up, the fisherman stops his reeling for a moment, feeling for the tugs of an entangled bass, hoping his quarry has not escaped and left him with a well-wrapped bundle of wet hay. He may have to wade to the scene, run a cautious hand down his line and grope hopefully for the bass's lower jaw, barely keeping his wader tops dry. It is likely that the water is in the 60's in February. When it reaches 80 degrees in late spring, fishing will be largely a morning, evening, and cloudy-day affair, except for deep sections of the canals.

A few miles away, below the holding dikes, the wide river of grass shallows and then splits into deeper runs for entry to salt water at the heads of the named rivers of the west Florida coast. With three years of good rain the flow of fresh water has temporarily halted the march of mangrove

Only a few miles distant from Gulf of Mexico, dark swamp water carries bass and panfish to meet coastal residents from tidal rivers.

trees. They grow ever farther inland as fresh water is used more and more and drawn off through man-made canals. A brackish solution with sufficient salinity favors their growth. Now they are lining a unique river head, a sector where the fresh water has temporarily blocked the tidal surges of the salt. The river's head has islands of water growth, dominated by widgeon grass, pondweed, bladderwort, and a dozen intertwined plants that tangle in outboard-motor propellers.

But the water level is falling, for the rain has ended, for a time at least. The black bass, products of the upstream sawgrass, are dropping down, living close to their enemy, salt water, which is coming ever nearer from the Gulf of Mexico, seven miles away.

The fishermen's outboard boat may be a little larger than that commonly used by bass fishermen, for the men have come up from the salt rivers, or perhaps from the Gulf itself, and they are thirty miles from a road. One of them poles the boat carefully and they look down through open avenues in the interlaced water growth, watching the clean bottom of gravel and sand four feet down. Now and then there are swirling clouds of tiny fish, shreds of water life unrecognizable as to species. Part of them are tiny black bass that have hatched over the scattered nests which appear as clean-brushed spots on the bottom. But at this size they are almost the same as several other kinds of swimming miniatures. Blue crabs nervously reach their arms for grass or bottom. Now and then a large moving shadow appears, generally seen sooner than its maker, a largemouth bass sliding boldly across an open space.

The fly-rod bug is cast long because of the clear water, and even with that precaution an occasional small bass can be seen darting away from the gently falling line. Some of the casts are directed at open spots in the vegetation at midstream, and some are dropped almost against the mangrove leaves and roots at the shoreline. The bug is worked slowly, allowed to lie a little, twitched gently, then popped more stridently if nothing has happened.

First sign of the bass is a gentle movement somewhere in the grass after a cast to a mid-river open spot. A tiny swirl shows just as the bug lands. When the angler moves his lure a distinct V moves toward it. It stops when the bug stops and moves again when the bug moves, soon coming close to the floating deception. Though the fish has stopped a foot away, the swell slightly bobs the bug, a cork thing with writhing rubber legs and a hair tail. Finally, the fish simply sucks the bug down in almost complete silence and turns slowly away toward a dark hole in the grass as the angler lifts his rod tip, then tries to force the fish's head up and away from the underwater tangles. The fish may well weigh two pounds, a good one for the river heads, and it will be a little while before it is in the boat. With the final splashes, a fast-moving wake approaches from somewhere near shore, skirting obstructions and stopping ten feet from the boat. It is a three-foot alligator, wearing the look of popeyed innocence common to little alligators, and wondering where the injured fish has disappeared to.

The alligator studies the boat and its occupants for several minutes, paddles to the mangrove shoreline and watches from comparative security, interested and befuddled by the antics of the popping bug, which it finally chases with a determined rush. It is ruining the fishing and one angler menaces it with a pushpole until it disappears in the green mangrove shadows with a sound, half squeak and half croak, difficult to associate with the vibrating bellow of a ten-foot bull.

The boat drifts downward in a current that goes so slowly there is only a slight tendency for the underwater growth to bend toward the Gulf. Most of the bass are quite small but there is an occasional two-pounder. The water is slightly deeper now, and the fishermen have seen the squirting streak of a ladyfish that passed the bug repeatedly and then pounced wildly upon it, to go leaping away in pinwheeling gyrations. When finally

1

2

3

Everglades World:
Wet season brings transient freshwater growth to brackish mangrove river (1). Gallinule (2) treads gingerly on aquatic plants. Angler (3) catches snook as dry weather brings fire to Everglades and saltwater fish invade land of sawgrass and cattails. Young raccoon (4) contemplates his ever-changing world. Alligator (5) is digger of wallows that become life-saving water holes in times of drought. Wading birds (6) are conspicuous feature of ponds, while for quail (7) camouflage is way of life.

7

4

6

5

caught, the gleaming arrow continues to twist and gasp, its large wild eyes contributing to its look of furious energy. Released, it is gone in an underwater blur.

Ladyfish are a sign of salt water nearby, for although able to live in either fresh or salt, they spend most of their life in salt. To the fishermen, another brackish-water intruder is more exciting.

The bug alights near the mangrove branches as it has hundreds of times before, throwing little flecks of water as the angler works it hard in a change of pace. There is a headlong rush from the mangrove roots, a dark back and jutting dorsal fin; the big snook comes without hesitation and takes the bug in a churning turn, slanting back for the cover to make a plunging fight that tows the boat toward the shoreline, while the poler tries vainly to change direction quickly. The end is inevitable and the twelve-pound leader snaps.

The snook spends much of its life on the fertile fringe of salt water; it can live for long periods in water that is fresh enough for humans to drink, but it can also live far out at sea.

The current is almost at a standstill now, held by the swelling shove of an incoming tide far away in the Gulf—fresh water halted by salt water. Evening approaches and curlews come twisting down the crooked river, flaring as they sight the boat. It is a long run to the dock and the fishermen prepare to leave. As the motor begins its hum, a big silver fish rolls in a deep pocket, showing a tarpon's large burnished scales, and a black-tipped shark glides away from the annoying exhaust.

There are pink thunderheads in the west, but there has been no rain and the bass's time may be short. If rain comes, the largemouths can return to their sawgrass homes. If the drought continues, their fresh water will be compressed and finally all of it will become too salty. The bass, once predators, will try to avoid the thunderous strikes of tarpon in this temporary habitat. It has happened for centuries.

It is different at the mouth of the Mississippi, four hundred miles away across the Gulf of Mexico. Here is another merging of fresh and salt water, although the transition is a muddy torrent that shoves far out to sea and spreads its color in an immense fan against the greens and blues of the Gulf. Silt, nutrients, and debris are deposited on a shallow shelf, an ever-building delta cut by deep ship channels.

On the older parts of the Delta, upstream, where the bayous and creeks are mostly fresh water, black bass and panfish are caught by careful shoreline casters who work the banks, framed by Spanish moss and hyacinth rafts. Muskrat trapping and catfishing are important industries, and the nutria, a giant rodent once feared as an invader, foolishly attempts to cross highways between bayous, or sits motionless on a heap of hyacinths. The pirogue, a needle of a boat, is paddled silently through marsh trails by native Cajuns.

So great is the Mississippi's discharge of water into the Gulf that its absorption creates one of the world's largest brackish communities. In some areas the shallows extend very far from land and the water goes back into thousands of shoreline crannies of the Delta. No angler knows them all. The land-and-water fan of confluence brings about the beds of shellfish, and the tiny organisms that attract and support shrimp, offshore billfish, and millions of migrating game fish that swing around the Gulf coast, including king mackerel, cobia, Spanish mackerel, and those less noted for travel—sea trout, amberjack, and the bottom-feeding species.

Where the Mississippi meets the Gulf a conservation question mark has appeared: offshore oil rigs. A platform may be a mile long and there are more than a thousand of them anchored to the Gulf bottom. They have changed the pattern of Gulf fishing for the better in the short run, but the long-term effect is questionable. Although the rigs have become artificial reefs for assorted game fish, including amberjack, cobia, snappers, sea

Too grassy for skiff and too watery for swamp buggy, inland bass habitat is traveled by airboat fisherman who goes hopefully from pond to pond.

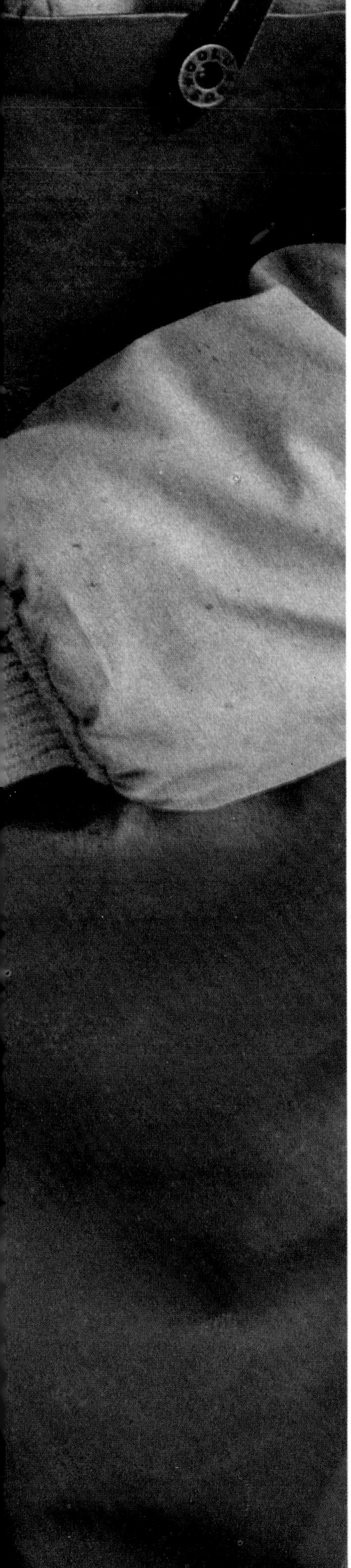
1

2

3

4

*Striped bass (1) travel Atlantic
and Pacific coasts alike.
Surf fisherman (2) meets noisy
sea with his casts,
finding schools of swift
nomadic fishes that skirt the
breakers. Oregon coast (3) is
broken by giant stones
into deep pools and channels
and foam-carpeted beaches.
On sandy beach (4) surfman
reads a changing tide
for sloughs and pockets, aided
by searching sea birds,
and sometimes wins his battle
with burly striped bass.*

Mississippi River's Head of Passes is giant work of sea, as building delta takes its toll of suspended soil and feeds the Gulf. In deeper San Francisco Bay, anglers drift for stripers.

trout, and many others, they have raised the specter of murderous oil spills that can destroy through pollution the fish life they have attracted.

The oil rigs by day are shade and shelter for bait-fish and their pursuers. By night they are immense attractors, with flickering fires of waste gas illuminating the bobbing boats of anglers, many of whom wonder if man may have outdone himself in this audacious challenge to sea and wind. In summer and fall there is the shadow of hurricane warnings. Present all year long is the threat of human error, and far down in the earth are the mighty pressures that can lay waste an ocean. The safeguards must keep pace with the drilling.

The Mississippi Delta and the river of grass are the extremes of transition from fresh to salt. In Chesapeake Bay, San Francisco Bay, and north to New England and Washington State are more typical river mouths, widening from brisk, mountain-fed currents into brackish marshes larger than most Americans imagine. Most have glimpsed the marshes only from highway bridges, where they appear as sluggish rivers, or from the air, where they appear as wastelands without life except for the bright specks of flying birds. The "warm-water rivers" overlap the "cold-water rivers" somewhat, for these are loose definitions. Generally it is the cold-water rivers that support anadromous trouts, and the warmer ones that carry the most sought-after brackish-water traveler of all, the striped bass. The stripers of the bays, estuaries, rivers, and landlocked lakes differ in many ways from the surf runners. Biologists have found resident populations of striped bass that never stray from their home estuaries, and they have also found marauding fish that sweep the coasts from Maine to the Caribbean and from Washington to southern California. Originally an Atlantic Coaster, the striper was introduced to San Francisco Bay in 1879.

The striped bass and the shad are the two best-known anadromous game fish, except for the salmons and trouts. Stripers, which have been caught on hook and line up to more than seventy pounds, get their name from the longitudinal pattern of their scales. They are powerful fish, given to explosive strikes—though they seldom jump—and they are followed with the same devotion as the trouts. Although much striped-bass fishing is relatively coarse, the fish has appealed to the wealthy sportsman since America was first settled. The golden age of striper fishing came between the Civil War and 1900, when exclusive striper clubs on the East Coast were maintained by business tycoons of the era, who used carrier pigeons for contact with their New York offices when stealing a few days off for fishing. They fished from "stands," structures built along the rock coasts in places where an angler might be thoroughly doused by a heavy sea, and they used elaborate systems of chumming. The great bass clubs faded away when the stripers mysteriously disappeared about 1900. It was more than thirty years later that the fish came back, to be greeted democratically by new fishermen with refined equipment; but these coastal prowlers are not our subject now. As we go from fresh water to the salt chuck, we meet the striped bass of the rivers, backwaters, and inland bays.

The striped bass spawns fifteen to thirty miles upstream from the salt line, a single female surrounded by a crowding little pod of male fish; the eggs are fertilized while suspended in the current. Generally the female fish is larger than the males.

Delicately suspended in water, the eggs will not hatch if they settle to the bottom, and it is thought that the river current is essential in maintaining the suspension for the thirty-six to forty-eight hours required for hatching in a temperature of some 62 to 65 degrees. In a week, the little bass, at first hardly more than an egg with eyes and tail, will be free-swimming and in a month it will begin its career as a true predator. Males are sexually mature at two to three years, females at from three to four years. At three years the fish

1

Inshore striped bass (1) falls to spinfisherman in light skiff. Flyfisherman (2) awaits opportune moment for landing catch in protected water. Striper (3) makes near-jump after dogged runs. Not an aerialist, fish will nevertheless "swim into air" if other tactics fail. Fish behave differently as migrants, spawners, and full-time residents of bays and rivers. Fly casters (4) catch many stripers by walking sod banks as tidal creeks form undercuts and bars.

2

3

 will be about 15 inches long.

Striped bass have done well in fresh water in most of the southeastern states, as well as in the Southwest, but most of these populations are put-and-take with no reproduction involved. There are exceptions, as in the Santee-Cooper reservoir of South Carolina, where bass-spawning rivers were dammed and the adults, confined by the reservoir, continued to spawn successfully in upper reaches of the streams—a complete life cycle in fresh water—while saltwater fish continued to migrate to waters just below the dam. There are other cases but less well-known.

In New Jersey's Barnegat Bay, fishermen have spent the night in a houseboat which sits now on dry land, although equipped to float with a hurricane tide. It is early spring. The day before a driving wind muddied some shallow areas, hiding subsurface activities from casters who called upon memory to find the holes along the shallow bars and against the sod banks. It was blind fishing, but could be successful for a student of the water who knew where the tidal current eddied just a little in a pocket, giving a heavy fish a chance to rest and wait for the tide to bring food.

While it will blow again today, at dawn there is almost a flat calm, chilly, and with a little mist on the water. The bay seems endless, running into the horizon without a demarcation, and the scattered houseboats and grassy islands seem very small. There are widely separated, wispy breezes making small ruffled patterns hard to distinguish from the wakes of small bait-fish schools, and there are hard-to-see current patterns around some of the bars.

It is quiet enough that the fishermen can hear the wing whispers of a low line of blunt-headed brant, soon to end their cold-weather stay on the New Jersey coast. It has been so long since gunning season that the brant's line lifts only slightly in deference to the men in the small outboard boat. They start the motor and move slowly across a flat that borders a known channel, peering through their polarized glasses for familiar shadows on the bottom, and when the motor operator, standing up as he steers, sights a school of stripers he cuts the engine instantly. He feels rather than sees the school, for all he actually sights is a pair of blurred shadows beneath the skiff. But he is right, for a series of dying whirlpools and wide swirls mark the alarmed passing of the fish, the swirls reaching the calm surface some seconds after the bass have left. He begins to pole the boat cautiously and his companion stands in the bow with powerful fly rod ready and running line coiled at his feet. A long cast to one side; there is a gentle surface disturbance, perhaps made as a big bass turns in his bottom feeding. The fishermen do not really believe the bass can hear them, yet they speak in half-whispers. The heavy line snakes out as if alive, coils purposefully in a single backcast, and slides forward to straighten its curling leader and drop the cork bug on the calm surface. Is that the direction the fish was headed?

The striper comes in an arc and his upper jaw makes a sharp plop as he takes, the actual strike minimized by the splash of his tail as he drives off with the hook in his jaw. The rod tip bows to his first confused run and the reel sings with muted complaint.

Later in the day the fishermen will lean a little against the wind and drive their spinning plugs into the choppy surface, but there is something special about the dawn striper of silent water, and there are similar mornings on San Francisco Bay with fog lying like silver foam over the coastal mountains.

Another of the few sporting fish that cross the salt line to spawn, the American or white shad occupies an even wider range than the striped bass. It was introduced to the Pacific before the striper, arriving in the Sacramento River in 1871 from its original Atlantic home, and it now runs from Alaska to Southern California and from the St. Lawrence to Florida's St. Johns. Its lesser relative, the hickory shad, receives less notice but has simi-

Anglers meet the American shad (3) on spawning migrations. Wader hooks wild leaper (1) in St. Johns River, Florida. Thrashing fish (2) takes fly.

1

2

3

New Jersey's Barnegat Bay meets sea at crossroads for striped bass and other game fish. Here stripers make seasonal spawning runs.

lar habits. The best-known of the shad grounds, perhaps, are the Connecticut rivers and the St. Johns.

With a life history to match either Atlantic or Pacific salmon, the shad has not acquired their glamour. It is a smaller, less colorful fish and appeals less to romantic writings. In the southeastern part of its range, at least, the shad usually dies after spawning, as does the Pacific salmon. In the northern parts, it appears to spawn more than once. It may spawn more than a hundred miles from the sea, but may spend most of its untraced career a hundred miles from the surf and four hundred feet beneath the surface. It passes pollution belts and commercial nets on its way upstream, and it departs from the Pacific salmon regimen only in that it may be careless as to just what stream it ascends for spawning.

In the Northeast and on the West Coast, shad are caught in swift-moving rivers and creeks by trolling, casting, or simply by dangling a weighted fly in swift waters that will keep it moving. Mainly a plankton feeder while at sea, the shad is seldom caught on bait but comes to a variety of bright and flashy little lures and flies.

In the South, the St. Johns River affords the largest catch of all. Most of the fish are landed more than a hundred miles from the river's mouth, so far upstream that the river is merely a wandering skein of sluggish current with sod banks grazed by Brahman cattle and patrolled by egrets and herons. During shad season, from December to late April, the teal, ringbills, and pintails pitch into the riverside sloughs, and Florida mallards, a nonmigrating species much like the black duck, make silent trips in small flocks.

A shad-spawning area is usually a bend in the river with a sandy bottom, and the fish may be located by their "washes," gentle rolls hard to distinguish at first from the surfacing of a small gar. Some of the shad areas are fruitful year after year; others may disappear after one season of spawning activity.

The trollers use two lures on a single monofilament line, set to run near the bottom, and the better anglers vary the depth by changes in trolling speed and lure weight. A tiny spoon and a colorful jig or "dart" is a prevailing combination. Colored beads have long been used in conjunction with shad lures. The strikes are gentle but the fish leap cleanly and run hard and repeatedly. They are difficult to land because of a paper mouth; landing nets are large. Shad fishing is a social pastime, for such productive grounds cannot be kept secret and voices rise above the gentle sputter of trolling outboards.

In the South, the fly rod is seldom used against shad, but a persistent steelheader, fresh from near-freezing Oregon rivers, uses steelhead methods for this very different fish, which is a herring rather than a trout. He casts across the slow current with sinking line and feels the gaudy, heavy fly's progress along the sand bottom, among the clam shells, eels, and gars. The shad makes a nudging strike, runs, and then leaps, and the transplanted steelheader is happily at home again beside a palm tree, his pleasure witnessed by a great wood stork on the far bank.

Across the saltwater line, on the side of the sea, are the fishes that depend heavily upon salinity for their life, some of them living part of their time in fresh waters, but only visitors there, not requiring fresh water for their reproduction as do the shad, striped bass, and salmons. They live on the edge of the true ocean, using the fresh water indirectly as a source of food, depending partly upon the great depths for their existence, but still vulnerable to the works of man on the border of their domain. Some of them have the size and power of deep-sea residents, and the fisherman regards them as a special challenge. He brings his freshwater tackle and methods to the salt, where a fish has the seven seas to run and hide in and the game is played on a larger scale. For some, the pleasures are the same as those of the trout stream—but magnified.

10.
The End of the River:

It is like a frayed rope — a mesh of bays, backwaters, and tidal creeks, where tarpon and snook lurk among the mangroves.

Frequently out of proportion to his surroundings, a big tarpon may live in a creek the width of an Adirondack trout brook, and he can be caught by trout-stream methods. It is true that the tackle is made stronger to meet his challenge, and the big streamers are as long as many a mountain trout, but the tarpon is truly a light-tackle fish, however large it may be.

Tarpon are basically inshore fish. Some of them are believed to live their entire lives in fresh water. The light-tackle fisherman knows them best along the mangrove coasts and Key flats of Florida. Where fresh water from the Everglades mixes with the Gulf of Mexico on Florida's southwest coast, a day's fishing for big tarpon is likely to be a long search—perhaps two hundred miles by boat in a web of bays, brackish creeks, and tidal rivers.

Fish are found largely by current study. At low tide they may be expected to move out of the shallow creeks and occupy deep holes. On swift tidal movements they are likely to travel, but the patterns may not be understood because of frequent change. Usually they go in and out with tides, and long observation will establish routines at least temporarily valid. Bays used regularly for decades may be inexplicably abandoned for years by schools of heavy fish, and it is these vagaries the professional guide and serious tarpon fisherman must follow.

In late spring the pattern of subtropical afternoon rain squalls has been established for the summer, and fishermen prefer a morning ebb, checking half a dozen known deep bays as the water level falls and finally sighting the slow arc of a dark back and pointed fin in a still cove within sight of the open Gulf. Loafing fish roll slowly and are not likely to go far. Reluctant to fish to what may be a single tarpon, the fishermen drift silently and wait for more appearances. Then there are more rolls, one so close to the boat that the fishermen hear the gentle sigh of the fish taking air and feel the cold stare of a single enormous eye. Below the gleaming black back is a great length and depth of scales, like overlapped plates of scoured silver, disappearing silently to leave only a few small bubbles, the silent trail of a hundred pounds of fish.

The caster in the bow of the boat throws hard with a powerful rod, the ropy line uncoiling lazily before the gaudy streamer, but despite the frequent appearances of rolling tarpon the first strike is a long while coming. When it comes the streamer is being stripped past the dying swirl where a fish has appeared and the angler's guess proves to have been good, for the lure has passed the fish's nose.

The subject takes it in a slow turn, his tail making a chugging splash and throwing water, and the fisherman waits, fearful that some of his stripped line may have tangled on the boat deck, but afraid to look down. He feels the strong tug, a sign the fish actually has turned away, and he strikes with rod arm and stripping hand, hoping to drive the hook into the near corner of the fish's mouth. There is a yank by the tarpon, too hard to be resisted with fly tackle. The angler feels his spare line flash through his hand and strike the rod and he expels his breath in relief that there is no tangle and the fish is on the reel.

Hooked deep, the tarpon leaves a chain of broad and curling swirls on the flat surface and then drives straight up into the sky, a great threshing, contorted silver thing that clatters its gill plates and falls back into a pool of foam, startling an anhinga from a driftwood perch on the muddy shoreline. If one of the fishermen takes a photograph at the moment of the jump he is likely to be disappointed. On the film will be the flat calm of the dark water reflecting the morning thunderheads, and there will be the white-rimmed, churning hole the fish left—but the writhing fish itself may be a shapeless gleaming blob, and the photographer will not recall any fractional instant when it looked just that way. A later jump, after the first fury has subsided, may be clean and classic with little or no convulsion.

Preceding pages: Tarpon, wildest leaper of all coastal fish, becomes twisting missile of polished silver as it feels the hook in a subtropical bay.

An angler is never quite prepared for that first leap, an event that seems to make his tackle puny and ridiculous, and for the moment the calculated attrition of light but steady pressure against such a fish seems inconsequential. As he settles to his sweaty work the man remembers the first jump best, humbled to see the fish actually higher than his head.

Yet, however strong it may be, it is not a superfish and crashing leaps soon give way to hard but random runs. Once the tarpon goes purposefully through a wide creek to another bay, riding a tidal current, and is followed by the boat for a quarter mile. When the tarpon surfaces slowly, head up, and sucks air with a bubbling sound, he is tired but may last a long while yet. The closing stages are tense wrestling at close range, with the ultimate in tackle strain.

But with all of his fierce power the tarpon is a light-tackle fish, for he can be taken in shallow water and his fighting tactics seldom include extremely long runs or bottom sulking. It is the unusual fish, one that leaves the scene in a straight-aimed series of greyhounding leaps, that can take all of the line unless followed instantly.

Although he may generally be a coastal resident, rather than a seagoer, the silver king remains a mysterious herring possessed of elementary lungs to supplement his gills, and despite his flashing exhibitionism he is capable of lying or feeding in stagnant ponds of warm water and rooting in odorous mud for his food. The adult fish favor crabs, or almost anything else that moves on the bottom, and they are equally willing to crash through schools of mullet or to gather drifting shrimp in a tidal pass. Even dead mullet will attract them, and almost any small fish can be used as bait in the deep island runs. Pinfish, sea catfish, and sardines are frequent food there.

It is estimated that the tarpon can tolerate water somewhat above 100 degrees but probably begins to suffer from cold in the mid-60's. Many small fish are cold-killed along the Florida coasts. Large fish either have a stronger sense of impending disaster or better equipment for seeking safety. As inshore water chills, big fish go offshore to deep water, or, if they can, find very deep holes closer in. The confusing part of their seasonal migrations is the question of whether fish actually travel north along the coasts as weather warms, or whether they simply move inshore from deep water, progressively farther north as the season advances.

In the western Atlantic the tarpon occurs regularly from Virginia south to Brazil, and in the eastern Atlantic it appears along much of the African coast. Although it has been almost sixty years since they first had access to the Panama Canal, there is no indication tarpon have become established in the Pacific. In any event, they are Atlantic wanderers, for they have been found as far north as Nova Scotia, and Florida Keys fishermen may find swarms of big tarpon over the flats before the fish work their way back out to sea and disappear. Huge schools of big fish have been seen well offshore, traveling steadily and rolling briskly. They must roll occasionally or die, evidently needing air when on the move but able to do without it for a considerable time when inactive. It has been difficult to determine the exact length of time resting fish can live without air, since tests of captive tarpon may not have provided true resting conditions.

There is no doubt that tarpon can live indefinitely in fresh water and it is quite common to find them more than a hundred miles above an estuarian tide line. The questions of their reproduction and complete life cycle in fresh water are more debatable. Lake Nicaragua in Central America is strongly believed to have a reproducing population of freshwater tarpon. The opinion that such a condition has existed in Deep Lake, Florida, a sinkhole type of natural impoundment, has weaker basis, since the fish seem to have disappeared from time to time there, and travel might be possible in times of high water. Those fish are near a tidal canal.

1

2

3

With jaw shaped for bottom scooping or surface slashing, tarpon (1) will take weighted lures from casting tackle. Successful skiff anglers (2) often find they have boatful of fish, and occasionally tarpon comes aboard uninvited. Fly angler (3) strains on tired fish from staked boat as companion gauges situation and awaits proper moment for sinking short gaff. Fumble could mean renewal of fight so nearly won.

It is in reproduction and juvenile life that the tarpon is most mysterious, having escaped the investigations applied to commercial food fish. It is believed that spawning may take place offshore, and it has been suggested that it occurs when the adults are milling in circular schools or "daisy chains" at the entrances of rivers and passes. However, efforts at collecting eggs or larvae forms from the circling schools have been largely unsuccessful. Spawning is believed to occur in late spring and summer, but the creature which emerges from the egg has little resemblance to a tarpon, a fact that once earned it a separate scientific classification. The larval tarpon is colorless and ribbon-like, with a very small head and fins, resembling an eel more than a game fish. Then, at the length of about an inch, it undergoes a metamorphosis in which it shrinks in size and takes on a fish-like appearance to begin a positive growth as a young tarpon.

Larval tarpon have been collected in shallow water of lagoons, rivers, beaches, and canals, generally from brackish areas, but one specimen of the first stage after hatching was found in the Gulf Stream, some one hundred and fifty miles east of Brunswick, Georgia. Larval and other very young tarpon feed first on planktonic crustaceans, small fishes, caridean shrimp, and mosquito larvae. The very small tarpon (under a foot in length) are strangely difficult for fishermen to find. There have been years when canals, barrow pits, and small creeks in some areas were full of fish in the one-foot class, only to be barren of them for years afterward. Few anglers have ever seen a tarpon of less than 10 inches, no matter how long they have

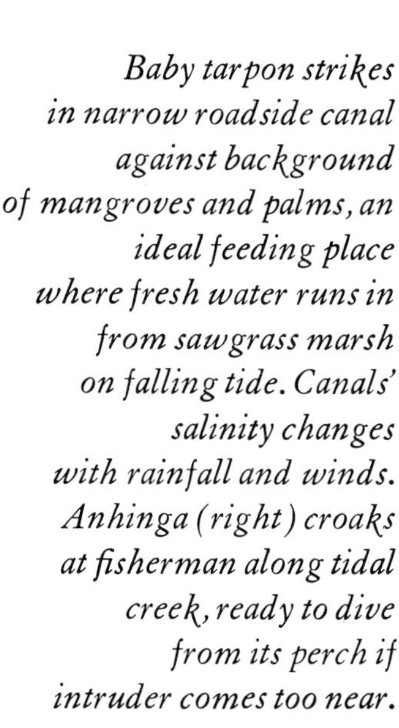

Baby tarpon strikes in narrow roadside canal against background of mangroves and palms, an ideal feeding place where fresh water runs in from sawgrass marsh on falling tide. Canals' salinity changes with rainfall and winds. Anhinga (right) croaks at fisherman along tidal creek, ready to dive from its perch if intruder comes too near.

Jumping tarpon can writhe with loud rattling of gill covers, tailwalk for long distances, or greyhound wildly in tackle-breaking escape.

followed the coastal watercourses. Fish from two to ten pounds are eager fly takers at times, but like their elders may stop feeding completely.

And tarpon seem to practice a strange selectivity according to their size. A given river or bay may be noted for years for young fish of a certain class—possibly ten or fifteen pounds—and the size will not change, proof that the much smaller fish do not move in and that the fish leave when they attain a certain growth. Fish that have rolled regularly at the same spot through decades have actually been used as landmarks by boat travelers.

Behavior patterns of tarpon may be inconsistent over the long term, but some performances are predictable, for a while at least. There are spots in tidal rivers where the fish will feed on certain tides, and even though they may be intercepted by a fisherman on their way to their feeding location they will refuse to strike until they are at the exact spot, be it a creek mouth, a mid-river shoal, or simply a deep pocket. And there are times when tarpon move beneath great schools of bait, taking what they want and refusing the fisherman's lures. Still, some fishermen say that any feeding fish can be caught if the proper presentation can be made.

Tarpon hunters look for signs other than the classic roll for air. They listen for the booming surface strike around the bend and watch the shorelines and bars for fish "lying up," or floating silent and inactive. A tarpon that lies still on the bottom will keep his undershot jaw almost flat against mud or sand and his tail somewhat higher than his head. In a such a pose he may be hard to attract to a lure unless it comes very near his head, and many a fisherman has nervously studied a long and indistinct shadow to learn which was the head end. A careless cast might scare the fish. The theory has been advanced that when tarpon are lying up they are asleep. If so, they are notably light sleepers.

Almost as subtle as the search for silent shadows in murky water is the analysis of bulging, generally slow surface motion. The course of a tarpon mildly alarmed is likely to include a series of half turns and pauses, and his movements may show in surface wake, for a big tarpon very frequently maneuvers in less than four feet of water. And occasionally a bottom-nosing fish will tip so steeply as to show part or all of its tail in the air.

In clear waters of the Florida Keys and near islands of the Caribbean, submerged fish are more visible, and the matter of finding them is simpler. Approaching them under such circumstances may be another matter.

Many tarpon are located by watching from bridges over heavy tidal runs, where they tend to feed upstream of the bridge. Some of the best tarpon fishing at such places is at night, a time for heavier tackle and large baits. A few bridge tarpon are permanent residents, others are seasonal visitors, disappearing after days or weeks beneath the spans, moved by weather or seasonal urges. For the most part, warm weather is tarpon weather.

❀

A heavy construction timber, partly waterlogged and with sawed edges rounded by a generation of contact with other floating objects and the roots of countless mangrove trees, is now drifting in the brackish inland channels of southwestern Florida. No one remembers for what purpose it was originally cut, or exactly where it came from, but it appears occasionally after a storm, then lodges in the mangrove roots of some narrow creek until a new flood moves it again. It is a perfect demonstration of the complexity of the currents of the mangrove coast, a wilderness, more water than land, where a light wind may cause the incoming tide to run north today and south tomorrow in a single creek. The old timber has apparently never reached the Gulf of Mexico in thirty years, although the open sea is less than ten miles away.

Much of the coast is a part of Everglades National Park, and the offshore slope is so gradual that there is little surf on the outer islands. Inland water routes are plentiful for small shallow-draft

1

Along offshore islands of Florida Gulf coast (1), snook anglers cast to mangrove roots and oyster bars on a falling tide. Fat snook (2) is taken from tidal pass by plug caster. Snook (3) lies on tattered chart of mangrove coast, a complex puzzle of tiny mangrove islands, brushy creeks, and inland bays of shallow water—giant estuary and nursery for sea life.

2

3

OYSTER BAY
HUSTON BAY
MORMON KEY

boats and the area has been used for hiding by Spanish pirates, Confederate blockade runners, rum boats, and an assortment of nameless fugitives.

The mangrove coast is a year-round home of the snook, a subtropical dramatist so varied in his modes of life that the literature has never really covered the fish. Researchers find themselves in the position of blind men studying an elephant that will not hold still.

Like the tarpon, the snook is a euryhaline fish, having a wide salinity range. A commercial fisherman, far offshore, may dredge a small snook from a deep reef. A small school of burly snook spends an entire winter in a boathouse one hundred miles from salt water, enjoying the warming influence of a huge spring, and refusing to strike at anything fishermen offer them. A row of bridge fishermen uses long calcutta poles, wire lines, and an assortment of fearsome lures. Some of these men seem to believe that snook bite only at night. For several years in succession, a single roadside ditch has produced contest winners in the fly-rod division. On some of the Gulf beaches on both the Florida and Texas sides the snook is a surf fish.

There are several snook species, some of them no more than a few inches long. They are similar in appearance, however, and the common variety may weigh as much as fifty pounds, although, as with the freshwater trouts, size seems related to habitat and tackle is adapted to size. In some back-country bays or rivers, a five-pounder is a prize. In a deep pass, Central American trollers would be disappointed in such a catch.

In summer the snook spawn in passes and river mouths along the southern Atlantic and Gulf coasts of Florida. The mating occurs in a spawning school, females and males emitting mature eggs and sperm into the water column, and fertilization occurs immediately. The eggs (a large female may produce two million or more) are semibuoyant and are carried by tidal currents until they hatch. Peak spawning activity is correlated with the heavy tides, and when the eggs hatch the larval snook go to extreme shallows. During the first few months they prefer a water depth of 1½ to 2 inches, waters often patrolled by bright-eyed herons, egrets, storks, and ibis. Small snook sometimes crowd the "mosquito ditches" dug for insect-control purposes on the east coast of Florida and often share that habitat with juvenile tarpon.

The mature snook carries a bold, dark, lateral stripe. Back-country snook may have nearly black backs and dark olive sides that show iridescent copper in some fishing areas. The "outside" snook from open water are silvery, and the fisherman who finds a light or dark snook in the wrong place assumes that he has come upon some sort of migration. The snook has an undershot jaw but no large teeth. The outside gill plates are razor-sharp, and there is a small retractable blade crosswise in the roof of the mouth which is thought to be used in holding food. As weapons, however, the gill plate and mouth blade hardly appear capable of the destruction to fishermen's nets often committed by snook. Commercial fishermen who have suffered expensive damage argue long as to just how the snook does it.

Small-creek fishing for snook in the mangrove country is a quest for an unusual fish in unusual surroundings, although the tools are the familiar ones of the black-bass plug caster, with the concessions of a heavy section of leader out of deference to the snook's abrasive mouth and cutting gill plates.

The fishermen go in against the brisk current of a falling tide, using a small boat capable of sliding beneath low-hanging branches. The open water of the creek may be thirty feet wide in some spots, but elsewhere it narrows until the mangrove trees are knitted together overhead and the sun comes through only in yellow streaks. Many mangrove roots are not attached to the bottom, but hang loosely in the water, waving in the current, carrying a trimming of barnacles and mossy growth. At very high tide they are mostly submerged and the mangrove branches are in or very

Hooked near offshore island and then played to open water, good snook makes escape as hook tears loose and rod kicks back in angler's hand.

near the surface, making it impossible to reach the snook that lie near the bank. Now that the tide is falling it is possible to see an occasional fiddler crab on the roots or soft mud at the shoreline. There are times when snook go on a splashy crab-hunting spree, but there are no fishy sounds today. The softly sputtering outboard motor startles an anhinga into a headlong dive from a buttonwood branch and its splash sends a green heron flying up the creek with complaining squawks. When the fishermen finally stop their motor there is a murmur of mosquitoes in the thick, muggy air and there are numerous golden deerflies—some of the reasons why the men have the fishing to themselves.

The big snook downstream from the buttonwood stump has lived there for several weeks. He is very near the bottom, in the edge of an undercut the current has made in the bank. The bottom itself is muddy along the edge, although in the center of the creek there is an area of solid rock eroded into edges and depressions, and invisible to the fishermen, for the water is darkly stained by vegetation. Along the shore the water is less than four feet deep; over the rock section it is a full seven. It is a pool slightly broader than the creek above and below it, and at the upper end there is a sand bar a boat cannot cross at low tide, although there is deeper water at one end of the bar. The creek is tidal and runs both ways during most days, but more water comes from the freshwater end. If there is a very heavy rain upstream

1

2

3

4

Daybreak fishermen (1) find striking snook in tidal Everglades canal. Ibis (2) feed on raft of greenery. Porpoise (3) are playful escorts of fishermen's boats. Channel bass (4) is found both in surf and back-country bays and rivers. Snook (5) churns surface when hooked.

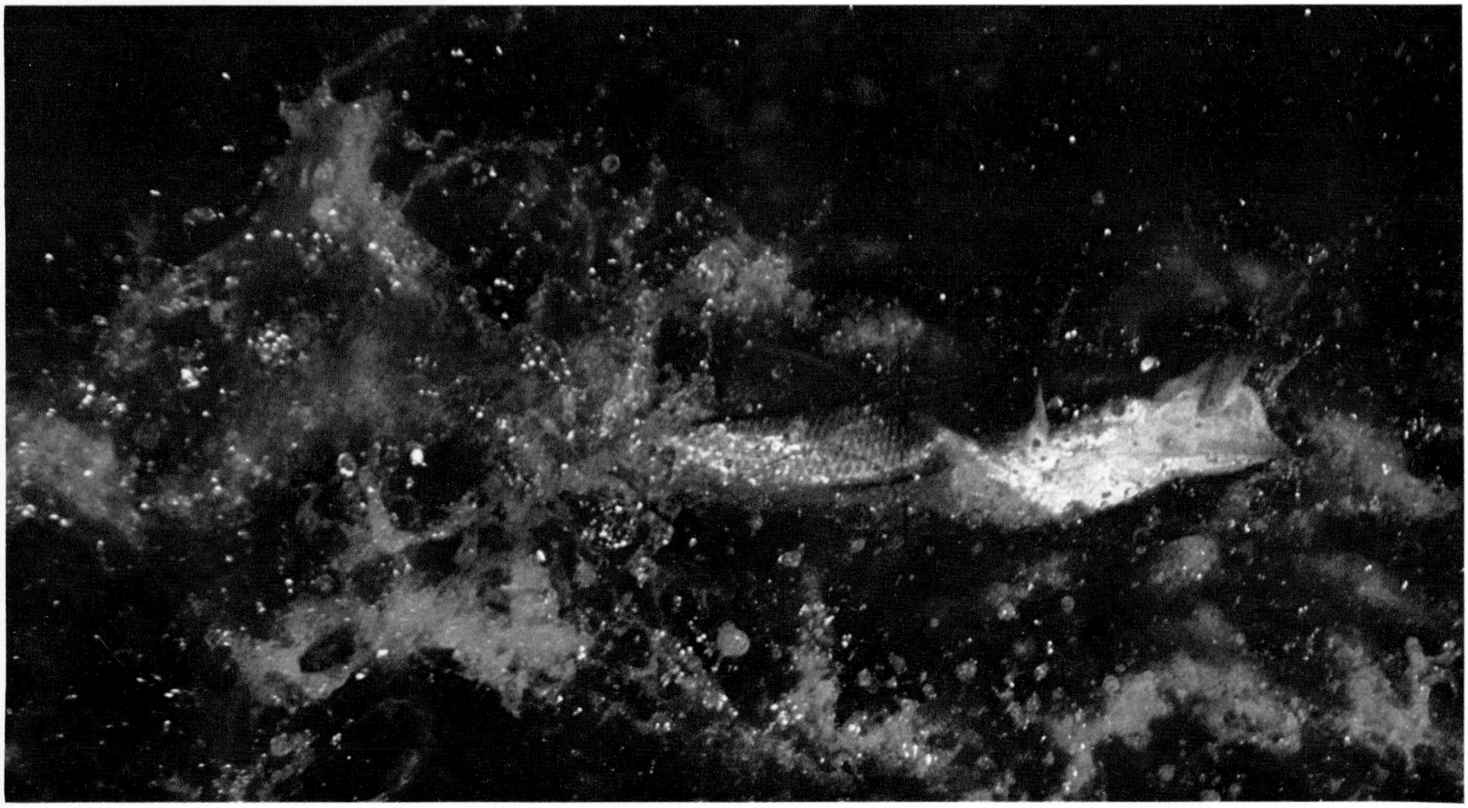

the water runs out all day, simply deepening as the current is impeded by rising tide downstream.

When the snook is feeding on an outgoing tide he can slide along downstream from the bar and intercept bait-fish that become scattered going over the shallows. When he is resting back of the buttonwood stump he can watch the main current while avoiding its pressure, and can shoot out into the midst of a school of finger mullet. When the tide changes he can move to the other side of the ancient black stump and be equally relaxed. For the past two years there has been a small treetop hanging against the stump, with some of the small branches staying in the water even at low tide. The tree was blown over in a storm and although the leaves have long since been washed away the small branches are durable and carry slim tendrils of moss imbedded with tiny crustaceans. Such a treetop offers a measure of safe hiding for schools of small fish and they can feed from the mossy growth. They are within striking distance of the snook, but the bait he slashes at today will be replaced by another school tomorrow.

The two fishermen have passed the pool and are now drifting back toward it, one of them occasionally catching hold of branches to slow the boat, then using his oars to keep it parallel to the current when it floats free again. The other fisherman is in the bow making short casts to the shoreline, moving his short plugging rod in deft underhand wrist-snaps, the tip barely missing the water and the plug going hard and flat to within inches of the rooty shore, sliding under branches that would foil a less skilled workman. It is a surface plug and it lands with a splat, skidding even closer to the bank in the deep shade. Almost as it strikes, the fisherman whips his rod tip and the lure pops loudly, throwing a little spray. He pops it several more times and then reels rapidly, causing it to dive erratically. In some places the fisherman is forced to kneel to avoid the overhead branches but he keeps up his rapid-fire attack against the banks, selecting the logical lies, eyeing a promising nook, eddy, or root structure for the next cast, even as he retrieves.

As the boat slides over the bar in barely enough water to float it, the fisherman makes a raking cast along the drop-off while looking ahead to the stained buttonwood stump and its accrued qualifications—the down branch, the rooty bank, the area he rightly suspects will contain what he calls a rock hole. As he casts a couple of inches downstream from the stump he straightens slightly and does not look for his next target.

The snook has not been feeding actively, but the current is brisk and it has been watching for food. At the first splash of the plug the fish rises ominously from the bottom with no noticeable swimming effort and without tipping his nose upward, his high-placed eyes noting what detail is not obscured by the splashing. With the angler's second whip the plug moves a foot and pops again, and this time the snook tips up and glides swiftly to just behind his quarry, pushing up a silent bulging promise, seen instantly by the fisherman, who pops his lure once more. When nothing happens he jerks it under and cranks furiously and the snook strikes. What appears as fast-escaping prey triggers instincts that overcome the snook's caution; he attacks from the side in a churning swirl and heads back toward his lie, the plug crosswise in his powerful jaws.

There is no time for aesthetic methods. As the snook heads for the stump the angler holds hard, then sees that the tackle will not take the strain. He sticks the rod tip deep into the water and gives line as slowly as possible. With the rod tip submerged the fisherman hopes his line will be kept low enough to escape the hanging roots along the shore. The snook reaches his holding area, fails to hang up the line there, then slants along the shoreline, jumping once in a tangle of roots. Somehow the line holds and pulls under the shoreline obstacles. The snook turns into midstream and is just another heavy fish once he is in open water.

A day after the fishermen and their catch have disappeared, a school of finger mullet showers over the sand bar at the head of the pool and there is the exaggerated bottle-cork pop of a feeding snook. It is a heavy fish and it drops back in the outgoing tide, pauses over the rocky bottom, and then fins out of the current's push, settling behind the old black buttonwood stump. The new resident is almost the size of the fish taken there the day before.

The fishing is different out in the wide passes. Sometimes the snook there are travelers new to the area and are caught and played in mid-channel. Most of the fishermen there prefer a fairly high tide, moving either in or out, and they pay special attention to areas where currents are diverted by oyster bars and eddy pockets are formed. There are porpoises occasionally, no help to fishing in confined quarters, and numerous sleepy sea-cows. A casting or trolling lure presented to an oyster bar drop-off may bring a channel bass as well as a snook, and the grass flats between islands are good for spotted sea trout. The snook fishing there is best in late spring and summer when resident populations are bolstered by the big migrants from unknown locations.

In early spring there is a migration of snook from salt water into some canals and roadside ditches. The smaller fish feed actively on the bait that comes from inland marshes with falling tides. There are a few large fish, sometimes addicted to "cruising," simply swimming along in mid-canal near the surface and pulling a swell that goads casters into violent although usually unproductive activity. The fish, of course, is actually well ahead of the apex of his swell, and even when the lure is properly applied the chances of a strike are poor; even so, such fish are occasionally caught. Many of them have remoras attached to their bodies and there is a popular theory that they travel inshore to rid themselves of unwanted guests. Although the remora is not properly a parasite, it can form a lesion where it has clung for a long while.

There is another kind of canal fishing for snook, thrilling to the handful of participants who make dawn patrols of highway ditches that border grassy marsh areas. Especially on a falling tide—whose effect is felt miles from salt water—bait will move from the sawgrass and cattail areas into canal edges where it is awaited by snook that sometimes line the grassy side and strike explosively. Such striking is known as "popping the banks," and an accurate fly caster from the road side of the ditch tries to put his streamer exactly where the fish will charge next. Dawn is usually best, preferably with the falling tide.

Herons and ibis mark the concentrations of bait, standing in the shallow run-ins, and at dawn the fishermen drive the road looking for the telltale bubbles left over from snook strikes. Occasionally, the canal is almost covered with them. First daylight is the conclusion of a busy time for raccoons, often threading their way along the sawgrass edge to get their share of the tiny gambusia, millies, or flagfish minnows that attract the snook's attention. Snook strikes bring showers of the small bait, some of it flying into the grass. Sometimes the shallows are filled with eager fish that have chased their quarry into 4 inches of water; the fish run against the legs of wading birds, producing indignant squalls.

The most efficient angler must decide whether the fish are driving bait against the grass or striking it as it parallels the shore. If it is the former the weedless fly must be cast completely into the grass and brought out. If the fish are striking farther out in the canal, the casting is less precise. Then there is the tactic of letting a heavy streamer sink to the bottom, masquerading as an injured or freshly killed minnow to be easily scooped up without the necessity of a topwater strike.

As the red sun goes higher and loses its color, traffic increases along the highway. The raccoon vanishes and the snook strikes stop as if on signal. The fishing is over for another day.

11.
At the Edge of the Ocean:

As the incoming tide covers the flats with warm, clear water, the hunt for the swift and skittish bonefish begins.

At low tide the flat appears calm, even on a windy day, and now only a light breeze is blowing. Large sections of the bottom are exposed, most of it putty colored. Other areas are brown or green, with uneven ridges of seaweed and grass.

Streaks of very shallow water feed into deeper channels that show green in the sun as they meander toward the end of the flat, where a gentle surf breaks over a ridge of bottom. Seaward of the surf line the water deepens immediately to a darker green, then a blue-green that becomes still darker toward the indigo Gulf Stream a few miles farther out. Where the flat breaks abruptly into the deeper water there are the remains of an old wreck, the flaking metal parts rounded off by the erosion of rust, wind, and salt water. At high tide there is no sign of it, but now a large part of the ship is visible, still in the spot where it first crunched against the land in some bygone storm. Year by year it seems to sink deeper into the sand and shattered coral. It is crumbling away from both top and bottom, and being gradually consumed by the shallow sea. It is scant shelter, but it gathers its own community.

On the exposed parts is a party of cormorants, crowding each other yet unwilling to forgo companionship for more comfortable perches. Most of the birds sit with necks drawn in and their heads tipped arrogantly upward. One sits a little apart, engaged in elaborate wing drying and conversational croaking. Underwater the old boat's engine still retains recognizable form although its compartment has long since disappeared. A little school of inch-long fish moves about it, never more than a foot from its rusty bulk, feeding on tiny things suspended in the water. The fish keep close formation, the little pod swinging slightly with the motion of the shallow swells that break over the wreck only three feet above. A few feet away are several gray (mangrove) snappers, the largest of them a foot long; they do not pursue the small fish since it is one of those periods when the sea's warfaring existence observes a truce. The snappers have their own cover of sorts in the blunt and broken ends of the old boat's ribs, but the giant barracuda ghosts along in the open, slowly following the deep side of the little reef and pausing as it reaches the wreck. The barracuda is four feet long and the dark blotches on its side appear to weave slightly in the changing patterns of light from above. The fish is cigar-shaped, a caricature of marine evil with multiple rows of teeth that can slice cleanly. Now, as it passes the familiar wreck—a regular stop on its low-tide patrol—it begins a rush at the snappers that stops the moment the smaller fish disappear in shadows. The barracuda turns slowly and lies silent for a time, well above the bottom, for a better study of the wreck, then slides away in the sunny water, its form lost in the changing reflections of surface waves and the distorted shadows of sea fans.

The upper Florida Keys are a dead coral reef with living reefs offshore between the flats and the Gulf Stream. The flats are strewn with the recognizable skeletons of various types of coral, though most of it has decomposed into marl or mud. Turtle grass covers large areas of the bottom, especially in the coves where the sea floor is soft and difficult for the fisherman to wade. Sea fans grow tall in the deeper parts of the flat, and basket sponges gape upward like funnels.

In its wide parts this flat is nearly half a mile across. The land lies low, with shallow sandy beaches and small mangroves that send roots twisting along the water's edge. There are a few tidal saltwater creeks, very deep in some spots but shallowed up where they spread their deltas onto the coastal flat. On the creek bottoms, plainly visible in the clear water, are schools of resting rays, undisturbed by boat traffic twenty feet above.

There is a constant deposit of sediment left by wave action, which contributes to construction of the land. On stormy days the flat is covered with "white water" carrying calcareous material washed out of the reefs. At those times it is impossible to see fish in the shallows.

Preceding pages: Hunter as well as angler, sportsman tensely shows fly to bonefish on a shallow marl bottom at edge of sea.

The red mangrove trees that line both the flat and the creeks are building land with the assistance of the offshore reefs, for their spidery roots catch quantities of sediment and make it into solid footing. A single mangrove tree that manages to survive at some distance from shore will become an island and then reach out for other land. The mangrove seedling, or "bean," drifts with the tide, eventually sends out a root structure, and floats upright in the water, feeling for an appropriate anchorage as a modest beginning of what may someday be an island. Tiny rooted mangroves are often taken for bonefish tails from a distance.

The mangrove contribution is complex, and when mangrove tangles are laboriously cleared for housing developments and highways the shoreline community suffers. Fallen and decomposing mangrove leaves provide food for a host of microorganisms which are an important part of the food chain affecting insect larvae, crabs, shrimp, and fish. The groping mangrove roots are a protective canopy for life at low tide. Among the most obvious residents then are the squads of fiddler crabs, each male having a single great pincer with which he carries on a program of formal saluting which seems to get a response from all other fiddlers in the vicinity.

Florida Keys flats are similar to hundreds of shallows throughout the Caribbean, waters with a part-time population that moves with the tide in an abruptly changing marine habitat. Now, with the low tide almost slack, there are faint snaps and pops from the barnacles and other small creatures newly exposed on the wet bottom. Herons and egrets watch trickling channels for bait-fish that have tarried too long in their move to deeper water, but larger fish have abandoned the flat. They are in the deeper water offshore, resting in an occasional pocket along the beach, or idling in the blue creeks. Today the flat's water temperature will be good, well into the 70's, and it will be a busy place.

The tide's change shows first in a few trickles of water filling slight indentations of the exposed bottom. At about this time there are some gentle wakes along a wandering channel that joins a creek mouth to the sea. They appear aimless but gradually work inshore, being made by a small school of bonefish waiting for the tide to cover the fertile flat. At first they nose about in grassy areas along the edges of the deeper channel, each fish doing its own foraging, but as the tide grows they move to the open flat, working gradually up the slightly sloping bottom.

Although it is noted for its invasion of the shallows, the bonefish lives much of its life in deeper water where it has habits that are less well known and where it may sometimes be caught on bait with heavy tackle. It is on the clear flats under a high sun and in scant inches of water that the bonefish becomes the gray ghost, the suspicious shadow, and the racing wake. Different instincts take command when the fish is barely covered by water, visible to any enemy above the surface and increasingly far from the depths where it is safe.

As the half-dozen fish move slowly from their entry channel they scatter slightly, though remaining within sight of each other, making a pod some thirty feet across. A gull swings low on a patrol of the shallows, its shadow striking near them momentarily, and they spurt back toward deep water, each fish leaving a puff of gray bottom mud where the thrust of its broad tail accelerated its departure. They are large fish, more than five pounds each, and it is unlikely any bird could harm them, but they are restless in the exposure of the shallows. They stop, indistinct forms beneath a slight ripple at the edge of deeper water, then return slowly in a tight group to the shallows, where they gradually spread out once more.

The bonefish is a bottom feeder. Its mouth is on the underside of its head, and it looks suckerlike at first glance. But the similarity ends there, for the sucker's tail waves while the bonefish's flicks hurriedly at the water and its high dorsal fin steers a hard-muscled torpedo. Though it is not

1

2

3

Herring gulls (1) crowd point of land near wide flats. Cormorants (2) can startle bonefish with their swift shadows. Mangrove snapper (3) is intellectual of the salt flats, hiding among mangrove roots for carefully gauged charge at passing bait or lure. Fiddler crabs (4) race over sand at low tide, cling to mangrove roots of newly formed islands. Flats fishermen (5) can see their targets best on calm days but need the sun; some live aboard cruiser and fish from skiff in thin water.

Using bait-casting tackle, angler throws to shallow-water target while guide poles gently from bow, vantage point for inspection of bottom.

the fastest offshore species, in the shallow flats the bonefish is a streak which leaves a churned wake far behind, a trail of swirling mud and sand with a great widening boil where the flight began. In this strange setting its speed is dramatized; twenty-five miles an hour can appear twice that.

The fish is best known as an angler's target in southern Florida and the Caribbean. It lives near tropical shallows around the world, but its lack of commercial value has left it an unknown species. It begins as a larva, ribbon-like and several stages from its final form. Very small specimens are seldom captured.

Certain areas are known for only a few large fish, while others have many smaller ones. Generally, a bonefish school is composed of fish of approximately the same size. The big trophy individuals, those of eight pounds or more, are likely to travel alone with the caution of long experience. The recluses lack the protection of numbers, a safeguard that causes an entire school to flush when one outrider sights real or imagined danger. Much bonefish feeding is between the high- and low-tide marks. However the fish seldom appear on the flats on cold winter days, and any water temperature below 70 degrees can mean poor fishing. Bonefishing is largely hunting, a special kind of sport, and flats fish are roughly classified, according to behavior, as feeders, tailers, and cruisers. Feeders are actively working the bottom in search of the tiny crabs or other crustaceans and mollusks that make up the bulk of bonefish diet. Tailers are foraging in such shallow areas that their tails show above the surface as they nose down. Cruisers are traveling to or from feeding areas or searching for food on bare bottom where it is scarce.

The ventral position of the mouth ill-adapts the bonefish to any form of surface feeding, although it will occasionally take from the surface, generally something that has been flushed from the bottom. Such striking is a difficult maneuver and is done awkwardly. The bonefish's powerful jaws are specially equipped to crush shellfish and crustaceans. When completely duped by an artificial lure the fish may take it slowly and be hooked far back. The violent strike is rare, for the bonefish does not pursue large bait-fish, but catches smaller tidbits at its leisure.

The little school of fish that we have been observing moves somewhat faster as the tide fills, going two hundred yards from deep water, and slows as it reaches a marl bottom scattered with grass, sponges, and bristly black sea urchins. As the fish investigate the bottom one occasionally stirs a small gray puff of mud particles, no larger than a tennis ball, that remains in suspension a few inches above the bottom, and the school can be trailed by these fading signs. As they move, the fish are seen as dark, wriggly shadows on the light bottom which disappear when the sun goes behind a cloud. Over some bottom there is so much vegetation the fish are hard to see. Their shadows are broken and they appear gray with an illusion of translucence. In the most shallow areas the fish leave little indistinct lines of surface wake, but such traceries are made by many types of swimmers and only the expert can be certain that a distant disturbance is made by bonefish instead of by a small barracuda or shovel-nosed shark.

A nurse shark, some four feet long, passes the foragers, swimming slowly with wide sweeps of the tail, dorsal fin breaking the surface. Even when it is not feeding, the shark stirs the bottom slightly, disturbing a variety of bottom residents and leaving a smoky mud trail. Out of place in such close quarters, it is easily seen. Two bonefish are close behind it, unlikely to be noticed in their effortless movement and taking advantage of the small water creatures disturbed by its bulk. Many a wading fisherman has turned to find a bonefish just behind him, investigating his mud trail.

The school of bonefish finds a concentration of tiny crabs on a soft bottom and their rooting produces a "mud," a solid blot of creamy water on the shimmering flat, visible to a fisherman from great distance and streaming slightly with the

Opposite: Its zipping runs slowed to feebly paddled circling, big bonefish is cautiously approached by fisherman on sandy bottom. Aborted landing attempt could break leader, set off new rush, or tangle fish and fisherman. Mouth of streamlined bonefish (above) is positioned for bottom feeding and has crushers in throat for crustaceans.

Shallow-water tarpon are known as leapers rather than runners or sounders. Spinfisherman's line slackens as fish rushes boat in frenzy of frustration.

building tide. It is a miniature of the great mud blotches sometimes stirred by large schools of bonefish—opaque sections that fill entire coves. The fisherman knows they contain feeding fish, but he must cast blindly for there is no way of telling where the individuals are.

At high tide the fish have worked their way to the shoreline. It is after midday and as the sun lowers, the fisherman's visibility will begin to fail; even his polarized glasses will not enable him to penetrate the glimmering reflective surface. The tide begins to fall and the bonefish now move on a more definite course up the shoreline, soon to be forced farther out by low water. There is a rocky point that narrows the flat to a mere hundred yards and all traffic following the shallows must be pinched to that narrow passage bounded by gentle breakers on one side and mangrove shore on the other.

The fishermen are in the narrow section of the flat, meeting a concentration of traffic moving in 18 inches of water. Their boat is driven very slowly, the pushpole used to search for soft spots and fend off grating rocks. Nurse and blacktip sharks go by slowly and a frightened ray flails water and bottom in its escape. A small turtle moves from the boat at furious speed, its frantic flippers setting up a blur as it banks and turns outward toward the surf line. Small trunkfish go away near the bottom, their bodies stiff in unyielding shells. Cruising bonefish pass in restless little pods, the larger ones appearing in pairs and singles. Sometimes it is possible to sight a moving bonefish a hundred yards away, a dark shadow that passes a light spot on the bottom. At other times the fisherman will never see the fish until it flushes in a boil of mud and water. Still again, the fish is suddenly present twenty feet from the boat, curious but restless and unseen until then, ready to flush at the lift of a casting arm, the flash of sun on a varnished rod shaft, or the swing of a pushpole. For success, the fish must be sighted farther away than that and its probable course must be plotted instantly, for the cast must be well ahead of cruising fish, far enough ahead that the splash of spinning lure or fly line will not frighten it. It must intersect the fish's course so that it is easily seen, but must be retrieved slowly and hesitantly to represent a blue crab, a pink shrimp, or simply a shapeless thing in erratic flight. In water of two feet or more it is essential that the lure sink quickly; where the water hardly covers the fish a slow-sinking fly is better, moved with spasmodic twitches just above the marl. Once seen and accepted, it may be plucked from the bottom as well as intercepted afloat.

A large school of bonefish approaches, more than twenty of them, and the fishermen watch the swarming shadows of the main pod, waiting for the exact range. They are startled by a fish they had not seen, an advance guardsman that swirls and spurts away almost at their feet to alarm the entire school. The fish scatter wildly but do not change their general direction and they swing wide on both sides of the boat, then regroup in their previous formation to continue up the coast.

The smaller school of fish, whose progress we have charted since the rising of the tide, now nears the fishermen's boat. It is going fairly steadily, though now and then a fish will turn aside to investigate something on the bottom, regaining position in the school with a hardly noticeable tail movement. Fifty yards from the skiff the school crosses a bare bottom patch and is silhouetted starkly for a moment, long enough for the bow fisherman to make a perfect cast when they are only fifty feet away. The spinning jig enters the water with a soft plop, well ahead and well past the fish. They ignore the gentle splash but one of them sees the lure wobbling slowly along the bottom with little darts and twitches. His tail moves sharply and he is over the lure, head tipped down an inch from the hook. The other fish mill about him and when he follows the bucktail jig toward the boat they crowd beside him, half a dozen fish in gill-to-gill formation, competing for

Bridges of Florida Keys provide easy access to great variety of game fish. Barracuda (below) is villain of flats and reefs, ambushing smaller fish.

the nearest position but unwilling to touch the laboring thing on the bottom. So, as bonefish often do, they follow the jig to within rod's length of the boat, then mill nervously and resume their course up the shoreline. The sun is getting low now and cruising fish are hard to see, but the anglers have another chance in a grassy cove.

A tailing bonefish is found as a distant flash of light where the sun reflects from a wet tail, or the fisherman may see the tail itself at closer range, very broad and curling slightly as the fish probes the bottom energetically. If the water is so shallow that the fish's sail-like dorsal shows too, the angler is somewhat handicapped in trying to keep his lure or fly off the bottom, yet the tailing fish is likely to be vulnerable for it is actively feeding and the ruse is to make the lure appear to be something stirred up by the fish itself. Tailers are difficult to approach with a boat and the fisherman usually wades, moving cautiously although often with great effort if the bottom is soft. He presents his lure or fly first at some distance from the fish to avoid startling it, and when the fish pays no attention he tries a closer cast, then moves nearer until the fish takes, follows, or flushes. Although the flyfisherman makes less splash with his lure than does the caster, he has the problem of a bulky line and a waving rod.

But there is added drama to the flyfisherman's strike, for he may have loose line in the water and must play the fish from the reel. He casts several times, and the fish finally stops its grubbing and lowers its tail in a silent moment of inspection, then it follows the twitching retrieve and takes the fly several feet from where it had been feeding. It is a quiet procedure, only a slow V showing the fish's leisurely pursuit, and when the fly stops and the hook is set there comes a tense moment before the fish runs. Then there is a quick swing around the fisherman, for a hooked bonefish aims for the open sea and this one has been approached from the seaward side.

The line sings and picks up a little sheet of water. Just behind its hissing streak is the muddy boil of the bonefish's wake, churned in frantic effort, and the reel screams, for bonefishermen let their fish run against a light drag. The run is fast but it goes in spurts, the reel's cry rising and falling, and the fish now running straight. It is a hundred yards before the first stop. After only a brief hesitation, there is a second run, this one much shorter, and the angler tightens his drag and follows a short way on foot. But the contest is not over —although the quarry has been held short of deeper water—for now the fish swings in a great circle against the pressure of the high rod tip, and the sagging line may pick up sea fans or grass. Sometimes a solid obstacle stops the line and the fish wraps both line and leader around a dozen things, while the fisherman flounders to free his equipment. Such a play ends with the fish breaking off, or resorting to rooting the bottom to disengage the hook. If it is landed it will be exhausted, its will gone, and the fisherman must move it gently back and forth in the water to revive it before the release. (The bonefish is aptly named and seldom eaten, although Bahama natives consider it a delicacy.) In bonefishing, finding the ghost is half the sport. Once hooked, its line-melting run leaves the issue in doubt until the last moment.

Here, as everywhere, it is the habitat that sets the pattern of fish behavior. On the wide flats nearly all fish will seek safety in deeper water, if not the open sea at least a deep channel or blue hole, and it is on the flats that fish acquire their reputation as runners. Even the channel bass, or redfish, known best as a deep, chugging bottom fighter, becomes a speedster on the flat. The redfish is usually found nearer murky outlets from the coastal swamps, waters that it often shares with weakfish or sea trout, where it is harder to see than if it lived over lighter bottom in clearer water. Channel bass work the bottom—with mouths very much like the bonefish's—and seem to retain some memory of its features. When hooked, they head for the nearest deep area. The run they make will be very different from anything they do in the depths, but once they reach their objective they become ordinary, head-shaking, tugging victims.

Barracuda are voracious feeders and will take gleaming lures readily, although they generally insist on a fast-moving target for their attacks unless the subject is natural bait. Most fishermen seldom hook the larger barracuda, which grow to something near a hundred pounds in many warm seas. The individuals that cruise the flats are residents of the edges, the wrecks, pilings, and reefs, and they have a curiosity that keeps them studying a wading fisherman for long periods, even when they disdain his lures. The barracuda lies motionless much of the time whereas many of his neighbors are constant travelers. And barracuda that fight over a bait trolled at high speed will simply follow a slower lure, tantalizing the fisherman into prolonged but fruitless casting.

The flats are a broadened edge of the sea with a taste of the fresh water from the rivers, and they hold their resident population while serving as hosts to great migrants like the giant tarpon that come and go with season and weather. The tarpon sometimes come in broad schools, sighted far out to sea, and their movements are complex. They can be found near the flats at any time of year, yet they seem to concentrate in spring, and the migration may come from far to the south. There is another theory that the fish habitually live in deep water and simply come near shore, progressively farther to the north as the water warms. Most biologists believe that tarpon movements are a mixture of the two procedures, moving inshore and northward with warm weather.

Along the Florida Keys are innumerable swift tidal channels that concentrate fish, including some tarpon that live most of their adult lives near the bridges. When there is an influx of big fish, the bridge areas may be crowded with rolling monsters, but when the travelers have disappeared there are still a few fish in permanent residence.

New mangrove island is haven for bird life as its probing roots seek materials for larger outpost. Pelicans are at critical stage in fight for survival against chemical pollutants. On ever-changing flat, anglers watch parade of underwater life and move to intercept game fish that sweep near shore on incoming tide.

Broad-sided permit, powerful flats adversary, feeds on bottom creatures, especially crab. Long runs are test of light gear, scraping lines, overheating reels.

Some of the more sporting tarpon fishing is done on the flats, often the same flats where the bonefish are found, but a hundred-pound fish requires more depth to swim in and the flats tarpon are usually found in water from two to eight feet deep. They are seldom the silent shadows cast to in rivers and back-country bays. Usually they are moving about to feed, scooping up crabs or crayfish or crashing headlong into a school of mullet.

There are routes about the flats followed regularly by tarpon, usually deep channels that take them near their feeding area. Moving tarpon usually roll frequently to supply increased amounts of oxygen for their dual breathing systems—lungs and gills. Fishing for them is partly a waiting game, partly a matter of cutting off a moving school. The fisherman seldom sees a complete fish. He watches the blue-chrome of a rolling back, or makes out a tail, or even the huge eye and jutting jaw of a tarpon's head. If he is after a record fish he must select his targets from these glimpses, and a school of tarpon may be simply a play of surface wakes, an occasional underwater gleam, and a scatter of shifting light. The presentation is even more complex in a strong tide where the fish are likely to move briskly and the boat is hard to pole except with the current.

The lure or fly is cast ahead of the moving fish and retrieved only a little beneath the surface. The fisherman may not even see the fish as it follows but when it prepares to take he is alerted by the sudden appearance of a large dark spot near his lure. The spot is the inside of the fish's mouth and generally means a strike. The fisherman simply continues his reeling if he uses plugging or spinning tackle, or, if it is a streamer fly, maintains his series of foot-long strips. Then the dark spot disappears, there is a surface heave as the fish turns, and the angler feels the pull and strikes back.

The permit has habits similar to the bonefish's, although it requires slightly deeper water due to its great body depth. While it ranges as far north as Massachusetts, it is primarily a prize of the warm waters. It is a member of the pompano family, and has the characteristic jutting forehead which Don McCarthy once called "the forehead of a philosopher"; its tail is shaped like two great finny scythes. When feeding on the shallow bottom, the permit often waves its great tail above water, and inexperienced viewers are likely to take it for some strange creature splashing in distress. Head down and busy with its bottom feeding, the permit may be approached quite closely and is often too engrossed to notice lures that land nearby. When on the move it is more easily alarmed. Nearly all rod-and-line permit are caught on bait, of which a small crab is most reliable. It is the permit's fight when hooked that makes the fish famous, for it not only runs longer and harder than the bonefish but employs its very broad sides to prolong the battle, even if deeper water is reached. The fish has a tough mouth, hard to penetrate with a hook, and it resorts to violent bottom rooting to free the barb. It can be deceptive when sighted in the shallows, a twenty-pound permit frequently appearing insignificant because of the flattening effect of refracted light. There is a hard core of flyfishermen whose common hope is to catch just one permit. But the great pompano is not truly a fly fish; it is only on rare occasions that they show any sustained receptivity to the fly, and the flyfishermen who hasten to the scene of the action find more often than not that the feeding plan has changed and that no more permit can be caught. If permit are often hooked in deeper water, it is their flats appearances that bring them fame.

Between the inshore and offshore flats is a succession of bridges and inlets. Where man has built his pillars and abutments, the fish of the flats meet those of the estuaries and rivers in heavy and changing currents that carry brackish products to residents of the sea. In these funnels the fish establish their feeding procedures and concentrate the eat-or-be-eaten process of life.

The bridge is not simply an obstruction. It

1

2

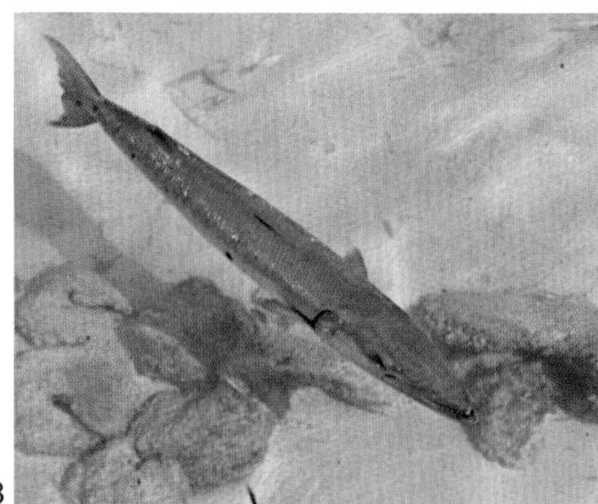

3

creates a special saltwater situation, different from anything encountered in nature. It is a protective roof that makes a shadow by day or night, more continual than the shadow cast by a marginal ocean cliff. Again, a bridge may be built away from the margin, with great tidal currents running under it from one flat to another. The bridge funnels the flow, breaks it into eddies and cushions, shelters it from above, and affords real or imagined protection for sea life of all sizes. Bridge fishing is a science, and the bridge waters have their long-time fish residents which have seen fishermen come and go, perhaps for years, as well as migrant fishes that pause for an hour or for weeks in the unique community. And because the bridge does not change and its structure is understood, the habits of its fishes can be learned through observation and their timetables established with tide charts and watches. So the bridge fisherman is developed by experience and study, and his performance becomes deft and objective.

The shadows of the bridge influence its residents almost as much as the broken current. In the broad light of a sunny day the shadows are instantly seen, but daytime seldom provides the best bridge fishing. At night the shadows are more subtle and the whole scene is in darkened tones. The surface movements of fish may then be outlined in bioluminescence from tiny dinoflagellates or touched by moonlight reflections. Lights from the bridge may show fish busily feeding near the surface, or pick up reflections of their splashing strikes. The artificial lights themselves, whether a part of the bridge structure or simply lanterns used by fishermen, stimulate feeding action, for they attract small bait-fish, easily seen in slower portions of the current. Sometimes bait-fish come in great swarms and crowd into the eddies behind pilings, giving off occasional pinpoints of reflection as they change position. In northerly waters their formations may be smashed by striped bass; far south the larger strikers will be snook or tarpon, and in either area there will be spotted sea trout or com-

Spotted sea trout (1) live in grassy bays and tidal rivers, seek deep holes in cold weather and migrate along outer beaches. Small shark (2) is predator on flats. Barracuda (3) is disturbing witness to stalking of bonefish. Anglers congregate (4) where bass are taking bait.

4

 mon weakfish. Truly booming strikes may come from very large tarpon which pursue fish that came to feed on the small bait, and even greater splashes can be caused by porpoises that ignore fishing lures with mammalian sophistication.

In spring there will be a night run of shrimp, thrown up in showers by their predators or skipping along the surface individually, the frantic hopping flight followed by an ominous wake and ending with a splash.

Whatever fish are present, the feeding pattern resembles that in other moving waters, from mountain brook to ocean current. Only the artificial roof of the bridge changes the procedure, and there are predictable spots where the feeding fish will work. As in a river, the predators seek current but will not face it constantly and, as elsewhere, it is the edges of the fast water that they prefer, though they employ the edges of the shadow, too. The favored feeding zone, whether for surface or bottom feeders, is upstream from the bridge and at the edge of the shadow it throws, a shadow that moves with the moon or remains stationary on dark nights. Perhaps it is a double shadow of both moonlight and bridge illumination.

The game fish is a stalker and he waits in the darker places for his prey to come downstream. The upstream side of the bridge is generally chosen and the fish appear to compete for the most forward positions. There is another favored spot downstream, but here the fish lie nosing against the shadow from the lighter side and meet bait-fish that are confused and blinded by the glare. Few game fish are found near the center of the shadow. The fish prefer to combine shadow position with eddies or cushioned current. Upstream they lie in line with pilings where the water slows to divide. Downstream they will be in the edge of the divided flow, able to see into the full current yet unwilling to swim against it constantly. These patterns must be solved by the fisherman, whether he casts from the bridge or from a boat.

The jig and its relatives are the favored lures of those who fish from the spans, for the lure is built to travel parallel to surface or bottom, even when retrieved from above. In using it, the fisherman who casts upstream hopes to throw across and above the fish's lie and then bring his offering in front of it as it noses the shadow line. When he fishes downstream he relies on the current to carry the lure to the fish in a swinging arc, beginning near the bridge itself after a cast that nearly parallels the span.

When large fish, regardless of species, are hooked from a bridge the percentage of landings is poor, for pilings are studded with barnacles which are almost sure to sever a line that scrapes them under tension. Even fishes that are not known for seeking cover when hooked may escape by accident if they pass under the span, and fishermen have devised schemes for lowering their rod and reel beneath the bridge to resume the fight on the other side when necessary. If the fish is too large to be hoisted with the line, and the fisherman has no flying gaff or bridge net, he tries to walk his catch to the end of the bridge and find a suitable landing spot on the bank. Beneath some southern bridges are giant residents which have been taking baits and lures for years, usually huge grouper which simply break off the catch in leisurely fashion after pulling the line across barnacles or sharp rock edges.

The bridge scene changes with its shadows, with its ingoing and outgoing tide, with the seasons and the temperatures, and its students know of the changes and keep carefully timed appointments with them. Betweentimes, they may be found in other promising places.

At the edges of the southern flats are the mangrove snappers, masters at taking cover, and believed by many to be the most intelligent fish of all. As found near the flats they are mostly small fish—a three-pounder is a large one there—and many anglers do not know that the mangrove snapper, or gray snapper, grows to much greater size along offshore reefs. Among mangrove roots, the smaller fish usually appear in schools and rush out at the fisherman's lure as if they were all eager to strike, but the school sometimes pulls up short after closer inspection of the bait. Another cast will bring only part of it, and a third cast may get no response at all. It is on the first attempt, when competition may overrule caution, that a catch is most likely to be made. The ideal snapper outpost is where a bit of current passes a mangrove point or island, and there may be snappers at the same spots every year. Almost every inshore wreck has its quota of snappers, ready to dart out for prey or flush farther back into the ruins for safety.

Where schools of the fish gather in boat basins for handouts of bait scraps or even bread crumbs, the fishermen may lay elaborate plans for their capture, but the morsel with the hook enclosed is usually left to sink alone while other food disappears in the school's churning rush. When a small fish is finally taken the rest are likely to disappear; the larger ones are seldom caught.

In warm weather, spotted sea trout cover wide flats, preferably those with abundant vegetation, and the fish prefer murky waters seldom visited by bonefish. Dawn is the best fishing hour of midsummer, a time when mosquitoes come and go in swarms, carried by light breezes, and the red sunrise promises a hot morning to be followed almost certainly by subtropical showers from immense thunderheads.

At night the sea trout have moved from their deep pockets and scoured the edges of shallow bars for shrimp or bait-fish, going generally in loose schools except for the large individuals which travel alone. The largest fish are generally found on the east coast of Florida; the most fish are found around the entire Gulf coast, where they meet a variety of fishing methods. The water they prefer is fairly salty, and although they visit inland bays they do not adapt to fresh water as well as do striped bass or snook.

The schools of fish can be sighted in the calm of daybreak, swirling against the surface for shrimp or minnows, often traveling very little. They can be remarkably selective and their tastes may change from day to day, although conditions may seem the same. The fish that insists on a dainty bucktail streamer today may be attracted to a loud popping plug tomorrow, and the "popping cork" has long been a sea trout deceiver. The fisherman uses natural bait, probably a shrimp, and drifts it just below a float shaped to make a popping sound when twitched with the rod tip. The theory is that the fish associates the popping sound with feeding neighbors, goes to investigate, and meets the bait and the hook.

The dawn fisherman casts a noisy plug, and he wades carefully across a grass bottom which is broken by deeper depressions of hard sand. Over the nearby mainland, the morning flight of crows is noisy and seemingly aimless, yet keeps to the same general direction. A small mangrove island is dotted with the white figures of egrets and white ibis, the birds restless and quarreling as they prepare for the day's feeding. Along a sandy strip of shore a raccoon putters, almost ready to find the proper spot for his daytime naps.

It is a pelican that helps the fisherman, skimming inches from the water and then turning into a higher glide for inspection of a wider area. Where the pelican has gone, there have been sudden splashes as schools of mullet left the surface, but those fish were evidently too large for the hunter. Now it turns and plunges to strike in a great splatter where there have been a number of disturbances, and the fisherman approaches the spot to find small bait with trout working. He casts his noisy plug, twitches it into strident plops, and bends his rod as the trout strikes loudly. He will catch a dozen fish before he loses the school, and later in the morning he will walk the edges of a spoil bank near a deep channel and fish for larger trout to be found in the pockets there.

To the fisherman, the estuaries and inland bays are the edge of the land, but the saltwater flats are the edge of the sea.

12.
The Deep Blue Sea:

The outer margin of the fisherman's world contains its giant game fish — and a trace of glacial water at its journey's end.

 Certain fishes belong to the shallow edges of the ocean. They are cruisers of the margins yet a part of the sea, seldom found in estuary or river. Thus they are set apart somewhat from the striped bass that runs the surf yet may live in fresh water, and the channel bass that shows his golden side against the shoulder of a clean wave ready to break upon the sand.

Some of the oceanic fish come so near the land that they may be sighted or caught from fishing piers and jetties. The bluefish almost qualifies as one of them, but the blue may take up residence in inland bays or deep canals, as much at home there as in the open sea. The fisherman may see the true oceangoing blue when they make their sweeps against the beach, following the fortunes of bait-fish and sometimes marked by gulls.

Another fish which comes close to land is the cobia. It prefers open but shallow sea, and migrates from Chesapeake Bay to the tropics, making visits very near to many beaches. A hard striker with strong flattened jaws, the cobia (or "ling") crushes plugs in a streaking rush. On a long fishing pier, migratory schools are awaited by early-morning casters taking advantage of calm seas and good visibility. Near the gentle breakers several boats appear, alternately hazy and brightly silhouetted as early mists begin to thin and disappear before a rising breeze.

The migrating school shows first as an irregularly bunched patch of indistinct shadows, bearing no resemblance to fish and changing shape constantly, but moving steadily almost parallel to shore, a little inside the far end of the pier. Over a shallow ridge of the sandy bottom the shadows are fish-like for an instant, but as they turn out to deeper water in rounding the pier they disappear almost completely and it takes a sharp eye to follow their progress. The fisherman throws his lure a little past and considerably ahead; it comes back slightly deeper than the fish are running, and one shadow disappears below the others just as the strike comes. As the fish runs, it comes very near the surface and suddenly the whole school of a dozen cobia is in plain view, following it, dark-brown backs fading to light-brown sides. The fisherman gives line grudgingly, for he has no boat with which to follow the fish. It will be some time before he can lower a net to bring it thrashing to the pier's deck.

The view is similar from the swaying cobia towers atop the boats that work tightly inshore, sometimes close to the breakers themselves. There are days when sea turtles lounge sleepily in the swells and hungry cobia are squirming shadows beneath them. At other times a scattered school of large rays loafs within sight of land and the cobia are under them to come streaming out after a lure. Occasionally, they lie in the water above the ray's back. But the run passes on and one day the watchers see no shadows. On some coasts migrant cobia pass only once a year and only in the spring.

Such elusive behavior is not for the mackerel. For weeks an enormous school of king mackerel may cover miles of sea, perhaps within easy view of beach cottages, sometimes farther out where the shore is a hazy dark line, often well out of sight of land. The school surges about in haphazard fashion, for it is temporarily at home with bait and temperatures to its liking. A change of weather can send it north or south. It separates into great segments and sometimes fishermen find a wad of fish so wide and so deep that the supply seems endless. They may be located by gulls or by the flying froth of surface striking, but if they are deep the clue to their presence will be a myriad of little marks on the recording fathometer.

Now and then a single fish will sail high into the air, higher than any hooked fish is likely to jump, and watchful fishermen will glimpse it as a bright glint fifteen feet above the water. It may jump to fall upon bait, or for some unknown reason—but this kingfish characteristic sometimes betrays the location of a school. When a boat trolls its spoons, feathers, or bait, a fish may jump again near the baits to come down on one or simply out

Preceding pages: Black marlin, giant of the Pacific, fights in landless vista of sky and ocean where currents are deep and taste of rivers is faint.

of interest in the lure. Paradoxically, once the fish is hooked it runs swiftly but does not jump.

While the thousands of kingfish mill contentedly with little movement to north or south, fishing seems simple and the concentrations of fish are marked by trolling or drifting boats. After the great schools move on, there are still many king mackerel, since it is the smaller fish that school and group, while the occasional very large king mackerel is a hermit, believed by most fishermen to appear among lesser fish by accident. Finding one now is done by studying the bottom contours and by locating the bait.

There are other mackerels similar to the king mackerel, such as the cero and Spanish mackerel, smaller fish with a similar range. When on the move most of them are easily provoked into striking. When they have settled in an area for a time, they become increasingly selective in their feeding. It was the popularity of lighter tackle in recent years that made game fish of all these mackerels.

Like mackerel, the dolphin comes often to baits intended for larger game and a big dolphin is an adversary for sailfish tackle. Any dolphin is a prize for very light equipment. Dolphin are found over deep water, often beneath any sort of shelter. Many a caster has hooked one from beneath an old vegetable crate or other flotsam from the steamship lanes, perhaps within sight of the ships themselves, and the fish lie under floating seaweed as well.

The dolphin's coloration, probably the most brilliant of all ocean fishes, is a transitory thing and few anglers will see it the same for more than a few seconds. In the warm sea, as the fish charges or circles bait, its colors are altered by the shade of the water and the depth of the fish—and the dolphin contributes to the chameleon effect by changing its tints with its moods. When first caught, it is likely to be purple or dark blue along the spine and dorsal fin, greenish along the upper side, and yellow flecked with dark spots on the belly. The death of a dolphin casts a fleeting shadow of sadness on a successful fishing trip for, even as the angler watches, the brilliant colors of life change to dull yellow or silver.

A school of dolphin will rush trolled baits on the surface, their dorsal fins throwing spurts of water as the fish accelerate—evidently in competition with each other—when nearing the targets. The females have a somewhat sloping brow, but the bull dolphin has a high, steep forehead and many a troller has been startled to see a watery plume marking the course of a big male speeding along the surface, his forehead cleaving the water like a prow. Once hooked, the dolphin is a leaping, racing fighter, without reserve or calculation.

Although they are found year-round in many southern waters, some dolphin schools move in ragged formations as if on invisible tracks, swinging north in spring and southward in fall. Anglers drifting along such a course find school after school, as if the ocean were full of these bright, speeding fish.

The modern fisherman watches both the surface of the sea and its bottom, seeing its conformation with the recording fathometer, and he carries on a ceaseless search for even small obstructions that can be rallying points for the schools of bait and the predators that follow them. The larger bottom obstructions may offer true hiding places, but some of the smaller ones seem to hold fish as reference points rather than as sanctuaries.

Where a ship sank many years ago the fathometer shows the wreck itself, as well as shifting clouds of small fish, busy schools of larger ones, and sometimes the firm mark of a single giant. On the bottom there may be warsaw grouper that could weigh in the hundreds of pounds. The mark nearer shore might be a jewfish, even larger. Many wrecks have their longtime residents of such great weight that they can simply retire to shelter where a fishing line cannot move them and the angler must break it to free it. The grouper can draw a large bait from the bottom with powerful suction, the bait simply

1

Birds of the sea (1) are informers to be watched by every fisherman. Jetty anglers (2) crowd to very edge of crashing seas. Handsome blue fish (3) is reeled ashore. Dolphin (4) is flashing speedster of Gulf Stream. Cobia (5) rushed to take plug thrown with light tackle.

3

2

4

going to the fish's mouth rather than being taken in a strike as the fisherman imagines.

Among the gamest fish of the wrecks and deep reefs are the greater amberjacks of the Atlantic, deep-digging fighters like the other jacks. Often, when one member of a school is hooked, the others abandon caution and follow the hooked fish up through the depths, willing to strike almost any lure that appears, their feeding stripes showing boldly on their heads. Like many other fish, the amberjack makes minor color changes when prepared to strike. In the Pacific, Southern California anglers pursue another amberjack, known simply as the yellowtail. It belongs to one of the largest families of fishes, whose members are often misnamed and confused.

The jacks are found both deep and shallow and there are reports of individuals, believed to be the greater amberjack of the Atlantic, being caught at a depth of more than a thousand feet. Some of the amberjacks are valued as food; some are coveted locally and considered second-rate in other areas. The jack crevalles, relatives of the amberjacks, are intruders when the angler seeks more glamorous species. Most of them prefer the shallower waters and they strike viciously at noisy surface lures, the explosive attack more dramatic because the mouth is located on the lower part of the head and the necessary lunging approach carries much of the fish above the surface.

All of the jacks have great power, and the smaller ones, weighing no more than three or four pounds, will strike and run like other species of much larger size, then turn sidewise against the pull of the line. The attack of the small jack crevalle is likely to show swift and churning swirls as the fish feints at the lure, sometimes passing it and plunging under the angler's boat as if demonstrating its speed and agility. In surface cruising, the fish may expose the tip of its dorsal fin like a finger tracing slow lines on gentle waves. In a contemplative attitude a larger jack crevalle will lie motionless studying a surface lure, an indistinct form of

Big jack crevalle (1) comes aboard after grudging, digging fight. Tuna team (2) works in harmony. Pacific yellowtail (3) are prime targets of California's offshore party and charter boats. Tuna tournament boats (4) are built for heavy fish, athletic fishermen, and battering waves.

1

3

2
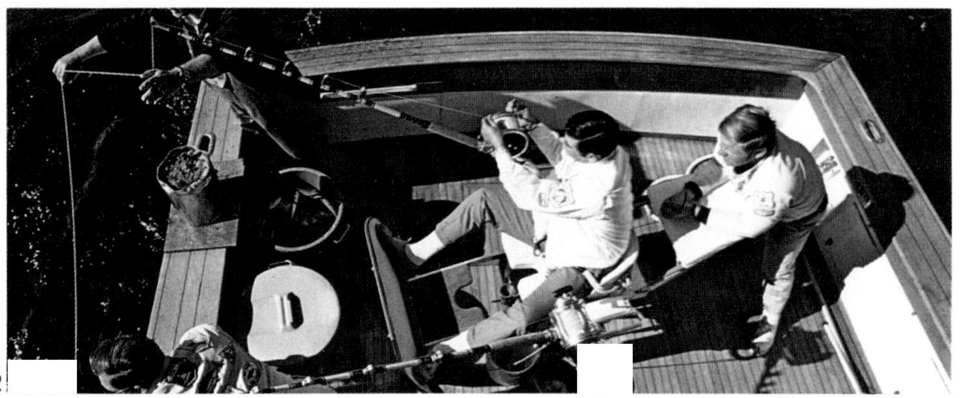

4

9
BOJEAN
BABYLON, N.Y.

Giant tuna travel Atlantic in complex migrations. They are found from tropics to Arctic Circle at appropriate seasons, and are caught far from land as well as within cliffed bays of Newfoundland. Vagaries of migrations have eliminated tuna ports after many years, caused new ones to prosper and brought competitive big-game anglers from points around the world.

olive green with a trim of bright yellow fins and tail. On quiet days the offshore fisherman will sometimes see schools of large jack crevalle moving slowly with negligible tail movements just inside the slow swells and turning together in slow motion; some schools are composed of fish of more than twenty pounds. The jacks, like most other fishes, group as to size, and a spattering surface disturbance may be the feeding of fish no larger than a hand. Once landed, a small jack gives forth petulant squeaky grunts, while a full-size jack can sound almost like an adult hog as the hook is removed. Sometimes the grunting is a part of the fight, the sound muffled and eerie as it comes up through the water from an unseen fish tugging below.

Off San Francisco's Golden Gate there is deep-sea fishing, truly deep fishing for the king, or chinook, salmon, a fish that knows a gamut of habitats, from mountain brook to offshore depths. Well offshore, the salmon is a true ocean fish caught both at great depths and near the surface. Here in the cold Pacific the fish is at its powerful best, but the deeper it is hooked the less sporting must be the method, and the lure or bait is hauled down through the fathoms by enormous sinkers which deaden the fish's fight. Some ingenious sportsmen have rigged the large and expensive weights so they are jettisoned once the fish is hooked, and thus the angler can feel the full fury of a forty-pound adversary in the dark world below, where large fish feed on herring and squid.

2

1

Outriggers tip gently on sunny seas (1) where green water gives way to blue. Marlin (2) can become giant arrow as it broad-jumps heaving seas and throws geyser with the line. Great fish loses (3), to die beside its captor's boat. Some marlin fights last for hours and fish can dive to great depth as well as jump. Once landed (4), marlin is catch of awesome size.

3

One of a tribe of colorful and unpredictable wanderers, sailfish has fought to wild finish (1 & 3) and is brought aboard with care (2).

1

2

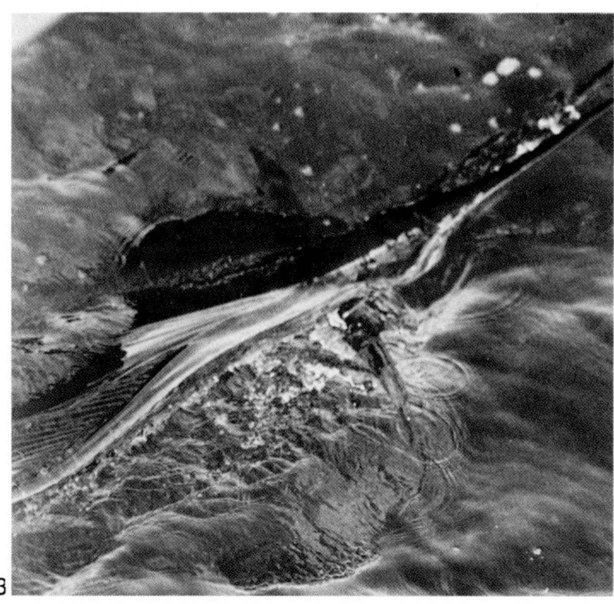
3

The chinooks are generally most active at dawn, feeding in the half-light before sun-up and continuing while the sun burns off the Pacific fogs heaving about the coastal range. The salmon are veterans of the deeps. They have escaped shark packs and seals in dramas during which large segments of the sea's population scatter and flee before the marauding destroyers. Later in the fishing day the boats may return to the wharf in brilliant sun and the sea is a different world from that of the chill dawn.

Bluefin tuna are citizens of the seven seas, their travels not bounded by restrictive migration routes, and although it is known that they move north and south with the seasons, they cannot be neatly scheduled. The fisherman must be content with the knowledge that large, medium, or small bluefin tuna are likely to be found in a certain area at certain times. He is unable to prove they are the same fish or descendants of the same fish each year. Although it has been assumed that there are separate western-Atlantic and eastern-Atlantic populations, fish tagged in American waters have been caught as frequently off European coasts as off the American coast. While record catches of other fish may be localized, the biggest tuna have come from widely separated places, including California, the Bahamas, Australia, Massachusetts, New York, Tasmania, and Prince Edward Island.

The bluefin is the largest of the tunas, and the hook-and-line record is more than a thousand pounds. Fish of more than six hundred pounds, while not easily come by, are still not unusual. The bigeye tuna is smaller, but can weigh more than four hundred pounds. It lives in warmer waters than the bluefin; so does the yellowfin, now considered the same as the Allison tuna. Both these travel less than the bluefin. In the Pacific the yellowfins appear mostly south of California, but in the Atlantic they are found as far north as New Jersey.

Conception Bay of Newfoundland is an extension of the deep Atlantic, its shores rising steeply for the most part; to it the huge bluefins come in late summer. It is nearly the northern boundary of their range, although they have occasionally reached the Arctic Circle. For all but a few months of the Newfoundland year the tuna boats are unused and tuna fishermen have little in the way of a second choice if the tuna fail them. It is a watchful but unproductive business at first, beginning early in July, and then the first fish are caught along the Newfoundland coast and the boats are busy.

1

2

Sailfish are seen frequently at edge of Gulf Stream, sometimes balling frantic schools of bait. They are caught as far north as Cape Hatteras, as well as in warmer waters of Atlantic. Pacific sailfish, probably same species, grow much larger. Huge dorsal fin, or "sail," may be flattened during fight (1 & 2), but is used for herding bait and receives admiration (3).

3

The fishing is mainly trolling. On a rainy summer morning a charter-boat mate unwraps his baits of squid and mullet, the latter flown from Florida, and the fishing begins as soon as the boat has left the little harbor. The sea is flattened by the rain and when the downpour slackens there are puffs of fog that hide sections of the green coastal hills, devoid of forest. On the slopes are brightly painted Newfoundland villages. The steep brooks are strengthened by the rain and appear as silver streaks, as much waterfalls as streams.

Here the tuna has no more power than it shows at sea, but it is more erratic in the shallower water against the shore and there are problems with boulders; the prize that wins its reputation in the open ocean is no easy catch in Conception Bay. If the fish are near the surface they may be located by gulls, but sometimes there is a huge lump of water and a wide swirl, made by a fish weighing hundreds of pounds. It is then that the boatman endeavors to present his trolled baits, turning cautiously to swing them to a target he can no longer see in most cases.

Bluefin-tuna fishing is a contest here, not only of man against fish, but of tuna teams against each other. There is hard work and heavy tackle in a test of both man and gear, and strikes are generally infrequent for big game is not killed in flocks. Through August and September the anglers troll the bay, coming from great distances, as they do on other tuna grounds. Some time later they learn that a new hook-and-line record has been set not far away, at Prince Edward Island. It is a fish weighing a thousand and forty pounds and more than ten feet long. The water cools in October and soon the fish are gone.

Tuna are mackerels, and have lesser relatives with the tuna's bullet shape and scaled-down power. The little bonito, scorned by a fisherman who expects a sailfish, strikes the lure and is hauled roughly aboard for bait. In the fishbox its dying throes are a tattoo of hard tail muscle that does not stop until it dies. Caught on very light tackle, it must be played to exhaustion. The bonito gives its best and dies as the angler tries to release it.

At the edge of the truly deep sea move the billfishes. The sailfishes are found in both Atlantic and Pacific. The Pacific fish are much larger, but it is questionable if they are a different species. Both blue and white marlins are found in the Atlantic, the white being smallest of their kind. The Pacific has the black, silver, and striped marlins, and the giant swordfish is found in many of the seas. Marlins have thicker bodies than the sailfishes, lack the enormous dorsal fin, and carry relatively shorter and thicker bills. Largest of all the billfishes, the record black marlin came from Cabo Blanco, Peru, and weighed 1560 pounds.

Although the sailfish is not one of the larger of the billfishes, it has the grace and beauty common to them all. It is even more streamlined than most, turning to a lance-like silhouette once its great sail is flattened into the slot along its back and its pectoral fins are fitted to their own groove along the belly. The sailfish lives in most of the warm seas of the world and is found at its largest in the Pacific. In Atlantic waters it is fished throughout the Caribbean and in summer as far north as Cape Hatteras. In the Gulf of Mexico it is far out over the gently sloping bottom and in the Pacific it is most energetically sought near Panama.

There are year-round residents in the warmer parts of the sailfish range, but there also are some migrations with warm weather. In the southern Atlantic, spawning comes in summer. The very small sailfish has little resemblance to the adult, although its toothed jaws are modified into beaks while it is only a few inches long.

With the outgoing tide the water has changed by dramatic stages. On the mainland side of the inlet it is slightly brownish, taking its coloration from sediment stirred by the high winds that preceded the cold front. In the inland waterway the spotted sea trout search for deep holes, where the water chills more slowly. The inlet itself has calmed with

Offshore fleet of deepwater boats gives fisherman his contact with ocean fishes, end of a quest that follows brook and river to deep blue water.

the dying wind, and the inlet channel is clearing. The tide carries out some shreds of grass loosened during the high wind and captured occasionally by small eddies along the heavy rock chunks of the jetties. In the deeper part, the inlet waters appear blue-green and are patrolled by brown pelicans sliding along at very low altitude or turning erratically higher up, their glides interrupted at intervals when they sight bait-fish near the surface. Their aerial plunges are deft and graceful strikes, although once the water is struck the birds appear disheveled and awkward, like poorly matched bundles of wings and beaks. The brown pelican is losing the battle for existence, a victim of chemical poisoning, as mortality gradually overbalances reproduction.

At the mouth of the inlet, the outgoing current meets swells from the sea. The breakers seem leisurely, an impression belied by the brisk swinging of a channel buoy. The seawater appears blue there and it is busy with gulls. On some days bluefish or Spanish mackerel mill about the inlet, and some species of fish are constant residents.

Little blue runners are nearly always there, darting members of the jack family and generally of the right size for sailfish bait. They are usually found about the buoys and the inshore reefs, sporting fish for very light tackle but generally caught with dispatch for use as live bait. Sometimes as a group they follow a small lure in a busy, whirling pattern, each fish seeming bound to catch the bait though somehow veering off at the last instant. The one that takes gives a solid tug and is cranked aboard as an attraction for amberjack or sailfish.

The Gulf Stream is an ocean river, its enormous current meandering much as lesser streams do, now swinging close to the land, now curving away from it. It is at the edge of the Gulf Stream that sailfish are expected, and it is there that the ocean suddenly seems very deep. The slightly muddy inshore water has changed to light green, then to deepening blue, and finally to the nearly purple cast of clear depths as the sailfishing grounds are approached. Floating tan streaks of seaweed move with the swells like great lazy sea snakes, and sea creatures live beneath them, especially the violent dolphin. Occasionally, on very calm days, close inspection will show really tiny dolphin no more than 3 inches long, feeding industriously in the shadow of the weed lines. Sometimes there are juvenile flying fish hardly larger than bumblebees.

The swells are still large, but the wind has gone down. It is early winter and sailfish are moving southward, an indistinct migration, for some of them remain in warm waters the year around while others venture north. Now, with the first really cold weather of the season, some of the sails travel on the surface in the bright winter sun. What wind there is comes from behind the fish, one of which has been picked up by probing binoculars from a flying bridge. The fish's sail, although not fully extended, is just above the surface as if it were actually being used to catch the north wind. The fish disappears in a wide trough, appears again on the shoulder of another wave while the boat swings wide to present a trolled bait.

When properly rigged, sailfish trolling baits —usually mullet or balao—are skipping lures, moving at a speed which causes a little spray of water ahead of each one, and if there are steep corrugations in the surfaces of the swells a bait will now and then leap clear of the water, plunge back in, and leave a bubbly track against the side of the wave. Most sailfishermen troll four lines, two from outriggers and two flat lines running directly from the rod tips or from stern clips. The mullet have most of the bones removed to give them added action. (The bait was caught in the early morning by a mate who waded the placid shallows of a small bay, carrying a leaded castnet and watching for the gentle breaks of mullet schools.)

Although the angler seldom sees the sailfish except at the surface, the boatman watches both the sky and depths, the one for gathering gulls, the other—with a fathometer—for the bottom irregularities he knows mean bait-fish and squid to be pursued by his quarry. They can move both near the surface as well as at considerable depth.

A striking sailfish may come suddenly or as a curious inspector of the skipping baits. It may snap an outrigger line from its clip without warning, or betray itself with its dark, erected sail as it trails one of the baits at the same speed. From the higher flying bridges such a fish will be a distorted dark shadow beneath his fin, occasionally flashing bronze or gold, sometimes showing his deep blue back and striped sides.

Strikes vary greatly. The fish may appear to hit the bait with its slender bill and then leave it dead in the water before taking. But there are other times when a sail comes with a rush and a gaping mouth to take the bait instantly, sometimes even to scoop in another bait before stopping its charge. For most sailfish strikes, the drop-back is accepted practice, slack line given instantly until it appears the fish has actually taken the bait, after which slack is retrieved and the hook set. The line clip of the outrigger is a sort of built-in drop-back mechanism, the fish having time to take the bait before the line comes taut again after leaving the outrigger.

The fish strikes and the line is slacked, the fisherman standing with rod in hand. The engines are out of gear, the boat coasting to a complete standstill. The angler winds his reel until he feels a slight tension and then sets the hook hard. He strikes against solid fish and he sets the hook again and again as the fish moves slowly, then dashes off in a swift run against the reel drag. The spool has whirred for some time before the fish shows itself, a glistening arrow atop a broad wave, a long way out and seemingly remote from the straining rod and reel. The fish walks erect across the sea, only its thrashing tail in the water, and it sounds while the reel gives off line in reluctant buzzes. Other jumps may be closer in as the angler gains line, and finally the combat is more intimate, fisherman and fish within a few yards of each other. Only fifty feet from the cockpit the sailfish moves slowly near the surface of a tall swell, and as the boat sinks into the trough the antagonists are at nearly the same level, the fish plainly seen as if it were frozen in a great block of blue ice. It is tired now and it is brought alongside. The fish swims with great effort, and a gloved hand closes over the rough bill.

There are days when the gulls find the ball of bait, marking it with their flicks of white against the blue sky, and the boats converge on the plunging birds. The gulls cry in their excitement and wheel in a tight funnel, so close together that they must swerve to avoid mid-air collisions. They make repeated dives to come up with small bait-fish and sometimes to sit high in the water and paddle about where the bait is thickest.

The sea is calm and small forage fish appear on the surface like raindrops, plainly audible with a simmering sound like grease beginning to fry in a huge skillet. There are periods when the sound is steady, and then it is broken as a section of the bait becomes frightened and darts downward with a light, thumping sound. The school is large, and now it is crowded for it is being balled by a group of sailfish, meticulous herdsmen whose approach is just close enough to make the flustered bait almost a solid wad, yet restrained enough to keep it from scattering. The great sails flutter above the water and the fish move back and forth at their task. Now and then a fish will thrust forward into the bait, mouth open, and then return to its herding duties.

The boat backs up to the bait, moving very slowly, and sailfish are on both sides of it when a line with live bait is slipped over the cockpit gunwale to be taken almost immediately. The boat moves forward, the boatman hopeful that the fish can be drawn away from the school of sailfish and their pod of bait without too much commotion. The hooked fish charges away against the light drag and jumps far out, leaving a spout of water on the wave crest where it re-enters. Now the fisherman applies pressure, for there are other sails to be found where the bait shimmers and he hurries the fight in his eagerness to try them.

When the fish is alongside and the leader is at hand the mate deftly snips it and the sailfish is free, lying awash in the sea. It turns slightly on its side, but rights itself in a slightly convulsive effort and the sharp bill turns downward. The gills work a little faster in a gulping action and the twin sickles of the tail move deliberately as the seven-foot fish goes down beside the boat, down into a hundred fathoms of darkness, the slender form fading into the deep blue, and the boat swings again toward the circling gulls.

Miles from shore the ocean currents still carry the traces of glacier water, diluted astronomically by the flow from mountain springs, and the chocolate run-off from hillsides where the harvested timber no longer holds the soil. Now, in early winter, many of the highest sources are frozen and unproductive. Part of the ocean is the polluted sludge of city refuse and the still-active chemicals of farmland which arrived by way of warm, shallow creeks and bigger rivers. There is the contribution of black, acid-stained water from the cypress swamps and the mangrove-tentacled islands of the South.

Most of the ocean's fishes are along its edges and they are often affected by man's additions to the water. Until very recently the deeper ocean was considered infinite and invulnerable, but now that the coastal shallows show their suffering and begin to repay man for his abuses there is the ominous thought that the great oceans themselves may be susceptible to damage. On the other hand, there is the hope that the seas contain immense resources yet untapped, a little-known immensity which is a last hope for despairing ecologists. Where our sailfish is released there is a sort of demarcation between known and unknown.

The tired fish goes deep and turns toward the deeper sea to rest, regain its power, and to feed another day. In its gills may be the taste of the fertile estuaries and the mountain brooks, but they are far away and the taste must be very faint.

Bibliography

Bates, Joseph D., Jr., *Atlantic Salmon Flies & Fishing.* Harrisburg, Pa., Stackpole Books, 1970.

Bergman, Ray, *Trout.* New York, Alfred A. Knopf, 1949.

Brooks, Joseph W., Jr., *Salt Water Fly Fishing.* New York, G. P. Putnam's Sons, 1950.

Coker, Robert E., *Streams, Lakes, Ponds.* Chapel Hill, N.C., University of North Carolina Press, 1954.

Farrington, S. Kip, Jr., *Fishing the Pacific.* New York, Coward-McCann, Inc., 1953.

Fennelly, John F., *Steelhead Paradise.* Vancouver, Canada, Mitchell Press, Limited, 1963.

Gabrielson, Ira N., *The New Fisherman's Encyclopedia.* Harrisburg, Pa., The Stackpole Company, 1950.

Haig-Brown, Roderick L., *Return to the River.* New York, William Morrow & Co., 1941.

Hewitt, Edward R., *A Trout and Salmon Fisherman for Seventy-five Years.* New York, Abercrombie & Fitch; Ann Arbor, University Microfilms Inc., 1966.

LaBranche, George M. L., *The Salmon and the Dry Fly.* New York, Arno Press, 1967.

Lyman, Henry, and Woolner, Frank, *Complete Book of Striped Bass Fishing.* New York, A. S. Barnes & Company, Inc., 1954.

———*Complete Book of Weakfishing.* New York, American Book-Stratford Press, Inc., 1959.

Marinaro, Vincent C., *A Modern Dry Fly Code.* New York, Crown Publishers, Inc., 1950, 1970.

Marshall, Arthur R., *A Survey of the Snook Fishery of Florida.* Miami, University of Miami thesis, 1956.

McClane, A. J., *Standard Fishing Encyclopedia.* New York, Holt, Rinehart & Winston, 1965.

Migdalski, Edward C., *Fresh Water Sport Fishes.* New York, The Ronald Press Company, 1962.

Needham, Paul R., *Trout Streams.* New York, Winchester Press, 1969.

Netboy, Anthony, *The Atlantic Salmon, A Vanishing Species* London, Faber and Faber, 1968.

Quick, Jim, *Fishing the Nymph.* New York, The Ronald Press Company, 1960.

Reinfelder, Al, *Bait Tail Fishing.* Cranbury, N.J., A. S. Barnes & Co., 1969.

Rice, F. Philip, *America's Favorite Fishing.* New York, Outdoor Life, Harper & Row, 1964.

Schwiebert, Ernest G., Jr., *Matching the Hatch.* Toronto, Collier-Macmillan, Ltd., 1955.

Skues, G. E. M., *Nymph Fishing for Chalk Stream Trout.* London, Adam & Charles Black, 1960.

Swisher, Doug, and Richards, Carl, *Selective Trout.* New York, Crown Publishers, Inc., 1971.

Walker, C. F., *The Art of Chalk Stream Fishing.* Harrisburg, Pa., Stackpole Books, 1969.

Wulff, Lee, *The Atlantic Salmon.* New York, A. S. Barnes & Co., 1958.

Picture Credits

EAB—Erwin A. Bauer
BB—Bill Browning
KHM—Karl H. Maslowski
PML—Pete McLain
MEN—Marvin E. Newman
LLR—Leonard Lee Rue
JVW—Joseph Van Wormer
CFW—Charles F. Waterman

Cover: Charles F. Waterman

CHAPTER 1
10–11, 13: BB. 14–15: CFW (*1*), BB (2), MEN (3), PML (*4*), Albert Squillace (5), BB (6), Bernard Kreh (7), EAB (*8*). 16: CFW.

CHAPTER 2
18–19: CFW. 22–23: CFW (*1,4*), BB (*2,5*), EAB (3). 24, 25: JVW. 26–27: CFW (*1,2*), BB (*3,4,5*), LLR (6). 29: EAB. 30: CFW (*1*), EAB (2,5), BB (*3,4*). 32: EAB. 34: BB. 35: BB (*1*), CFW (*2,3,4*).

CHAPTER 3
38–39: BB. 42–43: BB (*1,3*), CFW (*2,4*). 45: JVW (*top*), LLR. 46–47: JVW (*1,5*), CFW (*top, 2*), BB (*3,4*). 49: JVW. 50–51: BB (*1,2,4*), CFW (*3*). 53: JVW. 54–55: BB.

CHAPTER 4
58–59: EAB. 62–63: BB (*1,2,4*), JVW (*3*), CFW (5). 66–67: CFW (*1,2,5*), JVW (*3*), BB (4). 68: EAB. 70–71: LLR (*1,3*), JVW (*2,4,6*), EAB (5). 72–73: Michigan Department of Natural Resources (*1*), EAB (2), JVW (*3,4*).

CHAPTER 5
76–77, 80–81: MEN. 83: Albert Squillace. 84–85: CFW (*1,2,4,5*), BB (3). 86: CFW. 87: Nova Scotia Information Service. 89: Canadian Consulate General. 90: JVW. 93: CFW (*top*), JVW. 94–95: CFW. 97: JVW (*1*), CFW (2), LLR (*3,4*).

CHAPTER 6
100–101: EAB. 104–105: EAB (*1,2,4*), Albert Squillace (*3*). 107, 108: EAB. 110-111: KHM (*1*), EAB (*2,3,6*), BB (*4*), LLR (5). 112–113: EAB (*1,2*), CFW (*3*). 114–115: EAB (*1,3,4*), KHM (2), PML (*5*).

CHAPTER 7
118–119, 122: EAB. 123: CFW (*1*), KHM (*2,5*), EAB (*3*), BB (*4*). 126–127: CFW (*1,5*), BB (2), Albert Squillace (3), EAB (4). 128, 131-135: EAB. 130: KHM. 136: CFW. 138, 140-141: EAB (1), PML (2), CFW (*3,5*), KHM (*4*). 143: Walker, Missouri Tourism.

CHAPTER 8
146–147: EAB. 150–151: CFW (*1,3,5*), EAB (*2,4*), KHM (*6*). 153: CFW. 154–155: CFW (*1*), Lovett Williams (2), LLR (*3*), Wallace O. Hughes (*4*). 156–157: LLR (*1*), Wallace O. Hughes (2), Albert Squillace (*3*). 159: EAB. 160–161: CFW (*1,6*), EAB (2), Wallace O. Hughes (*3,4,5*).

CHAPTER 9
164–165: PML. 168: CFW. 170–171: CFW (*1,3,6*), EAB (*2,4*), LLR (5), Wallace O. Hughes (*7*). 173: EAB. 174–175: PML (*1,4*), JVW (*2,3*). 176: Department of the Army, Corps of Engineers, New Orleans District (*top*), California Department of Fish and Game. 178–179: PML. 181: CFW (*1,3*), PML (2). 182: New Jersey Department of Environmental Protection.

CHAPTER 10
184–185, 188–189: EAB. 190: CFW. 191, 192: EAB. 194–197: CFW. 198–199: CFW (*1*), EAB (2), PML (*3*), Joe Kenner (*4*), Patricia Caulfield (5).

CHAPTER 11
202: Bernard Kreh. 206–207: EAB (*1,5*), CFW (*3*), BB (2), Joe Kenner (*4*). 208: EAB. 210, 211: CFW. 213: EAB. 214: CFW. 215: EAB. 217: Patricia Caulfield (*top*), Bernard Kreh. 218: Bernard Kreh. 220: PML (*1,4*), KHM (*2,3*).

CHAPTER 12
224–225: EAB. 228–229: Albert Squillace (*1*), CFW (*2,5*), Fred Sammis (*3*), EAB (*4*). 230–231: EAB (*1,3*), Frank Eck (2), Rhode Island Development Council (*4*). 232: Nova Scotia Information Service. 233: Canadian Consulate General. 234–235: Frederick Baldwin. 236–237: EAB (*1*), CFW (*2,3*). 238–239, 241: EAB.

Index

T

W

Y